Compassion

Edited by Rodger Charlton

Compassion

Compassion, Continuity and Caring in the NHS

Edited by Rodger Charlton

Royal College of
General Practitioners

The Royal College of General Practitioners was founded in 1952 with this object:

'To encourage, foster and maintain the highest possible standards in general practice and for that purpose to take or join with others in taking steps consistent with the charitable nature of that object which may assist towards the same.'

Among its responsibilities under its Royal Charter the College is entitled to:

'Diffuse information on all matters affecting general practice and issue such publications as may assist the object of the College.'

British Library Cataloguing-in-Publication Data
A catalogue record for this book is available from the British Library

Published by the Royal College of General Practitioners, 2015
30 Euston Square, London NW1 2FB

Designed and typeset by Prepress Projects Ltd, Perth, UK

Printed by Hobbs the Printers

Indexed by Susan Leech

ISBN 978-0-85084-401-6

Contents

About the authors

Editor

Prof. Rodger Charlton BA MPhil MD FRCGP FRNZCGP is a GP and Training Programme Director in the West Midlands. He is Honorary Editor of RCGP Publications and Professor of Primary Care Education, the University of Nottingham.

Contributing authors

John Ballatt MA (Oxon) RCGP (Hon) worked for 30 years as a practitioner, trainer and manager in mental health services. He developed a core interest in the dynamics of human groups, and individuals, as they engage with ill-being and illness. John now works as a partner in People In Systems (www.peopleinsystems.com). He is co-author, with Dr Penelope Campling, of *Intelligent Kindness: reforming the culture of healthcare* (RCPsych Publications, 2011).

Dr Jenny Bennison MB BChir MClinEd FRCGP DCCH DFFP DGM DRCOG is a GP partner and trainer in Edinburgh, an Executive Officer (Quality Improvement) of RCGP Scotland and Vice-Chair of the Scottish Intercollegiate Guidelines Network (SIGN). She is also a training partner for GP Access, a company involved in helping practices improve access for their patients by using total telephone triage.

Dr Alastair Blake MB/BChir MA (Cantab) is one of the National Medical Director's Clinical Fellows (2014–15) working at the Care Quality Commission (CQC). His work at the CQC focuses on the use of regulation to promote better integration between providers. He has a strong interest in healthcare leadership and management, and interned at the management consultancy firm McKinsey & Co. in 2011. He subsequently founded a London-wide education network with over 500 junior doctor and medical student members called 'Lead-In'. From August 2015, he will continue his clinical training as a Core Medical Trainee at Barts Health in London, and he aspires to be a clinician who works at the interface of primary and secondary care.

Dr Rebecca Chellaswamy BMBS BMedSci MRCGP DRCOG is a GP and member of the RCGP's Adolescent Health Group and Expert Publishing Group.

She is currently studying for the Masters in Medical Education (MMedSci) at the University of Nottingham. Her special interests are medical education, mental health and adolescent health.

Dr Alys Cole-King MB BCh MSc FRCPsych DGM is Consultant Liaison Psychiatrist for Betsi Cadwaladr University Health Board and Director and co-founder of Connecting with People, a social enterprise. She is the Royal College of Psychiatrists (RCPscyh) spokesperson on suicide and self-harm, and a member of its Patient Safety Working Group, contributing to several College reports. Alys sits on the RCGP Mental Health Training Advisory Group and has contributed to both the RCGP and RCPsych curricula. She is primary author of the RCGP/RCPsych Suicide Mitigation in Primary Care factsheet, has written papers and book chapters, and has contributed to the RCGP e-learning module on suicide prevention.

Dr Samuel Finnikin MB ChB MA (Cantab) is a GP trainee and Academic Clinical Fellow at the University of Birmingham. He is an RCGP Midland Faculty board member and Vice-Chair of the West Midlands Associates-in-Training (AiT) committee. He is interested in understanding the implementation of clinical research and how policies and guidelines impact on clinical practice.

Prof. Simon Gregory MMEd FRCPEdin FRCGP FHEA FAcadMedEd is a GP and Director and Dean of Education and Quality, Midlands and East Health Education England. He was previously Postgraduate Dean, East of England, and before that GP Dean, East Midlands. He is a Fellow of Homerton College, Cambridge, and Visiting Professor Norwich Medical School, University of East Anglia, Anglia Ruskin University and the University of Pavia, Italy. Simon is also Chair of the RCGP Ethics Committee.

Dr Richard B. Gunderman MD PhD is Chancellor's Professor in the Schools of Medicine, Liberal Arts and Philanthropy at Indiana University.

Catherine Hall HND (Business Studies) is Head of Service at York St Health Practice, a service provided by Leeds Community Healthcare NHS Trust. She is manager of the Community Dental and TB nursing services and is currently studying for an MSc in Health Leadership.

Prof. Amanda Howe MD MEd FRCGP FAcadMed DCH DRCOG is a GP and Vice-Chair (Professional Development) for the RCGP. She has been Professor of Primary Care, Norwich Medical School, University of East Anglia, since 2001, when she joined as part of the Foundation Team. She is also President Elect of the World Organisation of Family Doctors (WONCA).

Dr Majid Khan MB ChB (Cantab) MRCGP is a GP in Birmingham with experience of working with substance misusers at HMP Birmingham. He is a fully trained

Breathworks 'Mindfulness for Stress' teacher and teaches the special study module 'Mindfulness in Medicine' at Warwick Medical School.

Dr Richard Knox BMedSc MB ChB MMedSc (Clinical Education) MRCGP DCH DRCOG is a GP in Leicester and a Clinical Associate Professor in Primary Care at the University of Nottingham School of Medicine. He is the School's academic lead for professionalism and ethics teaching, and chairs the Student Support and Professionalism committee. He is also a member of the School's Medicine Safety and Effective Healthcare Research Team.

Dr Iain Lawrie MRCGP FRCP is Consultant and Honorary Clinical Senior Lecturer in Palliative Medicine, the Pennine Acute Hospitals NHS Trust/the University of Manchester. Iain started his training as a physiotherapist for five years and then studied medicine at the University of Leicester. He entered palliative medicine through general practice, with a couple of years in a rural practice, and some time in a Category B Prison (as a doctor, rather than an inmate!). In addition to his very varied clinical work, he is actively involved in undergraduate education and palliative care research at Manchester Medical School.

Sister Kirsty Millard is a practice nurse and Clinical Commissioning Group Practice Nurse Development Lead, Solihull, West Midlands. She qualified in 1994 from the Queen Elizabeth School of Nursing, Birmingham, and has been working as a practice nurse (independent nurse prescriber) for 15 years. Kirsty is a passionate advocate of primary care.

Dr Tom Nolan MBBS BSc MRCGP is a London GP and member of the RCGP's Expert Publishing Panel. His GP training was at King's and included academic training within the eHealth department at UCL. He was a clinical editor at the BMJ before being lured back into GP training. He has written for the *Guardian* and the BMJ.

Dharmachari Padmakumāra has been a member of the Triratna Buddhist Order since 2004. His initial interests in philosophy and friendship were enflamed upon encountering meditation, mindfulness and the Buddhist path in 1996. Following ordination he has guided many people in mindful, compassionate and awakened living. He currently resides in Oxford where he helps run the Oxford Triratna Buddhist group.

Dr Mitesh Patel MB ChB BSc is an Academic Clinical Fellow in General Practice, Nottingham, with interests in cardiovascular medicine and mental health. He works to enhance the standards of patient care while always keeping the patient as the centre of his clinical and research practice.

Dr Dirk Pilat BSc (Open) FRCGP PgDipGp (Otago) is Medical Director for e-Learning at the RCGP. Dirk is a GP Principal in the East End of London where he is continuously amazed by the kindness, resilience and energy of his diverse patient population. He has a postgraduate degree from the University of Otago in Dunedin and undergraduate degrees from the University of Cologne and the Open University, of which he is particularly proud.

Dr Ryan Prince MB ChB MMedEd FRCGP CIDC is a part-time GP in Hampton-in-Arden, Solihull, and Associate Dean for GP Selection, Health Education West Midlands. He considers himself lucky to have had many opportunities in medical education, and has worked previously as a Clinical Lecturer in General Practice at the University of Warwick Medical School, a postgraduate GP tutor, and a VTS training programme director in the West Midlands. Other current positions held include Honorary Treasurer for the RCGP Midland Faculty, and membership of the academic teaching faculty of the Royal College of Physicians of London.

Dr Joanne Reeve BClinSci (Hons) MB ChB MPH PhD FRCGP DFPH PGCertLTHE is an academic GP – a non-principal in a busy inner-city Liverpool practice – and an Associate Professor at the University of Warwick. She leads an international collaboration (the School for Advancing Generalist Expertise [SAGE]) to develop, implement and evaluate the provision of expert generalist practice. She is also Chair of the Society for Academic Primary Care (SAPC), which works to enhance the capacity for advancing primary care through education and research.

Dr Rupal Shah MBBS (Hons) MRCGP DRCOG PGCert (Education) is a GP partner in Battersea and is Programme Director for assessment and retainers in South London. Rupal is an adviser to NHS Choices and is an e-Learning Development Fellow at the RCGP.

Prof. Nigel Sparrow OBE BSc (Hons) MB ChB DRCOG FRCP FRCGP FAcadMEd is Senior National GP Adviser and Responsible Officer at the Care Quality Commission. Until 2015 Nigel was also the Medical Director for Revalidation at the RCGP. He has been a GP for 30 years and has also been a GP appraiser and trainer. He was a member of the Standing Commission on Carers for seven years. He was previously Chair of RCGP Professional Development and was Vice-Chair of RCGP Council between 2004 and 2007. He is Visiting Professor in General Practice at the University of Lincoln. Nigel was presented with the Foundation Council Award at the RCGP in 2014 and awarded an OBE for services to primary care in the New Year's Honours List for 2015.

Dr Helen J. Stokes-Lampard PhD FRCGP is a GP partner in Lichfield, a Clinical Senior Lecturer at Birmingham Medical School and the Honorary Treasurer of the RCGP. She started as an academic GP trainee in 2000 and subsequently undertook a range of roles at the University of Birmingham; currently she is Academic Head of Community-Based Medicine and coordinates the highly successful academic GP trainee programme.

Prof. J.E. Thistlethwaite BSc MBBS PhD MMEd FRCGP FRACGP DRCOG is a Professor of Medical Education and adjunct at University Technology Sydney, a health professions education consultant and a GP. She trained in the UK and is now practising in Australia. Jill's main interest is in interprofessional education (IPE) and she has written widely on the topic, including books and book chapters. In 2014 she received a Fulbright senior scholarship and spent four months at the National Center for Interprofessional Practice and Education at the University of Minnesota, USA.

Dr Louise Warburton MB ChB FRCGP DFFP DM-SMed DRCOG has been a GP for 24 years and is currently a board member for Telford and Wrekin CCG. She is a Senior Lecturer in Primary Care at Keele University. Louise is a GP with a special interest in rheumatology and musculoskeletal medicine, has been the President of the Primary Care Rheumatology Society, was a member of the National Institute for Health and Care Excellence (NICE) guidelines development group for rheumatoid arthritis and is currently a member of the NICE guidelines group for spondyloarthropathy. She edited the book *Musculoskeletal Disorders in Primary Care* (RCGP, 2012). She is a trustee of the Arthritis and Musculoskeletal Alliance.

Harvey Ward BSc (Econ) MA (Hist) PgDip (Town Planning) is Lay Chair of the RCGP Patient and Carers Partnership Group (PCPG). He had had several careers between 1972 and 2008, all in public service, as a secondary school teacher, a town and country planner, a further education lecturer in town planning and finally as a carer support worker. Harvey retired from paid carer work in 2008 when his wife Patricia was diagnosed with incurable lung cancer and a brain tumour. They brought up three sons during their 36-year married life when Patricia had been a mainstream primary school teacher working with children with special needs and latterly a family historian. Harvey became deeply involved in patient participation group work after Patricia's death, hoping to disseminate knowledge about how compassion creates and encourages exemplary end-of-life care.

Dr Clive Weston MA MB BCh is Reader in Clinical Medicine, Deputy Head and Sub-Dean for Professional Practice on the Graduate Entry Medicine Programme at the Swansea University School of Medicine. He is a physician and cardiologist at Singleton Hospital, Swansea – where he continues to learn, teach and practise medicine.

Dr Eleanor Wilman MB ChB MA MRCGP is a GP at York St Health Practice, a service for people who are homeless, temporarily housed or seeking asylum in Leeds. She has an additional interest in medical ethics, previously holding a research post at the Centre for Excellence in Teaching and Learning, Interdisciplinary Ethics Applied, University of Leeds.

Prof. Rich Withnall MD MA MSc FRCGP is Defence Professor of General Practice and Primary Care at the Royal Centre for Defence Medicine in Birmingham. He joined the RAF as a Medical Cadet in 1990 and became the RAF's Adviser in General Practice in 2005. Following his doctorate in psychological medicine, he retains a keen clinical and research interest in community mental health. He is a GP trainer, RCGP examiner and the RCGP's Medical Director for International Accreditation and Training.

Dr Arnold Zermansky MA MB ChB FRCGP DRCOG is a GP and fair-weather cyclist in Leeds. He is also a Visiting Honorary Senior Research Fellow attached to the School of Healthcare, University of Leeds. He has been married to Pat for 45 years and has seven grandchildren.

Foreword 1

This book shouldn't be necessary. Why would anyone in health care need reminding that compassion is central, critical, essential? The humane quality of understanding suffering in others and wanting to do something about it must be one of the most profound drivers for anyone choosing to have a career in medicine – and yet all too often compassion can evaporate like mist in the morning.

Whatever your professional role might be, you are a patient too. As patients or as relatives we all know when care is delivered with compassion and when it is not. I have received care that has been of the highest quality, combining technical competence with great compassion. But I have also been treated with offhand arrogance that has taken my breath away. After leaving a consultation with one doctor who showed not a single microgram of compassion, I turned to my wife and said, 'I'm really frightened now. I don't want to need that man in my life.' Good doctors take away fear. Uncompassionate doctors worsen it. This matters – not just from a human and humane perspective. Confidence and trust produce better outcomes.

So if compassion is so central, why is it not the guaranteed norm in every single encounter with health care? Patients want and deserve to be treated with respect, dignity and compassion. Sometimes they experience care that is impersonally focused on the task, rather than the human being. We need to understand why that is.

I have my own evidence-free hunches, and I have long suspected that lack of continuity is a factor, both in primary and secondary care. Patients quite rightly stay in hospital for a very short time, but the unintended consequence is it is difficult for their doctors ever to get to know them as individuals. You have to be much more skilled to build up a caring relationship in a short space of time. A combination of shift work and rapid patient turnover in hospitals means that the doctor or nurse has no time to learn about the real human in front of them, and to take that learning into their careers.

And in recent years general practice has frequently become focused on access rather than continuity. Ask your non-medical friends who their doctor is and they will say, 'Whoever I can get to see.' All too often there is no real relationship, just a succession of isolated ten-minute snapshots seen by different doctors, rather than the full movie of a life.

On top of this there is the whole issue of our sheer busyness. It is extraordinarily difficult to be compassionate when the pressures on you are overwhelming. Exhaustion can so easily be dehumanising. And even the finest doctor can feel overwhelmed. The more caring the doctor, the more the risk of compassion fatigue. Some might fear

– either consciously or subconsciously – that if they share their patient's pain, they won't be able to bear it. And much of this is linked to the drivers that made us want to join the caring professions in the first place.

So what is to be done? We can start by valuing compassion, and care, and dignity. Everyone with any influence on the healthcare system has to recognise the absolute essential importance of these aspects of care. This isn't to denigrate the technical and the biomedical. It is to recognise the fact that these are synergistic – we absolutely need both.

The NHS's definition of quality now looks at safety, effectiveness and patient experience. The experience of compassion has a profound effect on every patient's experience of care. By focusing on this vital aspect of care, this book is reminding us of what matters. There is an old prayer that says 'Rekindle our compassion'. This book will do exactly that.

Prof. David Haslam CBE
Chair, National Institute for Health and Care Excellence, Past President and
Past Chairman, Royal College of General Practitioners

FOREWORD 2

For many years my local regional hospital had the technically best unit to which to refer a woman with a breast lump. However, I would always explain that the lead surgeon, who they would usually see, had no interpersonal skills. He was brusque, even rude, in his consultations. I would urge each woman to come back to me soon after being seen in the clinic for interpretation and discussion.

A few years ago a Primary Care Trust engaged me to review some of their more problematic GPs. One of these was a serious underperformer clinically, but his patient group loved him and described him as a true friend in their distress.

These two examples illustrate for me the importance of both technical competency and caring (‘*Cum scientia caritas*’) and how neither can be valuable without the other. Patients tend to take the competency of their doctor for granted – and hopefully that confidence is increasingly justified.

They are however much better able to assess their doctor’s interpersonal skills. They are co-producers of the relationship that lies at the heart of general practice, developed over time. The outcome of this is mutual trust and respect.

A key catalyst for this trust and respect comes from a skilled use of empathy and compassion. Sharing an understanding of feelings and circumstance, whether by conjecture or shared experience, is extremely powerful in developing mutual affinity.

Compassion is often instinctive, coming from concern for a fellow human being. Sometimes it has a learnt or practised aspect as can be the case with empathy. Whatever its roots, compassion is at the heart of good general practice, helping to create the long-term relationship that we and our patients prize so highly.

This book is a fascinating exploration of the importance of compassion in our clinical work and our lives in general. I commend it to all members of the RCGP.

Prof. Mike Pringle MD PRCGP
President of Council, Royal College of General Practitioners

Foreword 3

General practice is facing unprecedented pressures as family doctors try to manage an ageing population and rising numbers of patients against a backdrop of diminishing resources and a severe shortage of GPs. But in the scramble to balance budgets, tick boxes and achieve targets, we must never lose sight of the things that patients value most and which simply cannot be measured.

Kindness and compassion are the fundamentals of good patient care – and none of us working in the NHS must ever underestimate the importance of them. It is a great privilege to be a GP, to work with our patients, with their families, and with local communities. GPs have a unique role in the health service in that we are the only clinicians providing 'whole person' and continuous care for patients: care that considers the needs of the individual rather than treating medical problems in isolation.

The partnership between patient and GP develops over years, often from birth to death, and it gives us the opportunity to do good and to make a real difference to the lives of others. Over 1.3 million patients visit their GP surgery every single day. GPs and their teams are seeing 370m patients a year – 70m more than five years ago. We are also dealing with complex diseases that, even a decade ago, would have been referred automatically to hospital consultants. Yet as patient demand and the complexity of our caseloads has increased, the share of the NHS budget allocated to general practice has fallen and is now at an all-time low of just over 8%. As a consequence, we now have many doctors approaching retirement and not enough medical graduates going into general practice to replace them.

GPs go into general practice to care for patients. We listen and our patients share their feelings, their fears and their secrets with us. We must ensure that we have the support, time and resources necessary to focus our attention on what matters most.

General practice is the cornerstone of the health service and strong general practice enables the rest of the NHS to flourish. If properly funded and supported, general practice could provide the solution to so many of the problems currently besetting the health service. We can deliver more services in the communities where patients live and where they want to be treated, given the choice. With more GPs, we can deliver more appointments for our patients, give more time to those who need it – and demonstrate by example that kindness and compassion occupy their rightful place at the heart of the NHS.

Prof. Maureen Baker CBE DM FRCGP
Chair of Council, Royal College of General Practitioners

Preface

This book is an anthology of essays written by those who hold passionately that compassion is the central tenet of being a doctor and so of the consultation. It originally started as a project with the West Midlands Faculty and rapidly evolved to include the whole Royal College of General Practitioners (RCGP) (otherwise referred to as the College in this book). The title was debated regularly, and was originally to be *Compassion, Continuity and Caring* with the motto of the RCGP – '*Cum scientia caritas*' – as its subtitle. This is also the motto of the Royal New Zealand College of General Practitioners and the Royal Australian College of General Practitioners, and it captures the art and science of being a doctor with its definition of 'Scientific skill with loving-kindness'.[1]

Some of the authors in this book refer to Dr G.L. McCulloch (one of the original founders of the College) and his paper where he discusses in considerable detail the College motto. I assumed it would be possible to find out more about this GP, who it transpires also authored a book on physiology.[2] However, following careful research, little information remains about this man and his important work for the College. Others have defined *caritas* (and so compassion) as not meaning charity, but rather 'tender loving care'.[3] And, unlike science, it is 'unchanging'.[4]

For me, compassion became an abiding theme of this book, and one that will not date. This text is thus likely to become a seminal work of the College and medicine generally. Too often in medicine people try to measure outcomes with patients and forget or do not recognise that a lot of what happens in the consultation is not an exact science. Instead, it is a fine balance between *scientia* and *caritas*.

I have been privileged to learn from many colleagues who have written in this book that compassion is something that cannot be defined and is individual between patients and practitioners; where a practitioner can be one of many carers – both professional and informal. Those who are accountable for outcomes in the NHS such as politicians and managers should remember that, whatever compassion is, it is what matters most to people who are ill.

In my role as a medical teacher and regularly providing feedback to trainees on their consultation skills, I was shocked to hear one trainee say when feeding back to one of his peers, 'You perhaps should have turned on the empathy switch earlier.' Compassion is not something that you can learn or switch on. A definition of compassion that I found apt was provided by my research assistant, Jane Coomber. Jane, a nurse by training, described compassion as time-consuming emotional labour that does not fit well with a fast-moving world. So, when the effort is made in an ever busy and demanding health service, 'Compassion is like the sun, it just shines' (as written in the addendum to Dr Clive Weston's chapter). I commend this book to you. As editor, I have left largely unabridged the many personal views of my fellow authors. This is because they are speaking from the heart about something that is their own interpretation. These views are based on many years of experience and their understanding of their role in and towards the College and its motto, '*Cum scientia caritas*'.

Prof. Rodger Charlton BA MPhil MD FRCGP FRNZCGP

References

1. McCulloch GL. The James Dundas Simpson Address: *Cum scientia caritas*. *Journal of the Royal College of General Practitioners* 1969; **18**: 315–20.
2. McCulloch GL. Obituary. *British Medical Journal* 1983; **286**: 1986–7.
3. Abercrombie GF. Report of a symposium on the first year of life: the College motto. *Journal of the Royal College of General Practitioners* 1962; **5(Suppl 1)**: 45–6.
4. Clarke PS. *Cum scientia caritas*: 2. General practice as a caring discipline. *Medical Journal of Australia* 1992; **157**: 325–6.

Acknowledgements

I am indebted to everybody who has contributed to this book and to Helen Farrelly, RCGP Publications Manager, who has worked hard behind the scenes to ensure the book came to fruition.

Part I

Patients and the NHS

Chapter 1

Defining compassion in the new NHS

Harvey Ward

An account that is based on the personal experiences of NHS health care that he had in 2008 during his wife's end-of-life care.

I was thinking the other day about how I had the good fortune to become the Lay Chair of the Royal College of General Practitioners (RCGP) Patient and Carers Partnership Group (PCPG) in 2012. I realised that I owed it in great part to my wish nearly seven years ago to 'put something back into the NHS' after my wife Patricia decided on the catastrophic day we learned about her incurable lung cancer that she wanted to die at home with her family beside her. I agreed with her immediately, but had no idea if it was even possible. We had recently completed advance directives so there had been some discussion about our respective end-of-life wishes, but her diagnosis came out of the proverbial blue.

The fact that Patricia did die in our home with our three sons, their wives, our 3-month-old granddaughter and her mother present, and the fact that I had been well prepared for what was going to happen, was not only due to my wife's acceptance of her impending death but also the unfailing compassion of the NHS people that we met during her last three months of life.

About a year after Patricia's death I joined a local patient and public involvement group, and became involved in its activities motivated by a wish to ensure that other people could benefit from NHS compassion. I was alerted to a recruitment advertisement for lay members of the then RCGP Patient Partnership Group and soon after I had joined the RCGP in 2011 I realised that it was a very special organisation, unlike anything that I had ever previously encountered.

My working life before I finally retired in 2008 was mainly in public service as a teacher, then a local authority town planner, followed by ten years or so as a further education college lecturer and finally as a carer support worker. Generally these professional roles were focused upon personal advancement and also about dealing with groups of people – pupils and students and local communities. The exception was my intensely personal carer support role when providing regular one-to-one respite sessions for carers of people with Alzheimer's, Parkinson's and Huntington's diseases. The RCGP, on the other hand, being the professional membership body for family doctors in the UK and overseas, is populated by highly qualified professionals who spend their lives focused on worrying about creating health gain for people they do not know. My time as Lay Chair of the PCPG has made me realise that the RCGP's ethical foundation-stone is in fact 'compassion'.

The intimate relationship between 'compassion' and general practice is embodied in the College's '*Cum scientia caritas*' motto. As a lay person with no knowledge of Latin I am indebted to Dr D.L. Crombie, who translated the motto as 'Science with compassion' in his 1972 James Mackenzie Lecture.[1] He explained that the word 'compassion' has a complex meaning incorporating tenderness, loving care and what he described as 'feeling with' another human being. The authors of the 2009 King's Fund report *The Point of Care* define compassion as including 'empathy, respect, a recognition of the uniqueness of another individual and the willingness to enter into a relationship in which not only the knowledge but the intuitions, strengths, and emotions of both the patient and the physician can be fully engaged'.[2]

Dr Margaret McCartney in her book *The Patient Paradox* warns that 'doctors should [not] attempt to be priests or chaplains. Yet the understanding of what illness and disability mean to a person is fundamental to supporting and tailoring medical care to that person.'[3] Atul Gawande underlines an

> unresolved argument about what the function of medicine really is – the simple view is that medicine exists to fight death and disease, and that is, of course, its most basic task. Death is the enemy ... but the enemy has superior forces. Eventually it wins.[4]

I believe that Patricia's death was governed and guided by compassion that extended beyond herself to our whole family who, thanks to the NHS personnel we met, were included and welcomed as an essential part of the end-of-life care process. They understood what an incurable, then terminal, cancer diagnosis meant to a frightened family. We learned so much about palliative care from our GP and the oncology consultants, and in my wife's last week or so the palliative care team suggested that we embark upon the Liverpool Care Pathway. The processes involved in completing the various sections of that humane document enhanced every visiting health professional's knowledge of Patricia as a unique individual, about her advance directive and her personal wishes and beliefs.

Some months after Patricia's death I happened to meet one of the district nurses who had visited us several times and she commented that she and all her colleagues saw our family as something special and welcoming. I hope that the following vignettes will show how the compassion shown by members of the multidisciplinary team helped Patricia, myself and our family to cope with her 3-month-long final illness.

We had known our GP, Dr Woods, for over 30 years while we were bringing up our three sons and always respected him for straight talking, expertise and also a willingness to accept that our knowledge might even exceed his from time to time. Our three young sons contracted whooping cough one after the other and by the time that our youngest started he commented to Patricia –'Well, Mrs Ward, you are the expert so if you think that he has got whooping cough I'm sure you are right.'

I must admit though that I would not have described him as 'compassionate' until the week just before Christmas 2007 and thereafter until March 2008. He had been investigating Patricia's concerns about an incessant thirst through a series of inconclusive blood tests, but noted also that she had complained about 'flashing lights' before her eyes and then acute back pain. He arranged for an urgent X-ray at the local community hospital. Three days later Patricia visited the practice for another blood test and on her way out he rushed out of his office asking if she had ever had TB – 'because there is a shadow on your lung which could well be TB or a remnant of an old attack'.

Our immediate reaction was to cancel our usual big family Christmas because of the risk of passing on infection – especially for our first grandchild, born three weeks earlier. We shared a wonderful quiet Christmas – just my wife, myself and our youngest son who had only moved away a week before his mum became ill. We learned two months later from Dr Woods that he had decided to raise the possibility of TB rather than lung cancer. He explained that he thought that the GP's most difficult task was when and how to decide to break bad news. It is always so difficult to decide – shall I tell them today, are they in the right frame of mind or shall I leave it until next time? His thought in late December 2007 was, 'Why spoil their last Christmas?'

In January he started to visit us on alternate Saturday mornings purely to ask how we were coping and to discuss any problems that had arisen. I asked him on the first occasion, 'But isn't Saturday your day off?' He replied, 'Yes, yes, but it gives me a chance to do real doctoring away from the 10-minute consultations.' One important discussion was about our recent subscription to Dignitas in Switzerland prompted by Patricia's extreme pain, which could only be relieved for short periods. He listened carefully to our ideas and described the concept of palliative care. We had never heard of it so he was able to explain that pain control for cancer (Patricia's main desire) was relatively effective through palliative care rather more than for other illnesses like heart failure or COPD.

What was needed was to identify the most appropriate and amenable drug. This turned out to be oxycodone – a slow-release pill taken twice a day with liquid top-up as required. He was kind and compassionate enough later on to brief me on Fridays or Saturdays about the likely acceptable dosages that I could administer without reference to the out-of-hours service.

On other Saturday mornings we discussed Patricia's often very direct and penetrating questions – often about her likely life expectancy. He was able to tell us, two days after a brain tumour had been identified, that her likely life expectancy was less than three months. Patricia was really grateful to him because she valued unambiguous information, however uncomfortable it might seem. Some weeks later Patricia was bedbound but suffering new discomforts in her spine and legs. He offered to refer her for a scan and to consider possible radiotherapy, but readily accepted Patricia's opinion that there was no point in spending her last weeks undergoing fruitless treatment. We then had a long discussion about how doctors feel obliged to offer solutions in order to prolong life at any cost but how relieved he was that Patricia valued quality and not quantity of life. She and I had agreed that when sitting on the steps of the local hospital after learning about her incurable cancer.

Dr Woods referred Patricia immediately to the local respiratory clinic where we met the chest consultant on New Year's Eve. He briefly discussed the shadow on Patricia's X-ray and carried out a bronchoscopy three days later. Scans were organised quickly and we were soon asked to visit the oncology clinic. After an ultrasound kidney scan we were invited into a quiet side room off the main oncology outreach clinic where we met a young oncologist, Dr Faye Lim, and the hospital's Macmillan nurse. We were told sympathetically, calmly but with great clarity that Patricia had an incurable and inoperable lung cancer. The discussion was open with no rush for completion where we learned about chemotherapy and radiotherapy.

We were given the choice whether or not to accept treatment together with useful literature to take away and to let us know next week. Dr Lim made two light-hearted comments about drugs she was going to prescribe, including one she called 'Dynamite' for constipation and the other that we could probably make a fortune selling the unused drugs on Camden Market. Patricia really liked these direct jokes and told everyone about them.

Before the next clinic we were offered a PET scan but Patricia was so nauseous and ill during the weekend that we decided to refuse to attend. At the morning clinic Dr Lim was so concerned about Patricia's sickness that she arranged a brain scan for later the same afternoon. Normally the outreach clinic would close at lunchtime, but this time Dr Lim accompanied us to the scan unit, waited for the results and then, dragging a trolley of files behind her, ushered us into a side room. She told us quietly that a rapidly growing brain tumour had exacerbated Patricia's sickness. She was aware that we had decided against chemotherapy but also that Patricia valued quality of life over quantity.

The tumour would, within a week, take away Patricia's power of speech and her eyesight. The best way to avoid these terrible outcomes was five days of palliative radiotherapy starting the next afternoon at the regional cancer unit. In order to save time she wrote the directions to the cancer unit on the back of an envelope. Again, Patricia was buoyed up by the compassionate and direct care offered by Dr Lim. Next day, Patricia was extremely pleased to find her welcoming Patricia into the first registration session. My wife was prescribed steroids to take over the weekend but by Monday they had made Patricia agitated and shaky.

Once more, we were welcomed by Dr Lim, who immediately reduced the steroid dosages. Thereafter she checked with us every day until the completion of radiotherapy. The compassionate interest and personal involvement by Dr Lim was a great morale booster for Patricia, who was however exhausted after five radiotherapy sessions.

On our return home after the last session, our Macmillan nurse, who shared the direction of the palliative care team with Dr Woods, advised Patricia that she should have a 'duvet weekend', explaining that the exhaustion caused by five days of radiotherapy directed at Patricia's brain was only to be expected. In her subsequent weekly visits she took part in many difficult discussions including Patricia's question about how she would die. Quite accurately, she was told that she would get sleepier and sleepier.

Our friendly and resourceful Macmillan nurse added that it was her opinion that no one really dies until they are no longer talked about or remembered, and she was sure that our family would continue to talk about their mum for years. Even though Patricia and I had always been humanists this concept served to give us both some cheer.

A few weeks later Patricia asked the palliative care team leader to tell me when her death seemed to be imminent as we wanted all the family to be with us at that time. Three weeks before Patricia died our Macmillan nurse strongly recommended that I arrange Patricia's funeral as soon as possible in order to reassure her that her particular wishes (humanist funeral, woodland burial and a cardboard coffin painted by our youngest son) would be honoured. This seemed a daunting task but, just as the nurse had advised, it would have been impossible to arrange it after Patricia had died. In retrospect it seems incredible to me that these arrangements were made in Patricia's bedroom one morning in a discussion with the undertaker over cups of tea!

Carrying out the recommendation reassured my wife and contributed to the 'success' of her humanist funeral that is still talked about with our friends and neighbours. During Patricia's last week the palliative care team leader described the likely pattern of events to me – about the breathing problems and the tell-tale signs but especially how important it is to keep talking to a dying person because hearing is the last sense to go. She suggested certain topics that I might like to consider and be prepared for the last hours to keep talking, 'painting word pictures', and offering constant reassurances. Thanks to all this helpful advice my family was able to sit and listen, and share the experience of my speaking gently about our wonderful narrow-boat holidays during Patricia's last two hours of life.

Compassion is intimately involved with effective health care. Although my examples of compassionate health care are restricted to my wife's end-of-life palliative care I know, from speaking to them, that none of the healthcare professionals included in my story would see themselves as offering exceptional care. I am humbled by the thought that they produce these compassionate acts in their daily working life as a matter of course. They set a fine example for others to follow.

References

1. Crombie DL. *Practitioner* 1972; **22(114)**: 146–59. www.ncbi.nlm.nih.gov/pmc/articles/PMC2156513/ [accessed 4 December 2014].
2. Firth-Cozens J, Cornwell J. *The Point of Care: enabling compassionate care in acute hospital settings*. London: King's Fund, www.kingsfund.org.uk/sites/files/kf/field/field_publication_file/poc-enabling-compassionate-care-hospital-settings-apr09.pdf [accessed 4 December 2014].
3. McCartney M. *The Patient Paradox: why sexed-up medicine is bad for your health*. London: Pinter & Martin, 2012.
4. Gawande A. *Being Mortal: illness, medicine and what matters in the end*. London: Profile Books and Wellcome Collection, 2014.

Chapter 2

The NHS as the jewel in the national crown?

Helen J. Stokes-Lampard

The metaphor

The nostalgia, pomp and ceremony of the start of the Olympic Games in 2012 served as the perfect foil to the sense of justice and community that the whole games had brought to the UK following the worst period of financial austerity in recent memory. As the lighting dimmed in the stadium the world looked on faintly bemused as hospital beds whirled onto the arena floor and Britons' eyes brimmed with tears of pride at 'our NHS'. The collective sigh of contentment that 'Whatever else we may fail at, my goodness it's good to be British' accompanied a tacit acknowledgement that we do know that our NHS is one of the greatest jewels in our national crown. There was discreet, smug satisfaction in the knowledge that our international cousins would pause and wonder, and that we sleep well at night without worrying how we will fund our next brush with the medical profession.

The concept of 'a jewel in the crown' is a phrase borrowed from another time. In the twenty-first century, genuine crowns live in museums or remain locked securely in glass cases apart from occasional ceremonial occasions; they are not visible in the real world. Gems are things of beauty, rare, admirable and very precious. They are not accessible to the general population and do not serve great practical purpose. Thus the metaphor fails dismally to capture the essence of what the NHS has been, is and could be for the UK. To suggest that its value is based around admiration at a distance is selling it too short, and overstating its beauty – the NHS is so much more and so much less than a jewel in a national crown.

Accountants, management consultants and scientists argue that the NHS needs to be a sleek warship, a no-frills service, pared back, functional, efficient and good, really good, at meeting a pre-specified brief. However, humans are infinitely complex: in addition to multiple physical and functional limitations we are beset by mental fragility and our social constructs, new societies and environment are not conducive to managing the wellbeing of these elements. Thus the 'sleek warship' model of health care, although comparable to a working diamond, like a drill-bit tip, may be exactly right in the setting for acute trauma and medical/surgical emergencies, and may even suffice for early-stage cancer diagnosis and management, but holistic, patient-centred care and the sophistication of the human soul requires so much more from the NHS if we genuinely aspire to provide a service for the wellbeing of our UK population.

THE REALITY

The apparently insoluble dilemma for governments and policy-makers is the tension between scientific and medical advances pushing ever forward, an increasingly ageing and expanding population, and rising population expectations of what the NHS can and should provide. To provide for the wishes of every patient, healthcare professional and vested interest would rapidly lead to bankrupting the UK; rationing of care and services is not a potential threat in the distant future but is the very core of service delivery in the NHS now – it has to be. The multiplicity of guideline and protocol development agencies is a testimony to this. The new NHS contract, implemented in April 2013,[1] was an attempt to allow front-line clinicians to control the allocation and flow of resources. However, political and medical neurosis led to extensive modification and dilution of the bill so that what transpired was a seismic reorganisation but without the authority to make significant and necessary changes that could lead to improvement, and so the cycle continues.

So, can the NHS be legitimately described as a jewel in the national crown? It is certainly viewed that way by some, particularly when viewed through the rose-tinted spectacles of those who have had life-saving treatment or who have benefitted from long-term support from a trusted, respected healthcare professional. An Ipsos MORI poll in 2013 confirmed that the NHS is the UK institution that makes the general population proudest to be British.[2] Indeed the Commonwealth Fund report of 2014 is a stark reminder that, although we may bemoan the failings of the NHS, it is considerably better than many alternatives.[3] So what we have is an NHS that works better than other systems. However, all jewels benefit from regular cleaning and occasionally re-setting the gems to fit current requirements and future demands. Perhaps it is time to clean up our NHS and look afresh at the potential it contains.

When patients consult their GP with new concerns we know that their assortment of organic problems is invariably overlaid with their unique social and psychological dimensions. The complexity of real life in the twenty-first century means that the lack of trusted communities, lack of spiritual sustenance and lack of family networks have led to a famine of support for the psychological wellbeing of our patients, and that is where a successful NHS may indeed shine as a jewel to the vulnerable who seek help. However, the current GP consultation model no longer fits the needs of patients or their clinicians; to do justice to the holistic needs of our patients takes a remarkable set of skills but also requires sufficient time in which to utilise them appropriately.

The lack of time factored into current NHS systems to deliver the standard of care that most healthcare professionals aspire to deliver is a leading cause of disillusionment and burnout.[4] The ten-minute consultation, which has been standard practice throughout UK general practice since at least the introduction of the Quality and Outcomes Framework (QOF) of 2004, is no longer fit for purpose. In a primary healthcare service that attempts to shoehorn a host of standardised, protocol-driven questions and measurements into a 'standard appointment', something will be lost. The patient's full agenda and the provision of truly patient-centred care may involve areas that the patient had not envisaged (such as incidental findings and the exploration of psychosocial issues).

Applicants for medical school today are as idealistic, aspirational, intelligent and enthusiastic as ever, and the established, but increasingly cynical, profession needs their youth and vision to help retain both the professionalism and compassion that our patients deserve. Generation Y has a lot to teach Generation X and the Baby Boomers about how we work best together; we would do well to listen.[5]

Generational research has demonstrated interesting findings about the workforce. This has relevance to the NHS, which employs healthcare professionals across the full age range. The Baby Boomers, who, by dint of their experience and age, represent the majority of 'leaders' in the UK currently, are well suited to this responsibility with overall higher scores on strategic thinking and traditional leadership traits. However, there are notable differences between the generations that will inevitably affect working patterns and relationships in future: Generation X are frequently natural diplomats, educating upwards and innovating downwards. Generations X and Y are more individualist and are better at creative and abstract thinking, and are more socially responsive and people orientated, which is why they have embraced social media opportunities with such enthusiasm. Generation Y are more altruistic and people orientated than their elders. All of these attributes should be nurtured to ensure the NHS thrives and retains its 'sparkle'.

Note: Baby Boomers 1946–64; Generation X 1965–79; Generation Y 1980–94; Generation Z 1995. …

The future

With the release of the latest five-year plan for the NHS in England,[6] it is beholden on all healthcare professionals to think afresh about what models of care are appropriate and fit for the future. We are warned that '1000 flowers' cannot be permitted to bloom, but we are also encouraged to offer up creative solutions to fit the diverse needs of our nation, to manage demand and improve efficiency. In return NHS England has committed to stabilising core funding and upgrading primary care infrastructure.

The workforce crisis in general practice is symptomatic of problems throughout the NHS following a long period of austerity where healthcare budgets have been frozen or risen only marginally at a time of population growth, greater longevity and rising demand from patients. UK PLC may be back 'in the black' but the NHS and other public sectors are still being punished financially so the demoralised workforce fears yet more change and many are retiring prematurely or seeking opportunities abroad, with numbers applying for proof of registration prior to emigration from the General Medical Council rising every year since 2010.[7]

The NHS has historically been used as a political plaything. Politicians, keen to leave their mark in the short term between national elections, can't resist making attempts at 'improvement' and so are focused on 'quick wins'. However, increasingly, high-quality models of care are being demonstrated to require many years to have maximal impact. The Alzira model of health care in Valencia, Spain, has operated since 2003. It provides an integrated and efficient health service with a single provider responsible for the entire range of health care that is delivered to the population. However, this is on the understanding that there would be no political interference and a long-term payback for return on investment.

The Royal College of General Practitioners commissioned an independent inquiry into patient-centred care in the twenty-first century,[8] which confirmed that people with long-term conditions (rather than diseases that can be cured) are the main users of health care and this is predicted to grow considerably. One key finding is that patient care is not delivered consistently, often due to artificial barriers between services structured around a single disease focus rather than the needs of the individual. However, the report is also positive about the future if bold moves are made now to change the focus of our work:[8]

> Care that is holistic, empowering and that recognises the individual's priorities and needs is ... particularly vital to those with long term conditions ... re-orienting the health and care system around a patient centred approach has the potential not only to improve health outcomes and quality of life ... but also to reduce avoidable demand ... and thereby help place the NHS on a sustainable financial footing.

An inevitable consequence of change throughout the NHS will be the re-negotiation of the doctor–patient contract. The traditional paternalistic model of the patient giving up control to experts in exchange for medical care and professionalism no longer fits with the burden of illness the NHS is treating. Chronic disease management lends itself to greater patient autonomy, self-care and personal responsibility for health. Thus a new agenda that involves substantial empowerment of the patient needs to be embraced, not feared, by healthcare professionals. An NHS that can evolve to adopt this shift will thrive and survive; an NHS that clings to faded glories is destined for the museum.

Summary

A 'jewel in the national crown' is just a metaphor, imperfect and limited in scope, but it can provide a useful framework around which to consider the current relationship of the NHS with the British public. This is not an ancient set of gems locked behind glass, but working jewels that sparkle when viewed at their best. However, the NHS needs constant attention to ensure that it is fit for purpose in an ever-changing landscape.

It is now time to re-set the gems that comprise the NHS into a modern setting that will provide a service for the future that is run effectively and efficiently. This is a service that will fulfil the needs of patients and that provides the maximum amount of high-quality care for the resources available, and which is constantly learning from itself and other healthcare organisations.

The most distinctive gems, which are the true beauty of our NHS and set it apart from other healthcare services globally, include the continuity of care provided through trusted relationships between patients and their GPs over many years, the provision of highly qualified healthcare professionals throughout the service who understand and work to address the needs of the whole patient, and a universal healthcare service that remains free at the point of clinical need. To remove any of these gems would diminish the whole NHS and tarnish the crown.

References

1. The NHS structure explained. www.nhs.uk/NHSEngland/thenhs/about/Pages/nhsstructure.aspx [accessed 16 November 2014].
2. Ipsos MORI. *State of the Nation 2013*. www.ipsos-mori.com/researchpublications/researcharchive/3111/State-of-the-Nation-2013.aspx [accessed 29 October 2014].
3. Davis K, Stremikis K, Squires D, Schoen C. *Mirror, Mirror on the Wall: how the performance of the US health care system compares internationally*. New York, NY: The Commonwealth Fund, 2014, www.commonwealthfund.org/~/media/files/publications/fund-report/2014/jun/1755_davis_mirror_mirror_2014.pdf [accessed 29 October 14].
4. Orton P, Orton C, Pereira-Gray D. Depersonalised doctors: a cross-sectional study of 564 doctors, 760 consultations and 1876 patient reports in UK general practice. *BMJ Open* 2012; DOI: 10.1136/bmjopen-2011-000274.
5. Hudson. *The Great Generational Shift: why the difference between generations will reshape your workforce*. http://au.hudson.com/latest-thinking/the-generational-shift [accessed 21 April 2015].
6. Stephens S. *Five Year Forward View*. NHS, 2014, www.england.nhs.uk/wp-content/uploads/2014/10/5yfv-web.pdf [accessed 29 October 2014].
7. General Medical Council. *The State of Medical Education and Practice*. London: GMC, 2014, www.gmc-uk.org/SOMEP_2014_FINAL.pdf_58751753.pdf [accessed 21 April 2015].
8. Royal College of General Practitioners. *An Inquiry into Patient Centred Care in the 21st Century: implications for general practice and primary care*. London: RCGP, 2014, www.rcgp.org.uk/policy/rcgp-policy-areas/~/media/Files/Policy/A-Z-policy/RCGP-Inquiry-into-Patient-Centred-Care-in-the-21st-Century.ashx [accessed 21 April 2015].

Chapter 3

Access and the great socioeconomic divide

Dirk Pilat

If you would walk through the streets of Tower Hamlets – a severely deprived borough in East London – on a weekday at around 8 a.m. in the morning, you would frequently come across well-ordered queues of locals waiting patiently in front of the door of their GP practice. Some bring their chairs, some bring their breakfast, some both and make a picnic of it. The anxiety of not getting an appointment with their GP for either themselves or a family member is an incentive for them get up at seven (often after a night shift) and queue for an hour, often just to get that cough checked. If they don't make it to the very beginning of the queue, it is likely that they are being told to try again in a few days, take an appointment in a week or visit their local walk-in centre.

To paraphrase Norman Beale, there is overwhelming evidence that deprivation and good health do not share a duvet, even in 2015,[1] but this is a street scene that is not limited to Tower Hamlets but common across the four nations and likely to get worse.[2] Across the UK access to primary care has deteriorated even though individual GPs are offering more appointments than ever and the majority of us now see 40 to 60 patients per day.[2] Unfortunately the picture that some of our elected representatives and parts of the popular press paint about the efforts of GPs to give their patients access to services differs very much from the view at the coal face. Various political and press entities blame the existing primary care providers for a lackadaisical approach to access or even laziness.[3] It seems GPs just can't win.

Definitions of need

But what is it that makes access such a vexed issue for patients and GPs? There must be some sort of theoretical framework around the issue that could give the GP on the brink of burnout a leg up to redesign his (or more likely her) appointment system to make the punters happy? It comes as no surprise that the framework around need and demand for health care has already been visited by commentators from social scientists to health economists, and remains controversial. For the social policy scientist Jonathan Bradshaw, there are four separate definitions of need:[4]

- *Nominative Need* – which is the need that the experts (e.g. health policy-makers) decide is the actual, rational need for the services offered
- *Felt Need* – this is what the practice population feels is necessary
- *Expressed Need* – this is what the patients tell you should be provided for them
- *Comparative Need* – this factors in the impact of local characteristics such as deprivation and the other social determinants of health.

The health economists Roy Penchansky and William Thomas unsurprisingly define the variables around access as a market-orientated supply and demand model. They characterise care using five criteria:[5]

- *availability* – the relationship between available services and the volume of patients and their needs
- *accessibility* – the relationship between the location of the point of care and the means of patients to get there (and in 2014 primary care's ability to offer services online and via the phone)
- *accommodation* – the relationship between the operational set-up of the practice and the patient's perception of appropriateness of the provision
- *affordability* – the relationship between the cost of care and the ability of patients to pay for those. At present this is not such a problem for actual health provision in the UK, but transport costs, non-NHS fees and prescription surcharges can significantly limit a patient's ability to access appropriate health care
- *acceptability* – the relationship between a patient's perception of his or her health-care providers, and – just as important – the healthcare providers' perception of their clients.

Increased demand for primary care

There is an obvious connection between Bradshaw's explanation of need and Penchansky and Thomas's description of the variables that regulate access: all of them are intricately entangled and not easily separated; all are influenced by a vast range of factors only too familiar to every GP. These factors are the local socioeconomic and ethnic profile, health literacy, health-seeking behaviour and of course the provision of funds from their respective devolved governments. At a time when overall government spending for primary care has been declining since 2005 – hitting its lowest point in 2014[6] – it is unsurprisingly difficult for GPs to offer appropriate access just when the UK is bucking a European trend, delivering an uncharacteristic baby boom with an increase in population of 5 million since 2001. Add to that an increased demand for primary care due to an ageing patient load with an ever increasing range of co-morbidities, we have a perfect storm.

This doesn't mean that GPs aren't trying. The vast majority of primary care doctors joined the profession to follow the mandate of Aneurin Bevan and the Attlee government, which had a strong egalitarian ethos and initiated their radical changes to the UK's healthcare provision to deliver excellent, free health care for patients. And so we are continuing to put in the hours to meet these goals. Even the 2001 NHS Constitution reminds us to provide a comprehensive service to all, based on clinical need.[7]

The ever rising demand

Even though they might be trying their best, GPs are often not in control of the reasons for the ever rising demand in their area. Higher rates of GP consultations are associated with greater deprivation and with lower socioeconomic patient groups[8] but, to make things worse, patients living in the most deprived areas have a higher prevalence of multi-morbidity and longstanding conditions, creating a crisis for the local primary care services.[9] The immediacy of perception of educationally deprived patients puts a strain on appointment systems and greatly increases out-of-hours workload, which is often compounded by patients' lack of access to transport, the internet and a telephone.[10]

Due to the nature of primary care, GPs have few options to change the way their patients access their services. For some years now practices have made attempts to regulate access to appointments via either a GP- or nurse-led telephone triage scheme. Although phone triage can lead to a reduction in face-to-face consultations, it does not reduce overall workload. However, it changes the nature of the workload and does not offer any significant cost reductions.[11] Practices can attempt to divert patients with a limited spectrum of acute, self-limiting conditions to different providers of health care such as community pharmacies, and although this seems to reduce consultations for this limited spectrum of problems it again does not seem to reduce overall workload.[12]

Practices can try to further increase the number of appointments they offer by trimming personal development sessions and reducing consultation time. However, this is likely to be to the detriment of the quality and outcomes of the care delivered, and with negative consequences on perceived job stress by GPs.[13] The kind of desperate decisions made during partnership meetings in the face of overwhelming demand surfaced in 2014. In a rather dramatic gesture, one partnership in Yorkshire and another in Devon wrote to patients suggesting they stay away from the respective practices as, due to overwhelming patient demand, they were not able to provide safe care any more.[14,15]

Any solutions are complex

At this point in the chapter it is now pretty obvious that the issue of access to primary care services in the UK is a multifaceted one. There are no obvious solutions in the current financial climate as it is unlikely that we are going to be able to recruit ourselves out of the crisis. More success is likely to be had by reducing Bradshaw's 'Felt Need' and the health economists' 'acceptability' variables. Negative social determinants of health and lack of functional and critical health literacy are the likely reasons for the increased access rate. They should be the initial starting points in the search for a solution to address inadequate health-seeking behaviour. If central or local government's impact on the improvement of the social determinants of health is not adequate to influence local health-seeking behaviour, GPs are likely left to fend for themselves and change the lives of their patients for the better without an FP-10. This is of course in addition to the positive public health effect that having a GP practice within the vicinity of a neighbourhood already has.[16]

'DIY Health' sessions project

An interesting intervention was initiated by a practice in Tower Hamlets, which, with UCL Partners, started to introduce 'DIY Health' sessions in cooperation with parents who particularly frequently attended. Co-production was the chosen methodology as it gave patients the opportunity to work in partnership with professionals to build resilience in the community through education. Their aim was to place health promotion in a learning environment using participatory action learning techniques as the method of delivery. This ensures the effective transfer of knowledge, skills and capabilities that surround key child health messages to parents. They arranged group sessions to provide an opportunity to practise skills in a safe environment together with other parents. Their attempts at co-production also enabled the development of a shared curriculum that met the needs of both patients and health professionals. After the first cohort of the programme there was a significant increase in access to the Pharmacy First schemes, and parents who had attended the most sessions showed a reduced attendance pattern for GP, out-of-hours and A&E contacts.[17]

Targeting the needs of the local population

Initiatives like this do not have to be limited to child health but can extend to all social determinants of health, with the GP practice a hub for all of the neighbourhood's needs, from educational provision to help with legal, financial and housing issues. Initiatives such as those run by Bromley-by-Bow Centre have demonstrated that they can positively influence all aspects of a community's wellbeing in cooperation with local primary care. It has at its core services that target the needs of the local population as defined by a number of key indicators including local health indicators (on areas related to public health, lifestyle, wellbeing and mental health and clinical health) and indicators relating to the social determinants of health, including poverty, skills, employment, social connections, housing conditions and financial concerns. The Centre's programmes link clinical health as delivered in a primary care practice with a range of provision that supports healthy lifestyles, wellbeing and mental health improvement with a range of programmes that support the improvements in the social determinants of health.[18]

Social prescribing

So, could engagement with the third sector be the solution to our access problems? There is now growing anecdotal evidence that social prescribing in primary care can reduce attendance by giving patients a broader choice of services to engage with.[19] If practices, by starting to use social prescribing, could reduce the frequency of attendances of those patients with the most visits to the practice, a significant amount of appointments would be freed: frequent attenders, defined as those who consult their GP more than 12 times in a year, represent over 15% of the average GP's workload. If practices with access problems could reduce attendance of those frequent attenders by one visit a year, they would achieve a reduction of 1% of their workload,[20] certainly a number to ponder on.

Health-seeking behaviour – the future

In a time when even the Secretary of State for Health would rather take his children to A&E than wait for a GP appointment,[21] it is unlikely that central and local government are going to come to our and our patients' aid and solve the ever growing demand for primary care services. Only by tackling the roots of inappropriate health-seeking behaviour will the pressure on primary care in the UK reduce, and engagement with the local third-sector service providers looks like the most promising solution. Otherwise we will be sooner or later all writing letters to our patients, asking them to stay away if at all possible.

References

1. Beale N. Unequal to the task: deprivation, health and UK general practice at the millennium. *British Journal of General Practice* 2001; **51(467)**: 478–85.
2. Royal College of General Practitioners. Waiting times to see a GP now a 'national crisis'. 2014. www.rcgp.org.uk/news/2014/september/waiting-times-to-see-a-gp-now-a-national-crisis.aspx [accessed 25 October 2014].
3. Parsons S. Can no one force GPs to do their job properly? 2013. www.dailymail.co.uk/debate/article-2328709/SANDRA-PARSONS-Can-force-GPs-job-properly.html [accessed 25 October 2014].
4. Bradshaw J. The taxonomy of social need. In: R Cookson, R Sainsbury, C Glendinning (eds). *Jonathan Bradshaw on Social Policy: selected writings 1972–2011*. York: University of York, 2013, pp. 1–6.
5. Penchansky R, Thomas JW. The concept of access: definition and relationship to consumer satisfaction. *Medical Care* 1981; **19(2)**: 127–40.
6. Royal College of General Practitioners. *Put Patients First: back general practice*. London: RCGP, 2014.
7. Department of Health, 2013. Principles and values that guide the NHS. www.nhs.uk/NHSEngland/thenhs/about/Pages/nhscoreprinciples.aspx [accessed 20 October 2014].
8. Goddard M, Smith P. Equity of access to health care services: theory and evidence from the UK. *Social Science and Medicine* 2001; **53(9)**: 1149–62.
9. Barnett K, Mercer SW, Norbury M, *et al*. Epidemiology of multimorbidity and implications for health care, research, and medical education: a cross-sectional study. *Lancet* 2012; **380(9836)**: 37–43.
10. Main J, Main P. Jarman Index (Letter). *British Medical Journal* 1991; **302**: 850–1.
11. Campbell, D. Devon GP surgery accused of trying to deny treatments to patients. *Guardian*, 1 December 2014.
12. Hassel K, Whittington Z, Cantrill J, *et al*. Managing demand: transfer of management of self limiting conditions from general practice to community pharmacies. *British Medical Journal* 2001; **323(7305)**: 146–7.

13. van den Hombergh P, Künzi B, Elwyn G, *et al*. High workload and job stress are associated with lower practice performance in general practice: an observational study in 239 general practices in the Netherlands. *BMC Health Services Research* 2009; **9**: 118.
14. Perry K. It's not safe for you here, GP surgery tells patients. *Telegraph*, 7 August 2014.
15. Campbell JL, Fletcher E, Britten N, *et al*. Telephone triage for management of same-day consultation requests in general practice (the ESTEEM trial): a cluster-randomised controlled trial and cost-consequence analysis. *Lancet* 2014; **384(9957)**:1859–68.
16. Starfield B, Shi L, Macinko J. Contribution of primary care to health systems and health. *The Milbank Quarterly* 2005; **83(3)**: 457–502.
17. Self Care Forum. DIY Health: a coproduced health education delivery model to empower parents in managing children's health. 2011. www.selfcareforum.org/wp-content/uploads/2011/07/DIYHealthBBBHPcasestudy.pdf [accessed 11 November 2014].
18. Smith J, Holder H, Edwards H, *et al*. *Securing the Future of General Practice: new models of primary care*. London: Nuffield Trust, 2013.
19. Longwill A. *Independent Evaluation of the Hackney WellFamily Service*. London: Family Action, 2014.
20. Heywood PL, Blackie GC, Cameron IH, Dowell AC. An assessment of the attributes of frequent attenders to general practice. *Family Practice* 1998; **15(3)**: 198–204.
21. Donnelly L. Jeremy Hunt: I take my children to A&E because GP wait takes too long. *Telegraph*, 25 November 2014.

Chapter 4

What's love got to do with it?
Learning compassion for medical practice

Amanda Howe

Defining love

C.S. Lewis, in his book *The Four Loves*,[1] differentiates the love of family and kin, the mutuality of friendship, and the attractions of romantic love, from the fourth love '*agape*'. This is 'the highest level of love known to humanity – a selfless love, a love that is passionately committed to the well-being of the other, because they are human'.

Another word for such a love is compassion:

> made up of two words, 'co' meaning together and 'passion' meaning a strong feeling. And this is what compassion is. When we see someone in distress and we feel their pain as if it were our own, and strive to eliminate or lessen their pain, then this is compassion.[2]

Empathy

This resonates strongly with Stewart Mercer's definition of empathy,[3] though he focuses it more on the needs of the clinical encounter:

> Clinical empathy involves an ability to: (a) understand the patient's situation, perspective, and feelings (and their attached meanings); (b) to communicate that understanding and check its accuracy; and (c) to act on that understanding with the patient in a helpful (therapeutic) way.

The construct of empathy is routinely taught to most healthcare professionals, often linked with behavioural skills that allow patients to feel listened to and understood.[4] In most accounts compassion is broader than empathy, often being linked to a more value-driven aspect. Interestingly Mercer's work, which is now more than a decade old, also picks this up in his definition of the moral dimension involved in true empathy:[3]

1 *Emotive* – the ability to subjectively experience and share in another's psychological state or feelings
2 *Moral* – an internal altruistic orientation that motivates the practice of empathy
3 *Cognitive* – the helper's intellectual ability to identify and understand (analyse) another person's feelings and perspective from an objective stance
4 *Behavioural* – ability to convey understanding of another's perspective.

THE ROLE OF MEDICAL TEACHERS

My conclusion is that what we need to do as medical educators is to develop a professional kind of compassionate love, and that what we are trying to achieve is a routine practice where our learners get up to the top of Miller's hierarchy[5] – that they can be truly empathic with their patients, and their response is embedded and *professional* enough not to 'fault out' when the going gets tough. So if we want to help our learners learn to be compassionate, first of all, what do we know about how to do that? And then, what else must we do to enable them to sustain that in practice?

Maslow's hierarchy of needs[6] reminds us that learners will not deliver at this high level without first of all being made safe in their new identity. This means having built their confidence in their own actions through a supportive/caring set of relationships, which enables them to grow and develop to their maximum potential. We also know that they will look to us to act consistently with the goals that we expect them to achieve. So it is unlikely that they will attain a truly empathic state on a consistent level unless they see their trainers and senior colleagues around them delivering on this, and are themselves treated with empathy (indeed, compassion) as they go through their training cycle with its ups and downs.[7]

So what kind of love, or compassion, is needed in an educational relationship? There are probably elements of at least three of the four mentioned earlier. When a young person declares his or her intention to be a doctor, or enters training, we immediately treat this person as 'family' – a special bond engendered by our common identity, part of the same community. That leads to inclusion, attention, encouragement, social networks and the start of them being treated as 'a doctor'.

Then there is a degree of friendship – reciprocal give and take, sharing of experiences, and with some a warmer mutual relationship over time. But the greatest of these I think is *agape*, which is the respectful and unconditional love we have to give to any learner in our student group, our new trainee, our new team member – just because he or she is 'our learner' and we have a duty of care to help this person grow.

This of course is not unconditional love. Just as with patients, we have to set boundaries and challenges, and to make judgements, while still preserving our fundamental aim to nurture them and motivate them to be the best they can be – building self-esteem even if their capacity shows limits over time. This is a hard one, especially where summative judgements are concerned. But it is probably in those most vulnerable, defensive, confused moments when learners most benefit from a genuine compassion that waits and watches, and is persistent in its efforts to move things forward.

Compassion in clinical practice

So we need to be compassionate at the highest level with our learners for them to be compassionate in turn. Now this is a pretty big ask for both parties, especially faced with the significant workloads and demands of modern clinical practice. And clearly compassion, if it leads to endless giving, is actually a risk factor for the kinds of ill health we see in many health professionals.[8]

So we also need to build protective mechanisms that allow compassion to be sustained over time – in our work as educators, and in our work with patients. Three things can help here: the explicit building of resilience during training and career development;[9] the modelling of boundaries (including a work–life balance); and building compassion into organisations at a systems level, to maintain health for all.

A short selection of tactics at individual level are as follows:

- enhance self-efficacy – teach and practise coping with stress, give people meaningful tasks and feedback, and show them that persistence pays off
- mentoring/tutoring – focus on planning, managing anxiety, longer-term goals and feedback on coping skills
- design graded challenges – building resilience over time through increasing complexity of tasks
- develop individual motivation – allow some choice, control and autonomy
- role models – reflect on resilient individuals and show how it isn't easy!
- recognise and acknowledge stressors
- develop conscious coping strategies
- have medical care for yourself as a patient
- regular reflection on practice with supervision/support
- improve your workplace culture and work–life balance
- moderate over-idealistic professional expectations.[10]

Conclusion

The twenty-first century is not a place where compassion is part of the daily culture, and we have to learn what it means to care in a professional, selfless way. Medicine is intensely competitive at selection, it is a tough working environment, and there is a potentially risky culture where burnout and brutalisation can occur. It is also a wonderful job where, as Nelson Mandela foresaw:

> Our human compassion binds us the one to the other – not in pity or patronizingly, but as human beings who have learnt how to turn our common suffering into hope for the future.[11]

We need to be 'good enough parents'[12] to bring our learners through the stages of ego and insecurity to a stable, independent adulthood where they can, late at night and tired to the bone, be bothered to stop and listen to the unspoken question on the lips of the patient whose drip they are re-siting. Or even to hold their hand for comfort.

References

1. Lewis CS. *The Four Loves*. London: Geoffrey Bles, 1960.
2. Dhammasaavaka Mestre RJ. *The Buddhism Primer: an introduction to Buddhism*. 2005.
3. Mercer SW, Reynolds WJ. Empathy and quality of care. *British Journal of General Practice* 2002; **52(Suppl)**: S9–S12.
4. Silverman J, Kurtz S, Draper J. *Teaching and Learning Communication Skills in Medicine*. Oxford and San Francisco: Radcliffe, 1998.
5. Miller GE. The assessment of clinical skills/competence/performance. *Academic Medicine* 1990; **65(9 Suppl)**: S63–S67.
6. Maslow AH. A theory of human motivation. *Psychological Review* 1943; **50(4)**: 370–96.
7. Howe A. Patient-centred medicine through student-centred teaching: a student perspective on the key impacts of community-based learning in undergraduate medical education. *Medical Education* 2001; **35**: 666–72.
8. Department of Health. *Mental Health and Ill Health in Doctors*. London: DH, 2008, http://webarchive.nationalarchives.gov.uk/20130107105354/http://www.dh.gov.uk/prod_consum_dh/groups/dh_digitalassets/@dh/@en/documents/digitalasset/dh_083090.pdf [accessed 12 June 2015].
9. Howe A, Smajdor A, Stöckl A. Towards an understanding of resilience and its relevance to medical training. *Medical Education* 2012; DOI: 10.1111/j.1365-2923.2011.04188.x.
10. Howe A. Doctors' health and wellbeing. Keynote lecture, Wonca World Conference Prague, 26 June 2013, www.globalfamilydoctor.com/site/DefaultSite/filesystem/documents/miscellaneous/Prague/PragueAHowe.pdf [accessed 24 April 2015].
11. Mandela N. Thoughts on hope and overcoming adversity. www.jewelsofhappiness.com/thoughts-on-hope-and-overcoming-adversity-by-nelson-mandela/ [accessed 24 April 2015].
12. Bettelheim B. *The Good Enough Parent*. New York: Random House, 1987.

Chapter 5

Communication as the key to compassion

Rupal Shah

> May I never see in the patient anything but a fellow creature in pain. May I never consider him merely a vessel of disease.
>
> (Maimonides, a twelfth-century philosopher, rabbi and doctor)[1]

Compassion, a 'sympathetic pity and concern for the sufferings or misfortunes of others', is engendered by empathy. It relies on trying to understand what it is like to be in the other person's shoes, trying to understand what has brought the patient to see you, and why the patient's problem is causing him or her distress. In essence, compassion is the attempt to connect with the other person by acknowledging and affirming our common humanity.

Connecting with the patient

All doctors, but GPs in particular, rely on communication skills to help them understand why the patient in front of them is there at this particular time. Often there is the obvious problem but, underlying this, there are layers of subtext. A good doctor will try to explore this murkier ground, to get a better understanding of the patient.

Our communication skills are comprised of the non-verbal as well as the verbal. When we talk about the importance of 'connecting' with the patient at the beginning of the consultation, much of this is done without needing to say anything in particular, or perhaps anything at all.

A smile, eye contact, open body language – all the outward signs that show we are open to what the patient is going to tell us may set the scene better than words. Reinforcing this sense that we are on the patient's side, as the patient's advocate, is a good starting point in any consultation.

Perhaps it is worthwhile to reconsider our opening gambit? 'How can I help?' implies a linear pattern to the consultation, which will ideally end with the doctor finding a solution for the patient's problem.

Reality isn't always as neat, and allowing the patient to start the consultation or opening with something less directive may go some way towards acknowledging this inherent ambiguity.

Compassion in history taking

Many of the successful consultation models talk about the importance of establishing why the patient has come and working out a mutually agreeable management plan, which is understood by both parties, and with terms of follow-up specified. The RCGP's Consultation Observation Tool (COT) assessments for the MRCGP require the doctor to enquire about psychosocial aspects of the patient's problem. I have often seen trainees ask the right questions, but then fail to take into account what they have been told later on in the consultation. This is perhaps because the questions are being used to tick the requisite boxes for the purposes of assessment rather than emanating from a desire to understand.

There is a difference between asking questions and really taking an interest in the answers, using this knowledge to try to imagine how the problem might be affecting the patient. It all comes down to the practice of active listening, in which questions and comments from the doctor are said with the aim of helping the patient to tell his or her story. Active listening is likely to result in cues being picked up and the patient's agenda being discovered. This type of listening is ultimately a demonstration of respect for the patient and is different from superficial listening. In the latter the doctor decides the patient's story by making various assumptions about the underlying problem, regardless of what the patient has actually said, and uses gaps in the conversation to return to his or her own version of the narrative.

Narrative-based medicine

John Launer put forward the idea of narrative-based medicine – using conversation to explore the patient's story, which is so much more than the history of his or her presenting complaint.[2] Unless we have the background and a sense of the story of the person sitting in front of us, it is hard to feel empathy and therefore hard to feel compassion. When we are in a rush, running late or distracted by computer alerts popping up on our screens, the patient runs the risk of becoming reduced to his or her problem and nothing more. How can we feel compassion for a chest infection or osteoarthritis? We can only feel compassion if we actually see the patient, try to understand what it is like to be him or her, and become aware of how the patient's medical complaint is affecting the flow of his or her life.

Communication is the tool by which we gain this understanding and, importantly, make the patient feel that we are trying to understand. The mutual awareness of trying to establish understanding is a powerful determinant of how well the consultation will go, even if ultimately we can't solve the problem or explain it within a medical paradigm. We can help this process by not maintaining a degree of reserve/aloofness or hiding behind medical terminology, thereby creating an artificial distance between ourselves and the patient.

Authenticity is considered an important attribute of a good doctor and this quality seems to be one of the prerequisites of maintaining a compassionate approach. Not being afraid to reveal something of ourselves is a powerful way of creating trust.

The increasing importance of the doctor's agenda

There is the paradox of trying to show compassion in the face of what is the ever increasing importance of the doctor's agenda, with information to be captured for the Quality and Outcomes Framework, Quality and Productivity indicators and other Directed Enhanced Services and Local Enhanced Services. Even without these incentive schemes, the doctor has his or her own agenda – usually to understand the problem quickly and come up with a solution, so that the appointment flows within the constructs we are comfortable with and the doctor runs to time. Sometimes, though, it is necessary to suspend our own agenda, to stop looking for a solution, but to come alongside the patient. Perhaps we need to voice what we have sensed but tried to ignore in the interests of efficiency – for example, acknowledging that someone looks upset, worried or angry.

Launer talked about using the seven 'Cs' when taking a *narrative-based history*:

- conversation
- curiosity
- context
- complexity
- challenge
- care
- caution.

It is a change in mindset to think about the process of gathering information within history taking as being a conversation with the patient, but conversations can often be more informative than direct questioning. Reframing what we do in this way is likely to make us more compassionate to our patients and better doctors.

In terms of these seven Cs, doctors usually do care for their patients and are aware of when to exercise caution and when to challenge something. However, curiosity and complexity are sometimes forgotten. Being curious about the patient's motivations, thoughts and how the patient has tried to explain the problem to him or herself, and what the patient's family think about it, can all help to contextualise the problem. It also makes the job of being a doctor much more interesting. I mention complexity because it is so important to remember that everybody's story is complex, intricate and multifaceted. There are always many reasons why people end up in the situation they find themselves in, physically and mentally.

Communicating with compassion in difficult circumstances

It is a human characteristic to blame external factors for our own shortcomings and internal factors for those of others. When we make a mistake, or when our care for our patients falls short of what we might hope, we are quick to find a reason – time pressures, unusual presentation and stress. But when a patient makes a complaint or wants a sick note or referral we feel isn't justified, we may be less willing to give him or her the benefit of the doubt. Instead, we may blame the patient for being unreasonable or difficult, or having unrealistic expectations of the NHS – some or all of which may be true, but is only the end result of a long series of thoughts and events that have led the patient to where he or she is now.

Remembering this and avoiding the kneejerk irritation or even dislike is important. Being curious about why the patient is behaving as he or she does may be the key to compassion in these circumstances. So, for example, we may find that the woman demanding a gynaecology referral has been used to seeing a gynaecologist routinely in her own country and has been told this is necessary to detect early cancers or fertility problems. There may be a genuine misunderstanding about why the NHS doesn't fund these routine checks. It may of course still not be possible to meet the patient's requests, but at least, by understanding why they are being made, we avoid viewing the patient as an adversary.

THE HEARTSINK PATIENT

We all have people we don't look forward to seeing. These are the 'heartsink' patients, who have been characterised in various ways. 'Heartsink' in itself is not a helpful term, as it provides a degree of justification for us to act in a predetermined way towards these patients, allowing our communication with them to be coloured by the unfavourable response they provoke in us, rather than acknowledging that the patient is not entirely defined by his or her behaviour.

There are patterns of behaviour that are certainly challenging, but perhaps, as compassionate practitioners, we should make a more conscious effort to separate the behaviour from the person. Once a level of trust is established, it is often possible to challenge unreasonable behaviours and to enable the patient to understand the effect he or she may have on others.

CUM SCIENTIA CARITAS

The motto of the RCGP is '*Cum scientia caritas*'. This translates approximately to 'science with compassion'. The art of medicine is to relate our knowledge of disease to the story given by the patient. Communicating information about disease without compassion reduces the interaction to something akin to a business transaction. There is no doctoring involved.

It may seem unrealistic to think about sustaining a compassionate approach throughout decades of work as a GP. However, in the end, practising with compassion may make the job more fulfilling and go some way towards avoiding burnout. As the Dalai Lama said:

> If you want others to be happy, practise compassion. If you want to be happy, practise compassion.

References

1. Maimonides; Friedenwald H, trans. Oath and prayer of Maimonides. *Bulletin of the Johns Hopkins Hospital* 1917; **28**: 260–1.
2. Launer J. *Narrative-Based Primary Care: a practical guide*. Oxford: Radcliffe Medical Press, 2002.

Chapter 6

Compassion in health care for long-term conditions

Louise Warburton

A long-term condition is defined by the Department of Health as a condition that cannot, at present, be cured, but can be controlled by medication and other therapies. Examples of long-term conditions are diabetes, heart disease and chronic obstructive pulmonary disease. There are 15.4 million people living with a long-term condition in England. Numbers are expected to rise due to an ageing population and unhealthy lifestyle choices.[1]

Chronic diseases are now the most common cause of death and disability in England. These people tend to be heavy users of healthcare resources, accounting for at least 50% of all GP appointments, 64% of out-patient appointments and 70% of all in-patient bed days.[2]

Analysis of data from Scotland found that 42% of the population had at least one long-term condition and 23% had two or more.[3] Most people over 65 years had multi-morbidities, but, interestingly, the onset of multi-morbidity occurred 10–15 years earlier in deprived areas. People from these deprived areas are also likely to suffer from more mental health issues as well and suffer from low income due to inability to work.

Demographically, the number of people in England with long-term conditions are projected to be relatively stable over the next ten years, but the number of people with more than one condition, or multiple conditions, are likely to rise from 1.9 million in 2008 to 2.9 million in 2018.[1]

The NHS therefore has a crisis on its hands. The economic position in the UK is currently stretched due to banking problems dating back to 2009, which have resulted in a reduction in funding to hospitals and healthcare centres. The resources devoted to primary care have fallen in real terms in the past ten years, but the number of patient interactions have increased. There is also a recruitment crisis at present in primary care and this is not helping the care of patients with long-term conditions. There are fewer people entering medical schools and fewer graduates wishing to train in general practice because of the increasing workload and low morale of the workforce.

A 2011 King's Fund report concluded that:[4]

- the range of activities provided in general practice has increased. General practice plays an increasingly important role in coordinating care provided in other settings
- the availability of GPs is inequitable, ranging by Primary Care Trust from fewer than 50 to more than 80 per 100,000 population
- there are projected shortages in the general practice workforce due to an ageing workforce and changing working patterns
- the majority of care provided by general practice is good. However, there are wide variations in performance and gaps in the quality of care that suggest there is significant scope and opportunity for improvement
- more needs to be done to ensure that, where unacceptable variations exist, these are addressed so that a better and more consistent standard of care can be delivered to patients. Practices that perform poorly compared with others will need to be challenged to improve and, where appropriate, supported to do so
- there is considerable scope for improvement in ensuring that all patients receive all their recommended care as defined in clinical best-practice guidance, for example in the prescribing of low-cost statins and in delivering care to people with long-term chronic illness.

Clearly, the NHS does not have the financial or workforce resources to offer paternalistic health care to this growing body of clients. There is evidence that effective self-management of long-term conditions will improve outcomes for patients.[5] The NHS will have to employ more self-care strategies to work in a smarter way to tackle these long-term conditions.

People who are more 'activated' (that is who recognise that they have an important role in self-managing their condition and have the skills and confidence to do so) experience better health outcomes.[6] There is evidence that these skills can be developed and strengthened, even amongst those who are initially less confident, less motivated or have low levels of health literacy.[7] There is therefore scope to increase patient self-efficacy and self-management, which is a more person-centred approach to the problem.

Unfortunately, our health services have been challenged in the past few years by examples of poor care and lack of compassion. The best reported of these were the problems at Mid Staffordshire Hospital with high death rates, in the hundreds for in-patients, and many examples of poor care. This prompted a formal investigation into the events at Mid Staffs by the government under the leadership of Sir Robert Francis. The resulting 'Francis Report' has changed medical practice throughout the UK.[8]

The Francis Inquiry identified 'an unhealthy and dangerous culture' as a pervading cause of the failures at Mid Staffordshire NHS Foundation Trust. That culture was characterised by:

- bullying
- target-driven priorities
- disengagement by medical leaders
- discouragement of feedback from trainees
- low staff morale

- isolation
- lack of candour
- acceptance of poor behaviours
- reliance on external assessments
- denial.

As Francis said, 'It is a truism that organisational culture is informed by the nature of its leadership', noting that effective leadership at Mid Staffordshire was 'significantly lacking'.[8] The trust board was inexperienced and over-confident, preoccupied with achieving Foundation Trust status and meeting financial targets. Non-executives remained aloof from operational concerns even where they constituted a potential risk to patient safety. The trust's clinical leaders either lacked a voice at board level or did not make their concerns heard, while doctors were so disengaged from the trust's management that they failed to pursue their concerns, including those about the standard of patient care.

Francis also said that this kind of organisational culture, and the shortcomings identified in leadership, are not restricted to Mid Staffordshire: 'It is not possible to say that such deficiencies permeate to all organisations all of the time, but aspects of this negative culture have emerged throughout the system.'[8] In the wider NHS, the main features of this culture are:

- lack of consideration of risks for patients
- defensiveness
- looking inwards, not outwards
- secrecy
- misplaced assumptions of trust
- acceptance of poor standards
- failure to put the patient first in everything that is done.

According to Francis, these failings – in organisations that are generally staffed by caring and conscientious people – may be the result of mechanisms staff use to cope with the immense difficulties and challenges they encounter in their everyday work.

A top-down, command-and-control leadership style has given rise to a tendency to 'shame and blame'; this not only inhibits managers and staff from owning up to mistakes but also misses an opportunity for others to learn from those mistakes. Moreover, it is inimical to the openness, transparency and candour necessary to safeguard patient safety. As Francis put it: 'There lurks within the system an institutional instinct which, under pressure, will prefer concealment, formulaic responses and avoidance of public criticism.'[8]

At the beginning of our careers as doctors or healthcare workers, I am sure that we are idealistic and determined to care for our patients with compassion and consideration. However, as time progresses and we suffer from overwork and even burnout, many of us find it difficult to remain compassionate. The demands of the job and the target-based culture do not encourage us to sit down and spend time with our patients, and sometimes we have forgotten why we even decided to become healthcare workers. Under pressure, we tend to look inwards and try to conceal the difficulties within organisations, rather than reveal the problems. In some ways we are being asked to become 'whistle-blowers' to report examples of poor practice. However, this culture is difficult to develop, as many whistle-blowers have themselves suffered because of the disclosures they have made. Take for example the case of Dr Peter Wilmhurst, a cardiologist from Shrewsbury who uncovered alleged fraudulent practices by an American firm that was performing a research trial into the use of its medical device to treat congenital heart problems.[9] His own career and life have suffered as a result of this, as he was sued by the American firm NMT Medical.

Experiences like his do not encourage us to become whistle-blowers, but we need a culture of openness if we are to treat patients more fairly and with more compassion. The findings of the Francis Report illustrate very elegantly how and why we are failing in our roles as compassionate care-givers.

In an attempt to remedy this failing, the '6 Cs' campaign was devised by the Royal College of Nursing. A national campaign was launched to promote care with the six Cs and nurses were encouraged to report on examples of good practice. The 6 Cs are Care, Compassion, Competence, Communication, Courage and Commitment. A website is in existence and several national conferences have taken forward the message. GPs should be encouraged to read and understand the principles behind this initiative. Details can be found on the NHS England website.[10]

Taking into account the increasing incidence of long-term conditions and multimorbidity, NHS England has embraced the concept that care has to be redesigned to meet the needs of the twenty-first century. Its new initiative, which has looked to redesign the care of patients with long-term conditions, is the 'House of Care Model' (see Figure 6.1).[11]

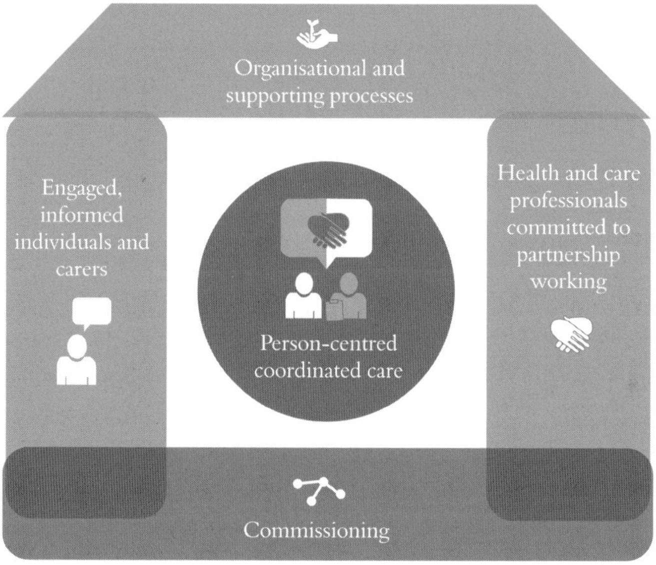

Figure 6.1 House of Care Model
Source: NHS England.[11] Contains public sector information licensed under the Open Government Licence v3.0.

The House of Care Model enhances the quality of life for people with long-term conditions, no matter what their conditions are. The concept places the patient in the centre of a virtual 'house' and they work in partnership with their carers and healthcare professionals, such as GPs and community nurses. Commissioners and local hospitals also provide a service to care for this individual.

Central to the care is an individualised care plan for each patient with a long-term condition; this is devised by joint working between the patient and the healthcare professionals. Of course, this care plan will be far more personalised than traditional models of care and can be far more compassionate, taking into account the individual requirements of that patient.

For example, a patient with local recurrence of breast cancer would traditionally have been referred back to the breast service and encouraged to have more surgery, radiotherapy and maybe medical therapy. Now, with an individualised care plan, the patient should be able to discuss her options with the breast surgeon, using the principles of 'shared decision making', and her views taken into account. If she does not wish to have any further aggressive treatment, then these views should be respected and care put into place to support her when she requires end-of-life care.

All too often, patients in this situation decline treatment in a hurry, and are discharged from hospital services because they do not understand the full implications of their decision. They are then cast adrift and lost to follow-up until their disease causes more major problems, which are much harder to sort out at this late stage.

Shared decision making involves the patient and doctor or nurse working together through a number of questions (in a decision aid). This helps them to explore the options available to them and should facilitate a discussion. Naturally this will enable the patient's views to be considered, and a more compassionate approach to his or her illness will be possible. Decision aids are already available on the NHS RightCare website: www.rightcare.nhs.uk. Use of decision aids has been shown to improve outcomes for patients.[12]

In conclusion

We often forget about compassionate care for our patients in the healthcare community of the twenty-first century. Long-term conditions are going to be the 'bread and butter' of general practice, and in order to extend limited resources and provide a better service for patients we must put the patients at the centre of their care and treat them with compassion! They will then become engaged in their own health issues and become more self-effective and self-sufficient.

References

1. Department of Health. Long term conditions. http://webarchive.nationalarchives.gov.uk/+/www.dh.gov.uk/en/Healthcare/Longtermconditions/DH_064569 [accessed 27 April 2015].
2. Coulter A, Roberts S, Dixon A. *Delivering Better Services for People with Long-Term Conditions: building the house of care*. London: King's Fund, 2013, www.kingsfund.org.uk/sites/files/kf/field/field_publication_file/delivering-better-services-for-people-with-long-term-conditions.pdf [accessed 12 June 2015]

3. Barnett K, Mercer SW, Norbury M, *et al*. Epidemiology of multimorbidity and implications for health care, research, and medical education; a cross sectional study. *Lancet* 2012; **380(9836)**: 37–43.
4. Goodwin N, Dixon A, Poole T, Raleigh V. *Improving the Quality of Care in General Practice*. London: King's Fund, 2011, www.kingsfund.org.uk/sites/files/kf/improving-quality-of-care-general-practice-independent-inquiry-report-kings-fund-march-2011_0.pdf [accessed 27 April 2015].
5. Epping-Jordan JE, Pruitt SD, Bengoa R, Wagner EH. Improving the quality of health-care for chronic conditions. *Quality and Safety in Healthcare* 2004; **13(4)**: 299–305.
6. Greene J, Hibbard JH. Why does patient activation matter? An examination of the relationship between patient activation and health-related outcomes. *Journal of General Internal Medicine* 2012; **27(5)**: 520–6.
7. Hibbard JH, Greene J. What the evidence shows about patient activation: better health outcomes and care experiences; fewer data on costs. *Health Affairs* (Millwood) 2013; **32(2)**: 207–14.
8. Francis R. *Report of the Mid Staffordshire NHS Foundation Trust Public Inquiry*. London: TSO, 2013, www.midstaffspublicinquiry.com/report [accessed 27 April 2015].
9. Dyer C. Cardiologist is sued for comments on potential migraine device. *British Medical Journal* 2008; DOI: 10.1136/bmj.a2412.
10. NHS. The 6 Cs. www.england.nhs.uk/wp-content/uploads/2012/12/6c-a5-leaflet.pdf [accessed 27 April 2015].
11. NHS England. Enhancing the quality of life for people living with long term conditions: the House of Care. www.england.nhs.uk/house-of-care/ [accessed 27 April 2015].
12. Mathers N, Ng CJ, Campbell MJ, *et al*. Clinical effectiveness of a patient decision aid to improve decision quality and glycaemic control in people with diabetes making treatment choices: a cluster randomised controlled trial (PANDAs) in general practice. *BMJ Open* 2012; DOI: 10.1136/bmjopen-2012-001469.

Chapter 7

End-of-life care

Iain Lawrie

Introduction

> How we care for the dying is an indicator of how we care for all sick and vulnerable people. It is a measure of society as a whole and it is a litmus test for health and social care services.[1]

End-of-life care has increasingly become part of our everyday language over the past decade or so, despite palliative and end-of-life care having been an integral component of the physician's remit for many centuries. Many clinicians see it as a central, defining aspect of their work, while some shy away from it, often for apparently justifiable reasons. However, as family physicians, we care for our patients and their families through the entirety of their lives, and death and dying is as much a part of that holistic, patient and family-centred care as all the myriad of other aspects that make up modern general practice.

Palliative care, with its roots in the hospice movement, has long since outgrown its original scope of specialised units with a focus on the care of people with cancer. Palliative care is now part of virtually all areas of clinical care, has widened its remit to include all life-limiting illnesses and is regarded as the responsibility of all doctors. Palliative medicine as a specialty has existed in the UK since 1987 and has been growing worldwide for just as long.

Context

Palliative care is not the sole domain of specialists. It should be recognised that more than 90% of patients spend the majority of their last year of life and receive palliative care at home, despite a significant proportion of patients dying in hospital.[2,3] This places GPs at the heart of palliative care provision and, indeed, they value this aspect of their work greatly.[4,5]

The central tenets of general practice are also those of palliative care: those of caring for the 'whole' patient and his or her family in the social context in which the patient lives.[6] The challenge for GPs in providing palliative care in the community can be that individual clinicians have, on average, few patients requiring such care each year (five dying with cancer and 15 dying from other causes),[7] which represents a further challenge in maintaining skills and expertise.[8] Both health services and the public have an increasing desire for patients to be able to choose to be cared for, and die, at home (which includes hospices, nursing and residential homes) should they wish, and this places additional responsibilities not only on GPs but also on specialist palliative care services to provide greater integration of care in the community.

Definitions and national drivers

How those approaching the end of their lives are cared for has been described as an indicator of how we care for all sick and vulnerable people.[1] The last decade has seen both an increasing awareness and interest in end-of-life care and a greater understanding of the importance of combining a palliative care approach with 'usual' clinical practice.

Definitions of palliative care have been variously promoted by national and global organisations, all with a common theme, but with many variations in both scope and emphasis. Although such definitions are all appropriate in their own way, one can tease these out to reveal the true essence of care intended. From various definitions, the most appropriate aspects appear to be the 'active, total care of patients whose disease is no longer responsive to curative treatment'[9] and 'You matter because you are you, and you matter to the end of your life. We will do all we can not only to help you die peacefully, but also to live until you die'.[10]

There are several points to emphasise here, but three are uppermost. First, clinicians often label patients as 'palliative', which may promote an approach of masterly inactivity. But 'active, total care' suggests otherwise, and is discussed further below, as palliative patients have the same right to care as any other patient.

The second is the recognition of which patients need referral to palliative care services. All patients with life-limiting illness are potentially eligible for palliative/end-of-life care. Referral should be based on need rather than on diagnosis or stage of illness. The traditional model of palliative care (Figure 7.1) is outdated and should now be largely ignored.

The newer, possibly more effective model of viewing end of life (Figure 7.2) is preferable, as it recognises the more complex relationship between traditional approaches

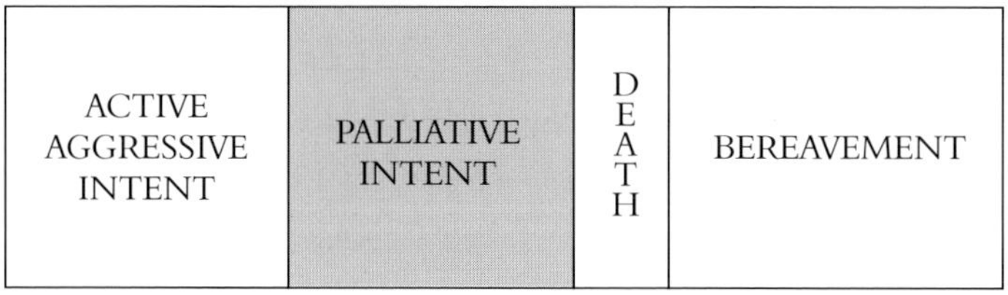

Figure 7.1: The traditional model of palliative/end-of-life care
Source: Frager G. Pediatric palliative care: building the model, bridging the gaps.[11]

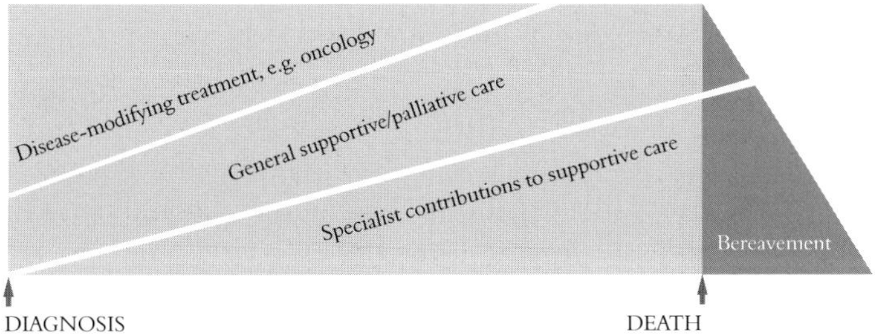

Figure 7.2: A more recent model of palliative care
Source: Watson M, Lucas C, Hoy A, Back I. *Oxford Handbook of Palliative Care*.[12]

to care, and the fact that palliative care principles can be utilised in any life-limiting illness from diagnosis where appropriate.

However, patients with non-malignant disease experience a much different trajectory of illness (Figure 7.3), and we should also consider how we manage them in the end-of-life care context, as their illness journey and required palliative care input will necessarily be intermittent and, to a large extent, unpredictable.

The last is that the words of Dame Cecily Saunders ring true throughout medical care, in whatever context. Good palliative end-of-life care is achieved through ensuring patients are symptom-free wherever possible, through anticipation, preparation and forward planning, and that we ensure they are encouraged, supported and enabled,

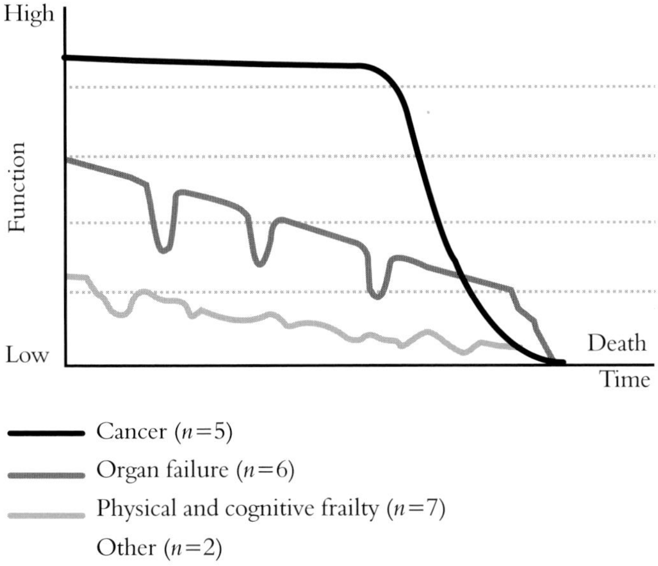

Figure 7.3: Palliative care and non-malignant disease trajectories
Source: reproduced from Murray SA, Sheikh A. Palliative care beyond cancer: care for all at the end of life. *British Medical Journal* 2008; **336(7650)**: 958–9 with permission from BMJ Publishing Group Ltd.[13]

through medical, pharmacological, psychological and social means, to have a fulfilling life until they actually die.

Nationally, palliative and end-of-life care has been growing in prominence on the healthcare agenda over the past decade.[1,14] We have recognised that patients wish to be cared for close to where they live, often in their own homes, and by people they know and trust. Such care has always been regarded as expensive but, compared with the costs of keeping a patient in an acute hospital bed, this argument doesn't appear to hold water, especially if care is well coordinated.[15]

With the introduction of the Health and Social Care Act (2012),[16] much greater emphasis has been placed on the integration of services across not only primary, secondary and third sector care provider organisations, but also social services. This is particularly relevant to palliative care, as patients with life-limiting illnesses often transfer between providers many times during their illness journey, and especially in the last year of life.

Assessment and provision

Another central feature of provision of high-quality palliative and end-of-life care is that of assessment – thorough, appropriate and continuous. Patients' conditions continually change, and so at no two consultations will the patient and those who care for the patient have the same symptoms, issues or questions. This is well worth noting, as attention to detail in assessment, and repeated assessment, not only contributes to excellent and appropriate care, but also has benefits in terms of patient experience and wellbeing, time management, job satisfaction and reduction of unexpected problems.

Symptom control is often seen as the most central aspect of the provision of palliative care, and, appropriately, management of potentially distressing symptoms such as pain, nausea and vomiting, constipation, anxiety, breathlessness, etc. is indeed an important aspect of improving quality of life and ensuring that the last few days, weeks or months of a patient's life are as comfortable as they can be. The aim is to optimise quality of life, both for patients and those who care for them, relative to their wishes, rather than what we consider appropriate.

Active, total care has been mentioned. Although 'palliative' patients may be nearing the end of their lives, it does not mean that they don't require or warrant active management. Antibiotics for chest infections, referral for consideration of supported ventilation, antidepressants for low mood (even where prognosis is short), referral to orthopaedic specialists for surgical stabilisation of bone metastases, etc. may all be appropriate symptom control measures for patients whose disease is not amenable to cure, no matter the stage of their underlying illness.

However, clinicians should always also remember the concept of 'total pain',[17] which recognises the interplay between the physical, social, psychological and spiritual aspects of the human condition. Simply managing physical symptoms well does not constitute good palliative or end-of-life care. Often, in addition to giving of oneself and using 'the doctor as the drug'[18] to support the patient and his or her carers, involving other members of the primary, secondary or third-sector health and social care teams to help address any of the four aspects of 'total pain' can be beneficial to overall management, and thus improve quality of life.

Advance care planning

Much more has been made of advance care planning recently – the process where the patient is able to express, have noted and ensure his or her preferences for care as the illness progresses and for end-of-life care – but it appears to be best placed as 'a golden thread', rather than a discrete consultation, that is part of continuous, holistic assessment of the patient, those who care for them and their needs.[19] However, although professionals should strive to ensure that an individual's plan of care is met wherever possible, it should always be made clear that circumstances may require adaptation of the plan.[20]

The advance care plan may stand on its own, or be part of a wider 'package' of preparation and planning that includes an Advance Decision to Refuse Treatment (remember, patients can refuse treatment but not demand it), preparation of Lasting Power of Attorney documents (property and financial affairs, or health and welfare, or both), or more simple preparation in the form of a will or funeral planning. It is important, no matter whether we as healthcare professionals see this as part of our role or not, that we support the patient and those who care for him or her in discussing such decisions, as this contributes to comprehensive and effective total patient care. Support and advice should always be available to GPs not only from national organisations such as Macmillan Cancer Care, but also from their local specialist palliative care services and hospices.

Coordination of care

The provision of palliative and end-of-life care is necessarily complex and involves a considerable number of professionals from a range of disciplines. Well-coordinated and seamless care is essential[21] and should be routine, but is often not achieved due to problems in accessing and communicating information between all parties, resulting in a fragmented approach. In the 2012 VOICES study, only 33% of participants felt that the care provided to their relative had been coordinated well.[22] Patients with cancer often receive much less disjointed care than those with non-malignant disease, despite representing only 30% of all deaths in England.[19]

Central to coordination of care is the multidisciplinary team (MDT), and the organisation, integration and effectiveness of this team will be reflected in the quality of care provided. Teams involving a district nurse, nurse specialist and GP provide much better care in terms of symptom control than a GP working in isolation.[23] The MDT approach is particularly well developed in cancer care, with the principles of key workers, guidelines, operational policies and communication systems being core elements. Provision for patients with non-malignant disease is less well developed, but is improving, and their care is a rapidly growing part of the work of specialist palliative care teams and site-specific clinical nurse specialists.

The MDT should operate in a way that addresses the core aspects of care for patients at the end of life, including: rapid discharge from hospital for care in the patient's preferred place; ease of access to care, which includes a single contact telephone number, appropriate response time in periods of crisis, and availability of equipment; effective involvement of health, social, statutory and voluntary care organisations; availability of anticipatory medicines in the home or community for symptom control; and use of electronic care coordination systems such as EPaCCS (Electronic Palliative Care Coordination Systems) or Coordinate My Care.

The key principles are those of care, compassion, communication, collaboration and common sense,[19] with no room for the historic approach of silo working. The challenges are numerous but, with careful consideration and cooperative strategic planning, excellent palliative and end-of-life care can be provided across sectors for patients with both malignant and non-malignant disease.

End of life, not end of care

It is often said that we have 'only one chance to get it right' when end of life approaches for our patients, and this drives all the initiatives and efforts to be able to provide a 'good death' in modern society. Often most difficult is the recognition that someone is dying, as discussions regarding place of care and death, and its organisation and coordination, cannot be finalised until this takes place, as preferences change, people delay discussions with those closest to them, and personal plans may not have been completed. Diagnosing dying can be particularly difficult in chronic, non-malignant illnesses, where the disease trajectory, as mentioned, can be much more uncertain.

Preparation for the 'dying phase' is essential in order to prevent distress and crisis, avoid unwanted hospital admission and to ensure patients, and those who care for them, remain informed and in control. Patients deserve dignity and privacy, as well as having their symptoms managed effectively. To achieve this, many members of the MDT may be involved, including occupational therapists for assessment and provision of equipment, district nurses for treatment and administration of medications, social carers for practical support, voluntary agencies to provide additional practical and emotional support, spiritual care services, specialist palliative care staff and, of course, the GP. The key word is 'preparation' in order that care can be proactive rather than reactive.

There may be reluctance from some about becoming involved in end-of-life care as a result of recent controversy surrounding tools designed to improve care, such as the Liverpool Care Pathway, which was withdrawn from use in July 2014. Such reluctance is understandable, but unfounded, and professionals from a broad range of disciplines have worked together to introduce guiding principles to support individualised care for dying people.[24]

Care at the end of life can require a considerable commitment on the part of the GP, both in terms of time and in professional knowledge and skills. This comes on top of an already heavy workload, and could be regarded as a burden to be devolved to other members of the MDT. However, patients value the care provided by GPs and prefer them to manage their care[25] and it represents a rewarding and satisfying part of primary care work.[26]

Care into bereavement

A doctor's responsibility of care doesn't end when his or her patient dies. This is particularly true in general practice, where a doctor may continue to be the practitioner for other members of the, now bereaved, family. Patients consider support in bereavement to be an important part of their GP's role, although few practitioners receive formal training in bereavement management.[27]

Good bereavement care doesn't simply refer to grieving and provision of emotional support. It starts at the moment of death, and involves how the patient's body is cared for, his or her wishes met and religious expectations respected, as well as responding to and supporting relatives as they travel along the grieving journey. The GP, although not necessarily an expert in all such matters, can be regarded as having a central role in supporting the family, signposting them to additional services or organisations as appropriate.

Barriers, opportunities and future direction

Many GPs do not like providing palliative and end-of-life care, and may not be comfortable with the MDT approach to this. Their knowledge about symptom control may be limited, they may fear prescribing controlled drugs in doses required, feel they don't have time and may avoid the emotional impact of providing such care.[28] However, GPs, trained and supported appropriately, are ideally placed both to provide palliative care and to extend its scope, especially to patients with non-malignant disease.[29]

The changing NHS in England, with the emphasis on integration and coordination of services, provides an excellent opportunity for further improvements in palliative and end-of-life care for all patients and those who care for them. General practice remains at the very centre of this provision and, with ongoing education, training and support, and with a drive for collaborative working, it will continue in its established role as the foundation of such care.

References

1. Department of Health. *End of Life Care Strategy: promoting high quality care for all adults at the end of life*. London: DH, 2008.
2. Barclay S. Palliative care in the community: the role of the primary health care team. *Palliative Care Today* 1997; **6**: 46–7.
3. Wiles R, Payne S, Jarrett N. Improving palliative care services: a pragmatic model for evaluating services and assessing unmet need. *Palliative Medicine* 1999; **13(2)**: 131–7.
4. Lloyd-Williams M, Wilkinson C, Lloyd-Williams F. General practitioners in North Wales: current experiences of palliative care. *European Journal of Cancer Care* 2000; **9(3)**: 138–43.
5. Meijler WJ, Van Heest F, Otter R, Sleijfer DT. Educational needs of general practitioners in palliative care: outcome of a focus group study. *Journal of Cancer Education* 2005; **20(1)**: 28–33.

6. Mitchell GK. How well do general practitioners deliver palliative care? A systematic review. *Palliative Medicine* 2002; **16(6)**: 457–64.
7. Barclay S. Palliative care for non-cancer patients: a UK perspective from primary care. In: JM Addington-Hall, IJ Higginson (eds). *Palliative Care for Non-cancer Patients*. Oxford: Oxford University Press, 2001, p. 176.
8. Grande GE, Barclay SIG, Todd CJ. Difficulty of symptom control and general practitioners' knowledge of patients' symptoms. *Palliative Medicine* 1997; **11**: 399–406.
9. World Health Organization. *Cancer Pain Relief and Palliative Care*. Technical Report Series 804. Geneva: WHO, 1990.
10. Saunders C. Care of the dying 1. The problem of euthanasia. *Nursing Times* 1976; **72(26)**: 1003–5.
11. Frager G. Pediatric palliative care: building the model, bridging the gaps. *Journal of Palliative Care* 1996; **12(3)**: 9–10.
12. Watson M, Lucas C, Hoy A, Back I. *Oxford Handbook of Palliative Care*. Oxford: Oxford University Press, 2005.
13. Murray SA, Sheikh A. Palliative care beyond cancer: care for all at the end of life. *British Medical Journal* 2008; **336(7650)**: 958–9.
14. National End of Life Care Programme. *Advance Care Planning: a guide for health and social care staff*. London: DH, 2008.
15. Raftery JP, Addington-Hall JM, MacDonald LD, *et al*. A randomized controlled trial of the cost-effectiveness of a district coordinating service for terminally ill cancer patients. *Palliative Medicine* 1996; **10(2)**: 151–61.
16. The Stationery Office. *The Health and Social Care Act 2012*. London: TSO, 2012.
17. Saunders C. Introduction: history and challenge. In: C Saunders, N Sykes (eds). *The Management of Terminal Malignant Disease*. London: Hodder & Stoughton, 1993, pp. 1–14.
18. Balint M. *The Doctor, His Patient and the Illness*. London: Tavistock Publications, 1957.
19. Hayes A, Henry C, Holloway M, *et al*. *Pathways Through Care at the End of Life: a guide to person-centred care*. London: Jessica Kingsley Publishers, 2014.
20. National End of Life Care Programme. *Advance Care Planning: it all ADSE up*. London: DH, 2012.
21. Bodenheimer T. Coordinating care: a perilous journey through the healthcare system. *New England Journal of Medicine* 2008; **358(10)**: 1064–71.
22. Department of Health. *First National VOICES Survey of Bereaved People*. London: DH, 2012.
23. Hearn J, Higginson I. Do specialist palliative care teams improve outcomes for cancer patients? A systematic literature review. *Palliative Medicine* 1998; **12(5)**: 317–32.
24. Leadership Alliance for the Care of Dying People. *One Chance to Get It Right: improving people's experience of care in the last few days and hours of life*. LACDP, 2014, www.gov.uk/government/uploads/system/uploads/attachment_data/file/323188/One_chance_to_get_it_right.pdf [accessed 1 May 2015].
25. Charlton RC. Attitudes towards care of the dying: a questionnaire survey of general practice attenders. *Family Practice* 1991; **8(4)**: 356–9.
26. Brown JB, Sangster M, Swift J. Factors influencing palliative care: qualitative study of family physicians' practices. *Canadian Family Physician* 1998; **44**: 1028–34.
27. Lemkau JP, Mann B, Little D, *et al*. A questionnaire survey of family practice physicians' perceptions of bereavement care. *Archives of Family Medicine* 2000; **9(9)**: 822–9.
28. Kenyon Z. Palliative care in general practice. *British Medical Journal* 1995; **311(7010)**: 888–9.
29. Burge FI, Latimer EJ. Palliative care in medical education at McMaster University. *Journal of Palliative Care* 1989; **5(1)**: 16–20.

Part II

Education and training

CHAPTER 8

THE EVOLUTION OF GP TRAINING

Equipping and preparing the next generation

Rebecca Chellaswamy

The past 60 years have seen huge advances in postgraduate training for doctors wishing to specialise in primary care, as well as a shifting direction of travel within the GP training landscape, and this chapter aims to reflect both of these things. This chapter provides an overview of how general practice training has developed over this period, including the development of the MRCGP examination and other methods of assessment.

The need for, and crucial importance of, formal training for GPs was one of the founding objectives of the Royal College of General Practitioners, and it is entirely possible that without the College there might still be no postgraduate training in general practice. The establishment of a compulsory, integrated and highly regarded training programme in general practice, as well as a rigorous, standardised assessment process for its trainees, is one of the College's greatest achievements in its first 60 years and one of which it should be justly proud.

THE HISTORY

EARLY IDEAS ABOUT GP TRAINING

The term 'general practitioner' was first used in the UK in 1840 and referred to medical practitioners who practised a combination of medicine, surgery, midwifery and pharmacy. Initially, control of general practice was handed to the specialists with the introduction of a joint diploma from the Royal Colleges of Surgeons and Physicians (the MRCS/LRCP conjoint diploma).[1]

An article in the *British Medical Journal* from the early 1950s stated:[2]

> The doctor of a family should be a privileged friend, with wide experience and up to date knowledge. … [The] overall and continuous responsibility for the care of patients is shouldered only by the general practitioner. Whenever a patient brings a problem, the doctor must feel that it is his duty to solve it himself, or to ask someone else to solve it for both of them, so that the patient is left with a lightened

> burden. The student who chooses general practice requires instruction in: (a) academic medical knowledge; (b) the application of the knowledge to conditions outside hospital; and (c) the doctor-patient relationship.

Despite this clear acknowledgement that GPs required a specific skill set and knowledge base, doctors wishing to go into general practice at that time had no formal training programme available to them. In addition to this, it was generally felt that the medical school training prior to 1960 was overwhelmingly focused on hospital specialties and did not produce doctors who were well placed to thrive in primary care.[3]

Plans for GP training

The British Medical Association published the Cohen Report in 1950, which set out the concept of GP training in detail; it was not, however, acted upon for many years.[4] A Trainee General Practitioner Scheme had been launched two years previously. This was felt to be a good idea in theory and it flourished in its early days.[5] However, it fell into disrepute due to poor organisation and wide variation in the quality of training received.[6]

The catalyst for rapid, sustained and coordinated development in GP training appears to have been the formation of the Royal College of General Practitioners. The Royal College of Physicians (www.rcplondon.ac.uk), the Royal College of Surgeons (www.rcseng.ac.uk) and the Royal College of Obstetrics and Gynaecology (www.rcog.org.uk) had been founded in 1518, 1800 and 1929 respectively, and all of these bodies initially opposed the formation of a college of GPs. This was primarily because of the fact that, before the early 1950s, general practice was barely recognised as a discipline in its own right;[7] it was widely regarded by hospital specialists as the sum of a number of specialties practised at a relatively superficial level. The College was essentially trying not only to found a new institution but also a new specialty.[8] Despite the opposition, the College of General Practitioners (CGP) finally burst onto the scene in 1952 – this had been a lengthy gestation, given that the first plans to found a college for GPs had been put forward in the 1840s.[8] It had to wait another 15 years until 1967, however, to be granted its 'Royal' charter.[9]

The early years of GP training

Education was high on the list of priorities for the new College and this is demonstrated by the fact that Undergraduate and Postgraduate Education Committees had been established within three months of its foundation.[9]

There had been experimental training schemes in Inverness and Wessex during the 1950s that provided a small number of trainees with integrated hospital and general practice experience. The feedback from these trainees was generally favourable;[5] however, by the end of the 1950s, there was still no formal GP training programme provided for the vast majority of trainees.

The College of GPs published a report in 1965[10] proposing a four-year training programme after the one-year registration period. There was a shortage of doctors in the 1960s and it was perhaps this factor, along with the fact that the undergraduate curriculum had been reformed to recognise the importance of general practice, which meant that this report was far better received than the BMA's report a decade and a half earlier.[11]

In 1966, the College of GPs provided detailed evidence to Lord Todd's Royal Commission on Medical Education, setting out the case for general practice to be considered a key specialty in its own right and deserving of its own postgraduate training programme. The Todd Report was published two years later and almost entirely endorsed the College's view, recommending a five-year training programme for general practice.[12] The College's Vocational Training Subcommittee was formed in 1968 and a number of training schemes started to spring up around the country. Despite the fact that there was an element of central coordination and a reasonable level of communication between the organisers of the various local training schemes by the end of the 1960s, there was still no consensus on what trainees should actually be taught.[6]

Standardisation of training

This issue was addressed by a landmark publication entitled *The Future General Practitioner: learning and teaching*,[13] which was released by the College in 1972. It included the College's 'job definition' for GPs, and extrapolated five key educational objectives from this that endured in varying forms for many years. A succinct version of this job description is provided below:[8]

> '[A general practitioner is] a doctor who provides personal primary and continuing care to individuals and families' and whose 'diagnoses are composed in physical, psychological and social terms'. Such doctors 'work in a team and delegate when necessary' and 'intervene educationally, preventatively and therapeutically to promote ... health'.

The Future General Practitioner report highlighted the importance of GPs developing good attitudes and consultation skills, in addition to detailing various areas of clinical knowledge that should be mastered. This seems to demonstrate the College's commitment to its motto (*Cum scientia caritas*) to prioritise and value the caring and compassionate aspects of general practice. This document set out the agenda and laid the foundations for the education of GPs, and it continued to have a wide-ranging influence in the field for decades afterwards.

In 1976, the Joint Committee on Postgraduate Training for General Practice (JCPTGP) was established[12] in an attempt to monitor the quality of training.[14]

Training becomes compulsory

Until 1981, it remained possible for doctors to enter general practice without any specific postgraduate training.[7] In order to make this training a requirement, it had to be approved by parliament, as GPs were self-employed independent contractors. The NHS Act was passed in 1977[15] and compulsory training for all new GPs was subsequently phased in;[12] a compulsory three-year post-registration programme was in place from 1982.[14]

EVOLUTION OF THE MRCGP EXAMINATION

Between 1952 and 1965, membership of the College was granted by assessment by the Board of Censors – all candidates were required to have been qualified for a minimum of seven years and have spent at least five of these years in general practice. They had to satisfy the Board that their GP work was of a high standard by providing reports from sponsors, and some were called for interviews.[16]

The first ever Membership of the CGP examination was held in 1965 and was undertaken by just five candidates, all of whom were successful.[16] This was, in fact, the first ever examination in general practice anywhere in Europe.[17] The MRCGP examination became the only method of entry to membership of the College from 1968, when the exam consisted of a multiple-choice question paper, a modified essay question paper, a traditional essay question and two oral examinations, one of which was based around a log diary created by the candidate.[16] Because membership was still very much optional, the qualification was widely regarded as simply a useful diploma and gold standard in the 1970s and 1980s.[12] Despite this, the number of candidates choosing to take the MRCGP rose dramatically over this period.[16]

In 1972, the College had formulated key areas of competence, which translated into seven areas for examination. These were: problem definition, management, prevention, practice organisation, communication, professional values, personal and professional growth.[16] Despite this, by the end of the 1980s there was still no MRCGP component that involved candidates being observed interacting with patients,[16] and this had been raised as an issue in a *Report to the Examination Board of the RCGP* in 1989.[18]

The MRCGP examination was still optional in 1990, although it was beginning to be regarded as a marker of quality both within the profession and by the general public.[8] Certificates of Prescribed or Equivalent Experience issued by the Joint Committee on Postgraduate Training for General Practice were awarded on the basis of satisfactory continuous work-based assessments made by trainers in both hospital posts and GP practice placements. The need for a formal evaluation of consultation skills was addressed during the following decade and, by the late 1990s, the MRCGP examination included an assessment of seven videotaped consultations.[8] There were still two three-hour written/multiple choice-based papers and two 20-minute oral examinations alongside this.[8]

In 2005 General Practitioner and Specialist Registers were set up in accordance with the General and Specialist Medical Practice (Education, Training and Qualifications) Order 2003. The Registers are kept by the General Medical Council (GMC) and it is the award of a Certificate of Completion of Training (CCT) that allows entry to the GP Register.

SUMMATIVE ASSESSMENT

Summative Assessment was introduced in 1996 as a way of ensuring a minimum level of competency amongst new entrants to independent general practice[19] and it became a legal requirement for all trainees to pass this assessment to obtain a licence to practise after the Vocational Training regulations were passed by the government in 1998.[14] It consisted of a multiple-choice question paper, a trainer's report, a piece of written work and a video assessment of consulting skills.[8] For several years, the MRCGP and the Summative Assessment system ran side by side and there was much debate regarding this. It was widely felt that the MRCGP exam standard was set at the optimum level, whereas the compulsory Summative Assessment was set at the minimum level.[20] From 2001 onwards, it was possible for candidates to submit a single set of videotaped consultations to satisfy the requirements for that component of Summative Assessment and MRCGP.

The present

The current system of recruitment to GP training

The GP National Recruitment Office (GPNRO) has coordinated a single national process for recruitment to GP specialty training since 2006.[21]

The short-listing method involves a computer-based assessment with two sections – professional dilemmas and clinical problem-solving. The professional dilemmas section attempts to assess the candidate's approach to practising medicine and is designed to allow demonstration of competencies such as professional integrity, coping with pressure, empathy and sensitivity. The clinical problem-solving section presents a number of clinical scenarios and the candidate is required to exercise judgement and problem-solving skills to determine appropriate diagnoses and management of patients. Short-listed applicants are matched in rank order to their highest available preferred Local Education Training Board (LETB)/deanery for the next stage of assessment.

The final stage of recruitment is run by individual LETBs/deaneries (overseen and standardised by the GPNRO) and involves candidates attending a Selection Centre and taking part in a number of exercises that are designed to test the following competencies: communication skills, empathy and sensitivity, conceptual thinking and problem-solving, and professional integrity.

The current GP training programme

The current training programme for general practice is the shortest of any of the specialties in the UK, still lasting only three years. Each trainee spends a minimum of 12 months in general practice, and the remaining time is spent in various secondary care placements. There is currently no requirement for trainees to spend any time in general practice prior to their final year. However, many local training schemes have chosen to provide their trainees with GP experience in their first and/or second years, and with far more than 12 months in primary care. There are no secondary care posts that are mandatory for all trainees,[22] so some trainees will not undertake a specialist post in child health, obstetrics and gynaecology or psychiatry during their GP training. This has been a concern for many trainees, particularly because up to 26% of consultations in primary care involve a paediatric element.[22]

The teaching and primary/secondary care placements are coordinated by each local training scheme with input, regulation and guidance from the LETB/deanery on behalf of the GMC. Formal teaching is delivered mainly via central lectures and small group teaching sessions, some of which are designed and facilitated by the trainees themselves. The trainee is allocated an educational supervisor for the duration of the training programme, along with a clinical supervisor for each individual post.[22]

The current MRCGP exam

The year 2007 saw the introduction of the first formal GP curriculum.[22] In the same year, the new MRCGP examination became the mandatory licensing examination for all new UK GPs.[23] The new MRCGP is an integrated and standardised assessment programme that is made up of three separate components – the Applied Knowledge Test (AKT), the Clinical Skills Assessment (CSA) and the Workplace-Based Assessment (WPBA). Each component aims to test different professional competences, and all three assessments have to be passed in order to be awarded the MRCGP, leading to the award of a CCT at the end of the training period following RCGP quality checks on meeting training standards and processes, and final approval by the GMC.[22]

The AKT is a three-hour-long online multiple-choice question assessment that predominantly tests the candidate's clinical knowledge base and other relevant areas such as understanding of statistics; an extra ten minutes was added in 2014 to provide more time for reflection and to assist those for whom English is not their first language. The CSA is a 13-case simulated surgery, in which each consultation lasts ten minutes. It is now held in the RCGP's purpose-built examination centre at 30 Euston Square, London, and assesses the candidate's ability to integrate and apply clinical, professional, communication and practical skills.[23] It cannot be undertaken until the final year of training. The 'patients' are portrayed by professional and specifically trained and standardised actors, and each case is assessed by a single examiner assessing in three domains: data-gathering, technical and assessment skills, clinical management skills, and interpersonal skills.[23]

The WPBA is a longitudinal assessment that aims to test attitudes and performance over the whole training programme using a variety of tools alongside information gathered in a structured electronic portfolio. The WPBA assessment tools are: Case-Based Discussion (CbD), Consultation Observation Tool (COT), Direct Observation of Procedural Skills (DOPS), miniCEX (Clinical Evaluation Exercise), Multi-Source Feedback (MSF), Patient Satisfaction Questionnaire (PSQ), Learning Log and Personal Development Plan (PDP). The trainee has responsibility for his or her own learning and must show evidence that this learning is taking place. The ePortfolio is reviewed at the end of each year of training and must be adequate in order for the trainee to continue to progress through the training programme.[22]

Membership by Assessment of Performance

Membership by Assessment of Performance (MAP) was introduced in 1999.[24] It was felt that this would provide an avenue to membership for established GPs (those who were licensed to practise before the introduction of the new version of the MRCGP as a licensing exam) who did not wish to undertake the MRCGP exam, but who felt their practice was of high enough quality to achieve the standards required for membership.[25] MAP involves submitting a comprehensive portfolio of 13 criteria covering all areas of practice within a year of making an application.[22]

The future

The proposed changes to GP training

The RCGP has for many years campaigned for major changes to the GP Specialty Training Programme and these changes were endorsed by Medical Education England (and other UK counterparts) in 2012. The most significant change would be a proposed increase in the duration of the training programme from three to four years, although this would still make it the shortest of the UK specialty training programmes. The College has also previously made the case for a possible further increase to five years once four-year training is established, and this would bring the duration in line with the radiology and public health specialty training programmes.[26]

It is proposed that the AKT and CSA exams would still need to be passed by the end of the third year of training, but the additional fourth year of the curriculum would provide the opportunity throughout training to consolidate and integrate previously learned skills and knowledge, as well as to provide a greater focus on the development of organisational and leadership skills. In addition to this, a new WPBA assessment would be undertaken in the fourth year – the Quality Improvement (QI) Project. This would involve an in-depth examination of an element of a local healthcare service, identifying ways in which it could be improved.[26]

The proposed plan is that every trainee would spend a minimum of 24 months in the primary care setting and that all trainees would be provided with direct exposure to child health and mental health. This would contribute to greater 'generalism' in training, as well as a greater focus on integrated care and possible new future models of care.

These changes would be accompanied by an expansion of the RCGP's successful 'First5' initiative for GPs in their first five years post-CCT, in order to provide extra support for development in the early years of independent practice. Additional support would also be provided to those in the final years of the existing three-year training programme during the transition process.

The agreed changes to GP training, for which the RCGP has strongly campaigned with significant support, have not yet been implemented pending the outcomes of the wider review of medical training ('Shape of Training' [SoT]), which has a particular focus on more generalist training, generic training pathways, moving the point of registration and introducing a system of post-Certificate of Specialty Training (CST) credentialing. The RCGP curriculum could easily be revised to address the potential outcomes of the SoT review, in particular to fit well with more generalist training.

Conclusion

Formal general practice training and assessment have evolved over the past 75 years from an almost non-existent arrangement to the comprehensive, integrated and highly respected training programme and examination of today. It is worth remembering that, when the majority of the 3355 candidates who sat the CSA exam once or more during the 2013–14 exam cycle were born, compulsory training for GPs was still in its infancy and the MRCGP was entirely optional.

It is clear that both *scientia* and *caritas* have always been at the heart of the development of GP training and assessment, particularly after the founding of the College.

General practice has evolved perhaps more than any other specialty within the past century, and GPs are now being encouraged to take on leadership and service redevelopment roles in addition to coping with the shift of many services from secondary to primary care.[26] It is essential that GP training evolves in parallel with these changes in order to produce a new generation of GPs who are able to thrive in the constantly transforming primary care landscape.

References

1. Cule J. A *Doctor for the People: 2000 years of general practice in Britain*. London: Update, 1980.
2. Barber GO, Abercrombie GF, Hunt JH, *et al*. The teaching of general practice by general practitioners. *British Medical Journal* 1953; **2(4826)**: 36–8.
3. Pereira Gray D. *A System of Training for General Practice* (RCGP Occasional Paper 4). London: RCGP, 1977.
4. Cohen H. *General Practice and the Training of the General Practitioner* (the Cohen Report). London: BMA, 1950.
5. Horder JP, Swift G. Vocational training 1: the history of vocational training for general practice. *Journal of the Royal College of General Practitioners* 1979; **29(200)**: 24–32.
6. Irvine D. Postgraduate education and vocational training. In: J Fry, Lord Hunt of Fawley, RJFH Pinsent (eds). *A History of the Royal College of General Practitioners: the first 25 years*. London: MTP Press, 1983, pp. 85–102.
7. Pereira Gray D. History of the Royal College of General Practitioners: the first 40 years. *British Journal of General Practice* 1992; **42(354)**: 29–35.
8. Moore R. The origin and development of the examination. In: R Moore (ed.). *The MRCGP Examination: a guide for candidates and teachers* (4th edn). London: RCGP, 2000, pp. 1–11.
9. Sturmberg JP. *The Foundations of Primary Care: daring to be different*. Abingdon: Radcliffe Publishing, 2007.
10. College of General Practitioners. *Reports from General Practice I: special vocational training for general practice*. London: CGP, 1965.
11. Royal College of General Practitioners. *Reports from General Practice VI: the implementation of vocational training*. London: RCGP, 1967.
12. Hasler JC. History of vocational training for general practice: the 1970s and 1980s. *Journal of the Royal College of General Practitioners* 1989; **39(325)**: 338–41.
13. A Working Party of the Royal College of General Practitioners. *The Future General Practitioner: learning and teaching*. London: BMA, 1972.
14. Field S. The story of general practice postgraduate training and education. In: M Lakhani (ed.). *A Celebration of General Practice*. Abingdon: Radcliffe Medical Press, 2003, pp. 117–30.
15. National Health Service. *Vocational Training Regulations*. London: HMSO, 1979.
16. Walker J. History of the MRCGP examination. In: C Lockie (ed.). *Examination for Membership of the Royal College of General Practitioners (MRCGP): development, current state and future trends* (RCGP Occasional Paper 46). London: RCGP, 1990, pp. 1–3.
17. Pereira Gray D. The creation and achievements of the RCGP. In: M Lakhani (ed.). *A Celebration of General Practice*. Abingdon: Radcliffe Medical Press, 2003, pp. 131–44.
18. Mulholland H, McAleer S. *Report to the Examination Board of the Royal College of General Practitioners*. Dundee: Centre for Medical Education, 1989.
19. *Joint Committee on Postgraduate Training for General Practice Report*. London: JCPTGP, 1993.
20. Haslam D. Why does the examination keep changing? In: R Moore (ed.). *The MRCGP Examination: a guide for candidates and teachers* (4th edn). London: RCGP, 2000, pp. 12–22.
21. GP National Recruitment Office, http://gprecruitment.hee.nhs.uk.
22. Hippisley-Cox, Fenty J, Heaps M, *et al*. *Trends in Consultation Rates in General Practice 1995 to 2006: analysis of the QRESEARCH database*. Leeds: The Information Centre, 2007.

23. Bartlett J. MRCGP in a nutshell. In: E Mehay (ed.). *The Essential Handbook for GP Training and Education*. London: Radcliffe Publishing, 2012, pp. 348–68.
24. Jackson C, Lakhani M. General practice: evolution or revolution? In: M Lakhani (ed.). *A Celebration of General Practice*. Abingdon: Radcliffe Medical Press, pp. 187–96.
25. Baker M, Pringle M. Membership of the RCGP by assessment: attitudes of members and non-members in one faculty area. *British Journal of General Practice* 1995; **45(397)**: 405–7.
26. Gerada C, Riley B, Simon C. *Preparing the Future GP: the case for enhanced GP training*. London: RCGP, 2012, www.rcgp.org.uk/policy/rcgp-policy-areas/~/media/Files/Policy/A-Z-policy/Case_for_enhanced_GP_training.ashx [accessed 5 May 2015].

CHAPTER 9

COMPASSION

A junior doctor's perspective

Mitesh Patel

DEFINING COMPASSION

Compassion means showing sympathy for how the patient is feeling. It means trying to alleviate the patient's burden, both physically and psychologically.

> Sadly, despite an increasing awareness of the need to be compassionate, compassion can easily be lost.

As a recent graduate, I have been instilled with an emphasis on communication with patients. Communication was stressed as much as clinical knowledge during my training. Compassion, a key facet of the General Medical Council principles that doctors abide by, was often discussed because of its obvious role in breaking bad news. However, I remember ascending through medical school without fully appreciating why we needed to be taught how to be compassionate. After all, it is a basic human element, an ingrained part of our personality that we should be able to demonstrate spontaneously when needed. So how can one be taught how to be compassionate? Since then, however, I have been surprised by how compassion is guided by three overlapping themes of place, time and the patient.

COMPASSION GUIDED BY PLACE

I remember an episode during my emergency medicine rotation in a busy trust serving a deprived population. I was told by my consultant that we did not have time to chase the blood results for a patient who was now under the care of the medical team but was staying in the department overnight until a medical bed became available. What if the blood test showed something that needed to be acted on urgently? I felt troubled by this. To me it seemed such a simple, quick thing to do and would ease the anxiety of the patient. To my consultant I showed inefficiency because this small task would not allow the patients in the corridor to be seen. I would not call my consultant uncompassionate. If anything he was showing compassion to the patients who had been waiting for hours to be seen.

This demonstrated to me that being compassionate can extend beyond the patient in front of you and to people who you have not yet even seen.

A deeper message perhaps is that unfortunately my consultant, like many other doctors, was faced with having his principles compromised because of the patient pressures faced by the NHS.

I could tell you of numerous occasions when compassion was questioned in the emergency department. But this is one specialty where compassion is classically guided by the place of work. Every late shift, the same alcohol-intoxicated, homeless patient would come to the department and was offered a bed to rest in for a few hours and he would then leave. Perhaps the sorrow of knowing that he had to endure another night in the cold environment outside triggered this compassionate act of offering short-term respite. But why feel compassion for this patient? This man chose to intoxicate himself and the decisions he made in his life eventually brought him to sit in front of me. Perhaps we are conforming to what society expects by showing compassion to a homeless person – someone in desperate need to escape his or her situation for a mere few hours?

The same night, I clerked a young female re-attender with multiple psychiatric issues. She repeatedly presented with superficial lacerations from self-harm and did not engage with community psychiatric support.

Compassion from those around me seemed to quickly dissipate when I would spend longer completing a psychiatric assessment.

Being in a department with a high patient turnover meant that frequently attending psychiatric patients requiring thorough assessment were often frowned upon.

Compassion guided by time

In general practice, my compassion has varied widely because of the time available for a consultation. I started my rotation with 30-minute consultations, so the patient who always came with five separate medical dilemmas or who finds it important to give the doctor every detail of his or her medical illness from 20 years ago was manageable because I did not run the risk of running late. I felt that you could discuss every small worry to avoid the patient being distressed and needing to see you again immediately, and your compassion was reciprocated by the patient thanking you. Now that I am seeing patients in half the time, my time available for compassion for the same list of patients has declined, as I divided up this available time for compassion to my other patients waiting. Interestingly, throughout my experience, I also think that the compassion shown towards me from my patients has increased as they appreciate that my time is more limited.

Being on a ward round also is a test of compassion driven by time.

The medical teams spend a lot longer than the surgical teams on the ward round and are certainly more thorough in their approach, although this is guided by the patient numbers. The general perception, reflected in patient views, is that surgeons are more 'straight to the point' and daunting to approach. However, my observation was that consultant surgeons showed as much compassion as medical consultants despite the limited time to review each patient. Patients were always asked how they were feeling post-procedure and examined to rule out complications.

I will always recall the on-call surgical consultant asking me for updates on the patients on the ward under her care at midnight on my first surgical night shift. This was likely a combination of compassion from the doctor and personal satisfaction, as is normal with all doctors, to make sure the patients have been treated and no complications will occur under his or her care.

Situation judgement tests (SJTs) are becoming a key form of assessment in medicine, especially with doctors faced with an armful of jobs created after a ward round or clinic. SJTs seem to be marked so that compassion needs to be included in your thought process and allows you to reflect on what you *should do* rather than what you would do in a certain situation. With limited time and the need to assign patients with urgent, life-threatening issues first, the tasks requiring compassion such as breaking bad news may have to be pushed to later in the day. However, this prioritisation actually also allows you to show compassion to the patient, who will require more time, and involves the need for a quiet, uninterrupted environment with loved ones present.

Compassion guided by the patient

The patient sitting in front of you can also determine the amount of compassion shown. The age of the patient is one part of this. Compassion should be universal and not specific to age, but I think we are all more compassionate to the 2-year-old boy or the 90-year-old woman. But why is this? Well, an aspect of this is uncertainty, especially in children. Recently I saw a 4-year-old boy with his mother who was concerned that her son was more lethargic than usual. All other observations were normal. Knowing how children can present with non-specific symptoms, despite a low risk of serious pathology, I called the mother the next day to find out how the child was. We do not want to miss a life-threatening rash or inadequately manage a child. Compassion in this instance is driven by the anxiety of the parents and therefore the environment that we are surrounded by. Our compassion here is shown by spending longer, being more meticulous in clinical assessment and having a lower threshold to review the patient.

In the elderly we again are more compassionate. However, this is driven by knowing that an elderly patient may be alone or unable to look after him or herself very well, and we want to improve the patient's health to limit any extra burden. Perhaps we can also relate to their care needs because we have close friends and family members in their position and appreciate that we too will be elderly one day.

Disability is an interesting topic and can range from minor to serious forms. Similarly to above, we will often be more thorough with our assessment, knowing that it may be difficult for disabled patients to seek medical help. Compassion for these patients includes having people around them they are familiar with and planning early to make the consultation as smooth as possible. But the key thing, which is easier to learn in primary care with patient follow-up, is that many with a disability do not want to be treated differently. This was a fundamental point that a carer of a patient with cerebral palsy once made to me. Trying to be sensitive by showing compassion may actually make the consultation more awkward and flow less freely.

Preparation for compassion

Compassion is trying to help patients with their symptoms but it is also specific to time, place and person. I am a firm believer that compassion is not something that can be learnt but can be developed. It is moulded by our own experiences, having different effects on our patients and is shown in different ways.

Before applying to medicine, I thought that compassion meant helping patients in every way possible.

> It was a buzz word to use in interviews without necessarily understanding the realistic role of compassion in the NHS.

I quickly learnt that how compassionate you can be and for how long varies, and with increasing responsibility compassion can unfortunately decline. The training that I received in the UK allowed early exposure to compassion in the NHS, albeit with limited responsibility while being a student.

But it is not until I started my first day of work as a doctor that I learnt I was actually under-prepared to maintain compassion in my work. I initially found preserving compassion while completing patient duties difficult and often had to be sacrificed. How could my preparation for work have been aided? This would have needed me to be have been in the decision-making situations with the junior doctors I was shadowing, which is easier said than done with learning needs also to be fulfilled. How can compassion be maintained? By re-emphasising the importance of compassion in patient care and remembering how fundamental this was in pursuing a life as a doctor, we can try to make sure it is not forgotten.

Sadly, the NHS's current situation – with high patient numbers, increasing co-morbidity and limited staff numbers – means that compassion may be compromised. However, by seeing every patient who walks through the door and offering management for diseases that can be prevented by simple lifestyle changes, the NHS has always upholded showing compassion irrespective of the patient's background. Having been brought up with the NHS and seen the benefits offered both to my personal family and to the patients I am now treating, it is sad to see the burden on our healthcare service. My teaching on compassion had one simple, key message that I think is important to always be aware of – that compassion should never be forgotten and always applied in our patient care.

CHAPTER 10

THE SELECTION OF GPs

Past, present and future

Ryan Prince

Note: the author acknowledges and thanks the General Practice National Recruitment Office and Work Psychology Group for much of the information and factual quotation within this chapter.

INTRODUCTION

Since 2009, I have worked for Health Education West Midlands (formerly West Midlands Deanery), as the Associate GP Dean responsible for overseeing the recruitment and selection procedure for our GP vocational training schemes (VTSs). My task, as part of the General Practice National Recruitment Office (GPNRO) steering group, is to help design and facilitate the assessment processes and procedures to select the doctors who are likely to go on to pass their Membership of the Royal College of General Practitioners (MRCGP) examination, and moreover enjoy their career, delivering safe and effective practice as a result of being happy and competent.

Being immersed in this process has often led me to reflect on my own route into GP training, and how different it used to be. I qualified from the University of Birmingham in 1995. I then secured 'house jobs' in two Black Country hospitals, after being advised by friends which posts were decent and not too onerous. My 'interview' process for both posts was a two-minute chat with the consultants (presumably just to make sure that I was not covered in scales like a crocodile), before being told what day I would start on their wards. These jobs were never advertised – they did not need to be – because posts were filled by word of mouth.

MY CAREER PATH

I moved away from Birmingham for six months, after getting an unpaid job playing my violin as leader of the orchestra pit in the Tommy Steel musical *Half a Sixpence* at the Edinburgh Festival. It was great fun, but after the month had passed my money had run out and I needed to find some gainful employment. So I moved down to London to rent a flat with some musician friends of mine who had also been in the show.

My plan was to do some locums, and try to get a Senior House Officer (SHO) post at a London teaching hospital to train as a surgeon. I went to visit Hammersmith Hospital, managed to get a tour around the department, and met a few consultants. Everything was showing great promise until they asked me which London hospital I had graduated from. It did not take the staff there long to work out that the Queen Elizabeth Hospital, Edgbaston, was not in London, and not even situated remotely within the Home Counties. The atmosphere quickly changed to one of mild uninterest. 'You can of course apply if you wish', said a surgical registrar, 'but I wouldn't waste my time if I were you. This place only takes London graduates and mostly ones who have been at the Hammersmith.' Sure enough – I was not shortlisted for any post I applied for. Presumably the same process as I had been through in Birmingham had happened – the informal chat with the local graduates, and the consultants wishing a junior doctor who would 'know how it all worked' in their locality.

After five months of doing various locums I moved back to the West Midlands, and this time actually went through a formal interview procedure to secure an A&E post. I then spent many years changing my mind as to what I wished to do with my medical career. Every six months, I interviewed for a new specialty, enjoyed it, tried something else, and got myself quite well known in the local hospitals for being a longstanding 'Journeyman' (as I believe professional footballers are now called who keep frequently swapping clubs). It suddenly dawned upon me that perhaps general practice would be a fine career for somebody who liked doing a bit of everything, so I started to investigate how one became a GP. A friend who was placed in Obstetrics and Gynaecology with me at the time told me that there was a great little village practice up the road with a young and dynamic GP trainer, and why didn't I go and knock on his door and see if he had a job going? This is exactly what I did, and a few months later I started as a GP registrar on the local VTS.

Getting my Joint Committee on Postgraduate Training for General Practice Certificate was a bit tricky at the end of 'Summative Assessment'. I had not failed the obligatory videos, audit or multiple-choice question exam, but I had omitted to obtain any signed 'VTR2' forms during my hospital posts – as at the time I did not realise that I wanted to be a GP. For those readers who did not go through this system, these forms had to be signed by consultants as proof that one had completed their hospital specialty satisfactorily, and then they were sent to the GP certification unit. A running scrabble over the next week ensued travelling around the local hospitals, convincing consultants who could sometimes barely remember me, to sign the forms that I needed.

In the end – as is often the case, even today – a year or so later I ended up joining my original training practice as a partner, where I have now been for 14 years.

If it is not broken, why fix it?

This seemed to be the mantra from the local GP trainers a few years after I had joined the profession, on hearing of the plans that the recruitment and selection of GP trainees would be centralised, and have a formal procedure for the first time. There was to be a regional selection procedure, followed by the offer of a three-year training programme (two years in hospital posts and one year in general practice).

Most of the trainers had come into general practice on 'DIY' VTSs like I had. A few of them had not done vocational training at all and started as GPs straight out of house jobs. Some thought that pre-ordained hospital rotations would be restrictive, and not allow for flexibility or choice. For example, when I had decided that I was going to be a GP, I arranged a rotation of dermatology, ophthalmology and ENT to augment my training. Some of the GP trainers were anxious and even annoyed that they would be sent GP registrars without ever having had the chance to interview them, or even meet them in person.

I remember complaining to the deanery recruitment and selection lead, saying that the quality of GP registrars we were being sent was questionable, and asking him what was he going to do about it. This was in annoyance that we had a bad experience with a registrar who we had not had the chance to interview, and who seemed completely incompatible for a career in primary care. His retort was appropriate – he enquired if I had volunteered to partake in the new GP trainee selection and assessment procedures, which had been clearly advertised to me, and he suggested that if I felt strongly enough to complain then perhaps I ought to get involved myself rather than leave it to others.

So was it 'broken', and did we need to 'fix it'?

There were advantages and disadvantages to the old system of having no procedures in place to select candidates for suitability to enter GP training, save them having GMC registration and the right to work in the UK. As far as I now can tell, the pros and cons of the 'old days' are summated as follows:

Advantages

- Training practices got to meet their prospective trainee, and presumably object if they felt that they would not be suitable.
- Trainees had the flexibility to choose their own hospital schemes that would best suit their educational needs.
- A lack of any formal recruitment structure was free of the running costs of administration for assessment.
- Local graduates seemed to apply for local GP training posts – thus possibly addressing local workforce needs.
- Trainees got to choose their training practice based upon reputation or locality to suit them.

Disadvantages

- This practice was in breach of equality and diversity regulations. At best, there was indirect discrimination as only local people would know about the unadvertised GP training posts. At worst, people simply chose whom they wanted.
- Anybody could join a GP training practice regardless of motivation or suitability for a career in general practice.
- Trainees often had the challenge of obtaining a new post by competitive interview every six months.

- Excellent candidates were not getting a fair chance to train.
- Poor candidates were causing training practices considerable stress.

The history of the development of our GP training selection procedure

Before the development of the national GP selection system, various or no selection methods were applied across different deaneries. Directors of Postgraduate GP Education were given the responsibility for developing a selection procedure that ensured open competition, and provided equal opportunities for all applicants. A commitment was made to work towards standardisation of recruitment methods across all deaneries, which eventually resulted in a national process. This process was broken down into three main areas:

Area one – job analysis

In keeping with selection procedures from other industries, a job analysis was conducted by Prof. Fiona Patterson (Work Psychology Group) and her colleagues in the year 2000 examining what a GP has to do in his or her working day, and then what attributes would make a good GP.[1] This outlined the relevant knowledge, skills, abilities and attitudes needed to perform competently as a GP, and now informs us to design our selection methods that are accurate (reliable), relevant (valid) and standardised across the country.

The original attributes thought to be necessary to be a good GP are summated in Table 10.1.

Area two – selection methodology

A selection procedure has to be different in design from an exit examination that gives a certificate of competency in a field. The difficulty in designing a selection procedure is that the question being asked is different, i.e. 'Does this person possess the personal attributes needed to successfully complete our training programme?' rather than 'Has this person gained the competencies and expertise required to safely exit our training programme?'

Once the job description and skills needed were agreed, selection methods needed to be designed to assess the candidate's capabilities against the relevant attributes, and the assessment piloted and finally implemented. It was decided that at selection for GP training there were five essential attributes from the table that needed to be present at the outset – the rest could be learned during the training process. The five chosen to be assessed at selection were:

- communication skills
- empathy and sensitivity
- conceptual thinking and problem solving
- professional integrity
- coping with pressure.

Table 10.1: A competency model for GPs with example behavioural descriptions

Attribute	Brief definition	Examples
Empathy and sensitivity	*Patient treated with empathy and personal understanding*	Doctor picks up on the patient's emotions and feelings
Communication skills	*Actively listens to patients, picks up body language and matches patient's language*	Is not patronising, can form relationships with patients
Clinical knowledge and expertise	*Able to apply and trust one's judgement*	Gives clear diagnosis and explains decisions
Conceptual thinking and problem solving	*Uses lateral thinking, can judge what is important from a mass of information*	Picks up on subtle cues, finds hidden agendas, uses probing questions
Personal attributes and desirable traits	*Flexible, sense of humour, passionate about the job, unselfish*	Warm, uses humour, innovative, changes plans depending on patient wishes
Personal organisation and administration skills	*Financially aware, uses IT systems well, can prioritise/ delegate*	Good time management, conscientious
Professional integrity	*Is open and honest, admits mistakes, acknowledges the contribution of others*	Takes responsibility, able to deal with all kinds of people, shows respect to patients and colleagues
Coping with pressure	*Remains calm, shares load with others, able to apologise or control anger*	Unhurried, doesn't get angry, self-awareness, ability to 'switch off' outside work
Managing others and team involvement	*Develops trust amongst peers, sees him or herself as a player in the organisation*	Pulls weight, compromises, negotiates, builds bridges
Legal, ethical and political awareness	*Demonstrates awareness of legal and ethical consequences of actions, can lobby on local and national level*	Aware of litigation and when to practise defensive medicine. Protects self legally
Learning and personal development	*Able to deal with change, updates skills*	Identifies what he or she doesn't know, deals with changing goalposts

Source: adapted from Patterson F, Ferguson E, Lane P, *et al.*[1]

The methodology and research used to do this is available at http://gprecruitment.hee.nhs.uk/ should the reader wish to know more. To summarise – the work showed that the most effective way to test these attributes was the combination of a long-listing procedure, a short-listing test in the form of a multiple-choice questionnaire (MCQ) paper, and a live exercise held at what was to become known as a selection and assessment centre (SAC).

Stage 1

The long-listing procedure confirms that he or she has the level of a satisfactory UK Foundation Year 2 doctor, has the right to work in the UK, and has no major unspent criminal convictions of relevance.

Stage 2

The short-listing MCQ is broken down into Clinical Problem Solving (CPS) questions, and a Situational Judgement Test (SJT) where ethical dilemmas are posed to the candidates to measure the appropriateness of their responses. An example of an SJT question is given in Box 10.1.

Box 10.1: Situational Judgement Test question

You are a second-year Foundation doctor (F2 or FY2) working in general practice.

At the baby clinic the nurse gives you a syringe with fluid already drawn up, an immunisation (MMR) to give to a baby. After the parent and child have gone home you realise that the syringe contained only diluent; the ampoule of active powder is intact.

Rank in order the following actions in response to this situation.

A. Contact the parent immediately and explain what has happened
B. Inform the practice manager of the nurse's mistake
C. Fill in a critical incident form
D. Send a further appointment without delay
E. Take no action

(A, D, C, B, E was deemed the correct order of actions to choose.)

An example of a Clinical Problem Solving question is given in Box 10.2, and was deemed necessary to ensure the applicants had the clinical acumen of a competent Foundation Year doctor:

Box 10.2: Clinical Problem Solving question

A 25-year-old woman has a mucopurulent discharge, pelvic pain, cervicitis and urethritis. Which is the **SINGLE** most likely cause of her symptoms? Choose **ONE** option only.

A. Bacterial vaginosis
B. *Candida albicans*
C. *Chlamydia trachomatis*
D. Herpes simplex
E. Trichomoniasis

(Answer is C.)

There is a national written paper working group whose responsibility it is to write, pilot and quality assure these questions, with great input from the Work Psychology Group. The final output paper comes from a two-day residential meeting where questions are peer-reviewed and discussed. All questions are piloted before appearing in a 'live' paper and statistically analysed for reliability.

Following later research, it became apparent that the SJT score was to be the most powerful predictor of future performance in later GP training of all the assessments performed at recruitment.

Stage 3

The SAC involves each candidate being subjected to an hour of assessments. These originally included a written paper, a group exercise (to assess performance in a team) and a simulated patient scenario. The group assessment has now been discarded in favour of two further simulated scenarios, which assess the candidate's performance with a patient's carer/relative, and a colleague who may not be a doctor (e.g. a nurse, or a ward cleaner).

Each written paper tests four of our chosen entry competencies, and the simulation stations test three. The highly trained examiners are calibrated to assess the competencies against a set of criteria, then award a mark from 1–4 in each competency based on a rating scale, as outlined below:

Box 10.3: Rating scale for competencies

4 – Strong display of specified positive behavioural indicators (and possibly others). Few negative indicators displayed, and these considered *minor in impact.*

3 – Satisfactory display of specified positive behavioural indicators. Some negative indicators displayed, but *none causing concern*.

2 – Limited number of specified positive behavioural indicators displayed. Many negative indicators displayed, *one or more causing concern.*

1 – Little evidence of specified positive behavioural indicators. Mostly negative indicators displayed, *one or more decisively*.

Written paper

The written paper generally describes a situation where a doctor has to leave the ward for another task within a specified timescale, and there are five simultaneous situations occurring. The challenge for the candidate is to prioritise the order in which he or she would deal with the issues, justifying his or her responses (see Box 10.4).

Box 10.4: Candidate instructions

You are a junior doctor working on a busy hospital ward. It is now 12 noon. You must leave by 1 p.m. to attend an interview for specialty training (cancellation of the interview is not an option). The various issues below remain outstanding and need to be prioritised for action.

Your task (30 minutes in total for the exercise)

1. To rank each issue in the order in which you intend to deal with it.
2. To justify your decisions and describe what action you will take.
3. To reflect on the challenges posed by this exercise.

Issues to be ranked

A. One of your female patients has dementia and severe Parkinson's disease. Her son has travelled 200 miles to meet with you. He is waiting to discuss his mother's future care.

B. You overhear a student nurse repeatedly shouting at a patient with dementia in the bed next to the nursing station where you are working.

C. The oncology nurse contacts you to inform you that one of the patients who is neutropenic has developed a temperature of 40.2°C.

D. The ward nurse-in-charge informs you that a patient who was diagnosed with multiple pulmonary emboli two days ago is refusing to take their warfarin.

E. You receive a text message from a colleague, whom you are due to hand over to, informing you that they will be late for their shift again (this is the third time in three weeks), and asking if you will cover them.

There is not deemed to be a correct or incorrect order of prioritisation. However, the examiners are instructed to assess the justifications for their choices, and categorise them against the tested competencies earlier outlined (e.g. empathy and sensitivity, coping with pressure).

Simulation scenarios

There are three simulated patient scenarios that aim to test our competencies in different ways. As stated before, the candidates are challenged with ten-minute consultations with a patient, a patient's carer or representative, and a colleague who usually will normally not be a doctor. The doctor/colleague scenario (anecdotally) seems to occasionally allow the poorer candidates to show their 'true colours' when speaking with somebody that they may feel is not their social or intellectual equal.

An example of a simulation scenario with a colleague is found in Box 10.5:

Box 10.5: Simulation C: candidate instructions

Context

In this exercise you will be consulted by a colleague in an acute hospital setting. The role of the colleague will be taken by somebody who is not directly involved in the assessment process.

Your task (ten minutes including reading time)

You are a Foundation (F2) doctor working in an obstetric unit. The hospital where you work has around 1000 births per year.

You have agreed to meet a midwife colleague in your ten-minute coffee break. She said she wanted to ask you something about work.

To increase face validity, we have started asking GP trainees to describe instances when a non-doctor colleague has had cause to speak to them about something that has been troubling them. A recollection that I had from being a junior doctor was when a rather irate cleaning lady accosted me in a covered outdoor walkway between hospital buildings. She complained about the fact that she was constantly being delayed getting to her ward cleaning duties, as the doctor's mess common-room was always full of last night's takeaway cartons, general detritus and dirty washing-up. She asked me what I was going to do about this – presumably identifying me as one of the culprits as I was wearing a rather grubby white coat with the pockets bulging with *Oxford Handbooks* and overhanging tourniquets.

I thought it best to apologise on behalf of the doctors for her distress, and assure her that I would have a word with my colleagues to try to assist in keeping the place a bit tidier. She seemed happy with that, so I suggested that I meet with her in a few weeks to see if things had indeed improved.

In similar examination scenarios I have come across candidates who seem to have no interest whatsoever in the problems of non-doctor colleagues, and state this quite frankly in front of the examiner who is marking! Working with colleagues and in teams is now one of our main tested competency areas for the MRCGP Workplace-Based Assessment – so I am pleased we have the opportunity to challenge them at the selection assessment.

How do we put the assessment results together and make a decision?

The quartile score of the SJT and the scores from the four tested exercises at the selection centre are put into a computerised matrix, which is projected onto a screen once the assessors have finished examining each cohort or candidates. Each matrix has a candidate photograph attached. Based upon the scores the candidate has received, the mathematical programme within the matrix can make a decision that the candidate has done well enough to enter training, has done poorly and should not enter training, or it is unsure and asks that only the examiners who had contact during the process should discuss the performance and give evidence to one of the day's assessment leads who acts as a moderator. The moderator weighs up the evidence presented and makes the final judgement as to whether a borderline candidate has demonstrated the competencies required to enter training.

Evaluation of our current system, and the future

Candidates fill in a post-assessment questionnaire each year. Trainees overwhelmingly feel that our current national GP selection procedure is fair, and that the scenarios have face validity. This year in the West Midlands we did not have any candidates out of the 500+ who applied appeal against their selection decision. Most candidates who are admitted to GP training successfully complete the MRCGP examination. Many other specialties are looking to the GP system of selection to revamp and improve their own selection procedures.

So – what of testing compassion in this system? Can we select for the compassionate? Of course, this is an attribute that is highly desirable for us to discover. I feel that our tested competency of empathy and sensitivity at least gives the candidate the chance to demonstrate this. They have many scenarios in the SJT and the simulated patient stations questions that are really asking them, 'Do you actually care? Can you be bothered to get involved in somebody else's problems?' We also instruct our examiners how to spot the 'coached' candidate, i.e. the one who can 'walk the walk and talk the talk' – as they have been advised what to do and say in the tests by other parties. A cardinal sign of not caring would be when the patient tells a candidate that their husband died last year, and the non-compassionate would then say that they were sorry to hear about that, before moving directly on to ask how their blood pressure was treated without so much as a glimmer of being interested in the circumstances.

However, the GP national recruitment office with the Work Psychology Group recognises that there is always room for improvement and refinement to our systems. The role of the GP has changed hugely since the original 'person specification' was published in the year 2000. Thus a new job analysis study was published in 2013 that acknowledged the changing demands on the modern GP. Fiona Patterson *et al.* concluded that the original assessed competencies remained important, but the domains of competency have broadened significantly to include balancing multiple agendas (e.g. the patient choice agenda versus commissioning restraints).[1] It is planned to keep the selection procedure up to speed with changes by modifying our methods to incorporate assessing the trainees' potential of gaining these new skills during training. Patients deserve the very best GPs at the crisis moments of their lives, and we intend to recruit the best possible candidates into our training programmes to fulfil this aim.

Reference

1. Patterson F, Ferguson E, Lane P, *et al.* A competency model for general practice: implications for selection, training, and development. *British Journal of General Practice* 2000; **50(452)**: 188–93.

Chapter 11

Reflections of a new GP

Tom Nolan

What does the college motto '*Cum scientia caritas*' mean to a newly qualified GP in 2014? To many of us, I suspect, it means very little: a Latin phrase belonging to an ancient world that, even if you did understand what it meant, you would never dare say out loud for fear of humiliation. But leaving aside whether Latin mottos are acceptable as topics of conversation, is 'science with compassion' relevant to a GP released from his or her training into modern primary care, a world of walk-in-centres, federations and Clinical Commissioning Groups?

If you believe the narrative of the GP press and the messages coming from the British Medical Association and the Royal College of General Practitioners, we are a profession in crisis. Recently qualified GPs are flocking to Australia, experienced GPs are retiring in their droves, and powerful secondary care organisations loom over struggling practices ready to take over lists and turn us all into salaried doctors. Those of us who decide to stay in the UK after we qualify are surely only thinking about survival, rather than pondering over whether they practise science with compassion? But is the current crisis really any different from the last one? Or the one before that?

Many of the more experienced GPs (considered by us more recently qualified as both oracles of wisdom or long in the tooth depending on how we're feeling) will tell you that this is the way it's always been. Giving them the benefit of the doubt then, let us take a break from panicking about the imminent death of general practice and reflect on *Cum scientia caritas* like many GPs have over the 60 years since the RCGP was formed.

General practice is very different from what it was when the College's motto was chosen. When Dr McCulloch, one of the founder members of the RCGP, gave his talk, '*Cum scientia caritas*', to the East Anglia RCGP faculty 17 years into the motto's life in 1969, his account of being a newly qualified GP could scarcely be more different from my own experience.[1]

> In 1922, on the very morning after I had graduated and registered – a simultaneous process in those distant days – I plunged straight into general practice armed with a thermometer and a stethoscope, and precariously buoyed up with faith, hope and charity – faith in whatever knowledge I had succeeded in acquiring from my

> excellent teachers, hope that I should remember the dose of strychnine and which forceps blade to insert first, plus my inborn but, so far, undeveloped caritas.

How times have changed. For me, in 2013, on the morning after I had registered as a fully qualified GP (seven years after graduating from medical school) I plunged straight into general practice armed not with a thermometer but a smartcard. Although I too was buoyed up with faith and hope, my faith was in Google and BNF Online, and my hope was that as the only male GP at the practice I wouldn't be called on to do too many smear tests.

But what about my *caritas*? Had four years of GP training, two Foundation years and six years of medical school made me a compassionate doctor? I had certainly learned the techniques: I was asking about ideas, concerns and expectations long before I could take blood or write a prescription, and I had later learned the value of connecting with patients so convincingly described by Neighbour.[2] To any observer, or Clinical Skills Assessment examiner, I was a caring, compassionate doctor. But inwardly, did I experience a 'feeling with' my patients that would allow me to see them as something more than a *piñata* to be hit in such a way that their symptoms fall out in a form that I could apply my accumulated knowledge to?

Perhaps evidence-based medicine has removed the need for compassion, which in McCulloch's account of his work in the 1920s seems to have been a sort of god of the gaps, filling in where contemporary medicine was failing.[1]

> Here was almost no science at all. ... We had opium and morphia and caritas. The battle against disease itself was a losing one, but we were able to win some mastery over the worst of physical suffering.

Now that we have a better understanding of disease and more effective treatments, our patients are less obviously suffering (at least physically) than they were in 1920. McCulloch described how quickly things had changed from the 1920s to the 1960s so that patients in the 1960s were 'for the most part in very good shape physically', meaning that GPs were 'faced with the more exacting task of considering the person as a whole than of simply dealing with a physical syndrome'.[1] Five decades later, the diagnosis and treatment of cardiovascular disease, malignancy and other leading causes of morbidity and mortality have completely changed. People are healthier and present earlier, meaning that our opportunities for 'simply dealing with a physical syndrome' are few and far between.

Newly qualified GPs of the 1960s were, according to McCulloch, full of the latest knowledge, but 'every patient they set eyes upon', he remarked, was 'at once a potential candidate for the operating theatre, the laboratory or, at the very least, the radiology department'.[1] How many of us newly qualified GPs wonder why we seem to refer more patients than our more experienced colleagues? We like to think it's our more up-to-date knowledge, but perhaps sometimes it's because we're missing the point.

McCulloch argued that his junior colleagues, in unnecessarily investigating patients rather than acknowledging and addressing their suffering, were depriving them of their martyrdom badge. Although wonderfully old fashioned in its name, the martyrdom badge seems very much a relevant idea in modern primary care. The bottles of brightly coloured, hideously flavoured medicine that McCulloch dispensed were the martyrdom badge that they required to gain 'that sympathy of which they have been starved'. He went on: 'whatever these things contain, our giving them to the patient, short of poisoning him, is good therapy. Indeed, nowadays they are an absolute necessity.'

But can we, or should we, find room for the martyrdom badge in a world dominated by evidence-based medicine? Fifty years on from McCulloch's talk, the demands on GPs to be up to date with scientific and clinical knowledge are greater than ever. Guidance exists for practically every condition and symptom, giving an objective judgement on everything from the common cold to end-of-life care.

How many of us newly qualified GPs recite these guidelines to our patients, saying (perhaps with a satisfying sense of our superior knowledge) things like, 'I can't prescribe you that because there's no evidence that it works', while remaining completely oblivious to the underlying request for McCulloch's martyrdom badge. I can hear myself saying these words, and can recall my sense of bewilderment in the disappointed or sometimes angry response from my patient. What is the solution though? To prescribe drugs that we know are no more effective than sugar pills for the sake of providing a compassionate rather than scientific response to patients' circumstances? The modern-day preoccupation with quantitative, evidence-based medicine does not seem to have an answer to this problem. The modern-day preoccupation with access to primary care doesn't even realise there is a problem.

Unconditional doctoring

For a two-week period this year, on returning home from work each day, my wife would tell me about the latest chapter from a book called *Unconditional Parenting*.[3] It was my role, I felt, to scoff at this parenting technique that says that punishments and rewards aimed at getting children to do what you want only serve to make children want to earn your approval.

Unconditional Parenting says you have to show your child that you will love them no matter what by never withdrawing your approval, and using other methods to teach them right from wrong. One evening, as she described the latest chapter, my mind began to wander onto one of the more challenging patients I had seen that day. Every time I saw this particular patient, currently on a weekly basis, she had some new crisis that would be described through floods of tears. Over the weeks I'd discovered that each of this patient's loved ones had given up on her: parents, siblings, friends and partners. I had increasingly got the feeling that I was being challenged to do the same. As my wife's words about unconditional parenting filtered through, and as I continued to nod and say yes at the appropriate moments, I realised that by refusing to withdraw my approval and willingness to help I had been using the technique of the unconditional parent with my patient (although hopefully in an adult-to-adult rather than a parent-to-child manner).

I have seen unconditional doctoring, as you might call it, being practised by each of the doctors whom I have looked up to throughout my training for their compassion and commitment to their patients. The patience, understanding and care that these doctors give must surely be borne out of a sense of compassion rather than any scientific calculation that this approach will statistically be most likely to benefit the patient.

Time to care

Many of us newly qualified GPs have been on the training treadmill since medical school (and in education of one sort or another since before we could hold a pen). Leaving this sheltered world behind and becoming an independent practitioner can be daunting. But being launched into the big wide world of general practice can also come at a time of great change in our personal lives. It is around this time that the grim truth that we are no longer in our early twenties dawns on us all. The priorities of one life are gradually replaced by those of a new one. Revision, parties, dating, exams, holidays and next month's rent become buying a house, pensions, life insurance, marriage and children. Parties and holidays remain but with the prefixes of dinner and family respectively.

Aged 31, with more than a few grey hairs already, married and expecting our first baby, I was just coming to terms with these shifting priorities when I started work as a fully qualified GP. One of the unexpected benefits of being a new dad and a GP was a newfound understanding of the anxieties of first-time parents. I'd previously done my best to reassure the mums and dads of snotty children with coughs, but often fallen short. 'Sorry for wasting your time' were the departing words of many a parent, as they left the surgery, crossed the road, and waited for a bus to take them to A&E for a second opinion.

Having a child means that I know what it's like to see a spot on my baby's skin and worry that it's meningitis, and I've had a glimpse of the desperation a parent can feel when a newborn just won't stop crying (although we got off lightly compared with many). Having these recent memories means I know exactly what it feels like to be worried about these things, and it's made me more compassionate towards this group of patients. I can show that I know how it feels, show genuine empathy and truly connect with the problem. This is compassion as described by Peter Toon in his recent book *A Flourishing Practice?*[4]

> Compassion is a natural response to suffering that motivates what we do as clinicians. ... We don't share the suffering of the patient, but we see it and that involves its own suffering. Obviously we feel less for a patient than we would for a son or a close friend, but if we don't feel sad when we see suffering ... we are less than fully human.

But does how I feel inside really matter? Can I be compassionate without feeling sympathy or empathy, or suffering alongside the patient?

Recently a patient thanked me as she was leaving my consulting room and said that I was a compassionate doctor. I was at once flattered, wary and confused. Confused as I felt I'd done little in the consultation apart from sit opposite her, nod my head and reflected back to her some of what she'd said. I didn't recall feeling moved by her problem, or saddened by her suffering. I felt that I wanted to help her with her problem and I had the means to do so thanks to numerous years of training, a reasonable night's sleep the previous night and an empty bladder. But there was one other key ingredient that allowed me to behave in a compassionate manner: time. For however we define compassion, either as a feeling or behaviour, we know that in a ten-minute consultation it rarely gets the chance to emerge.

Compassion requires time. Time to listen, time to explain, time to let someone finish telling his or her story, time to offer sympathy rather than antibiotics as a martyrdom badge, time to look up the evidence, time to let the tears dry, time to think, and time to clear your head before the next patient. When we're overworked and have no time we stop feeling and acting compassionately.

This is seen on an individual basis in the growing numbers of burnt-out GPs and in whole institutions as described in the Francis Report into the failings at Mid Staffordshire hospital.[5] In project management there is a useful rule to aid time management: the 60:20:20 rule.[6] That's 60% of time allocated for planned work, 20% for unplanned work and 20% for socialising. What a difference to compassion and caring would it make to use these ratios in general practice? Where I work we undoubtedly fall short of this standard but we offer 15-minute appointments and try to find half an hour a day to have lunch or a chat with each other. It seems to work.

As the motto '*Cum scientia caritas*' reaches its sixtieth birthday, perhaps it's time for it to retire and be replaced by a motto we can all understand: science with time.

References

1. McCulloch GL. *Cum scientia caritas*. *Journal of the Royal College of General Practitioners* 1969; **18(89)**: 315–20.
2. Neighbour R. *The Inner Consultation: how to develop an effective and intuitive consulting style*. Abingdon: Radcliffe Publishing, 2005.
3. Kohn A. *Unconditional Parenting: moving from rewards and punishments to love and reason*. New York: Atria Books, 2006.
4. Toon PD. *A Flourishing Practice?* London: RCGP, 2014.
5. Francis R. *Report of the Mid Staffordshire NHS Foundation Trust Public Inquiry*. London: TSO, 2013, www.midstaffspublicinquiry.com/report [accessed 27 April 2015].
6. Klanten R. *The Little Know-it-all: common sense for designers*. Berlin: Die Gestalten Verlag, 2007.

Chapter 12

The role of the multidisciplinary team and interprofessional learning

J.E. Thistlethwaite

Quality standards for the NHS state that 'patients are treated with dignity, kindness, compassion, courtesy, respect, understanding and honesty' and that they 'are introduced to all healthcare professionals involved in their care, and are made aware of the roles and responsibilities of the members of the healthcare team'.[1] Teams of health professionals play a major role in healthcare delivery in the twenty-first century. Such teams have various titles such as *the multidisciplinary team* (common in palliative and child care), the *primary healthcare team* and the *multiprofessional team*. They are formed of a diverse range of health and social care professionals, each of whom have different, though sometimes overlapping, roles and responsibilities. In primary care a core team may be comprised of one or more GPs, practice nurses, nurse practitioners, community nurses, etc., as well as a physiotherapist, psychologist and podiatrist, for example, depending on the nature of the general practice or community health centre. Added to this core group is a wider collaboration of practitioners who at certain times share responsibility for the care of a patient or a family. These may include hospital specialists through referral processes.

Patients (or service users) within the NHS thus frequently interact with more than one health professional during their 'patient journey', where that journey may be defined as their experience of and movement through the health service during the course of an illness or condition. In particular people with complex and long-term conditions will consult with many different health and social care professionals and move between services and locations many times. One British study focusing on patients with cancer found that 28 doctors were involved in the first year after diagnosis.[2] This figure did not include all the other professionals encountered during this time. Similarly, an observational study of interactions in an emergency department reported that between eight and 15 health professionals were involved with each patient's visit, whereas one patient, whose face-to-face interactions with staff lasted 47 minutes in total, had 62 separate encounters in that time.[3] Obviously, the more people involved in care, the more possibility that it becomes fragmented and that there is a lack of communication and continuity between all involved. Patients and families may receive conflicting advice, leading to misunderstandings and poor adherence to management plans. It may not be clear who has overall responsibility for their care. This causes frustrations for both those receiving and providing health services, a situation that is not conducive to compassionate care and empathic understanding.

The process of teamwork

Although there are many definitions of a team across all literatures, I prefer this one of teamwork:[4]

> Teamwork represents a set of values that encourage behaviours such as listening and constructively responding to points of view expressed by others, giving others the benefit of the doubt, providing support to those who need it, and recognizing the interests and achievements of others.

One interesting question is the status of the patient in relation to the healthcare team. Is he or she a member? In the interprofessional literature we read of the patient as being at the centre of the team, resonating with the concept of patient-centred care and the suggestion that 'medical care without compassion cannot be truly patient-centred'.[5] But what does this mean in practice? And how does this equate to team meetings to which patients and families aren't invited?

Three conditions have been defined as being necessary for teams to function optimally.[6] These include that clear objectives (goals) are set and known by all members, that the members work closely together to achieve the objectives, and that the team meets regularly to review progress and discuss performance and how it may be improved. The shared decision-making approach to clinical practice advocates that patients and their healthcare professionals do reach consensus about a management plan,[7] but still too often patients do not feel that they are involved in decisions. Team meetings take place at which decisions are made without the patient present. The patient subsequently may not be informed of the thinking behind such decisions. They 'may be in the best interests of the patient' but who is the best judge of those interests? Patients are thus really not team members in the same sense as the professionals.

Values-based collaborative practice

Values-based practice (VBP) aims to involve the patient, family, professionals and the team in decision-making and management.[8] For professionals it should complement evidence-based practice and facilitate patient partnership. Indeed part of the original definition of evidence-based medicine includes the following:[9]

> the conscientious, explicit, and judicious use of current best evidence in making decisions about the care of individual patients. The practice of evidence based

> medicine means integrating individual clinical expertise with the best available external clinical evidence from systematic research. By individual clinical expertise we mean the proficiency and judgment that individual clinicians acquire through clinical experience and clinical practice. Increased expertise is reflected in many ways, but especially in more effective and efficient diagnosis and in the more thoughtful identification and *compassionate use* [my emphasis] of individual patients' predicaments, rights, and preferences in making clinical decisions about their care.

In health care values may be defined as 'the unique preferences, concerns and expectations each patient brings to a clinical encounter and which must be integrated into clinical decisions if they are to serve the patient',[10] whereas VBP is 'a blending of the values of both the service user and the health and social care professional, thus creating a true, as opposed to a tokenistic partnership'. [11]

VBP is included in the curriculum of the Royal College of General Practitioners (RCGP), which states that all GPs should be able to understand and respect values and how their own values may impact on patient care and decision-making.[12] In a team the personal values of individuals also have an impact on patient care, team dynamics and the collaborative process.[8] Collaborative practice, a priority of the World Health Organization (WHO), not only includes teamwork but also acknowledges the importance of working with others who are not co-located and do not meet regularly. Furthermore the WHO suggests that there is now sufficient evidence to show that collaborative practice enhances health services and improves health outcomes, particularly for patients with long-term conditions.[13] The following definition stresses respect and trust between collaborators, conditions that require an understanding of each other's knowledge, skills and values.[14]

> Interprofessional collaboration is the process of developing and maintaining effective interprofessional working relationships with learners, practitioners, patients/clients/families and communities to enable optimal health outcomes. Elements of collaboration include respect, trust, shared decision making, and partnerships.

Professional values and personal values may conflict. Good collaborative practice for patient-centred care therefore requires skills of negotiation, conflict resolution and compromise. How often do team members discuss their values and how these may affect their interactions? In addition, in relation to the focus of this book, can compassion be a shared value of the team? How is compassion demonstrated through team processes? Orientation for new members to the team, the wider collaboration and the new working environments are important. Although some of the knowledge necessary will be gained through working together, this cannot be assumed. The new member should be encouraged to discuss his or her own values within the context of a team discussion on shared values. Such sharing and reaching consensus may not come naturally: it may involve conflict and negotiation, the conflict arising sometimes due to conflicting values and lack of communication.

Interprofessional learning

Contemporary health professional education at the undergraduate and postgraduate level is still predominantly carried out as a uniprofessional enterprise. Although curricula do frequently include learning outcomes related to teamwork, students rarely work in multidisciplinary teams and therefore may graduate with little practical experience of collaborative practice. General practice-based education can certainly be delivered interprofessionally. Interprofessional education (IPE) is defined as occasions when two or more professions learn with, from and about each other to improve collaboration and the quality of care,[15] whereas interprofessional learning (IPL) arises from interaction between members of two or more professions. IPL may be a product of formalised interprofessional education or happen spontaneously in the workplace.[16]

For teams to perform well, they must also be continuously learning.[17] To be effective as learners, teams must engage in learning processes that include collaborative problem solving, reflection and work practice improvement.[18] We learn teamwork best by observation and practice, and reflection on that observation and practice, with feedback from others if possible. For IPE this observation and reflection is no longer an individual process but also involves other team members.[19] A key need for successful learning teams is the concept of psychological safety, which means that team members can take interpersonal risks without repercussions. When team members perceive a level of respect and acceptance, they experience higher levels of psychological safety, which, in turn, allows them to speak freely, facilitating the learning process and a discussion and sharing of values.[20] The health professionals involved are less likely to be concerned about bringing up errors or discussing their concerns.

An IPL session can focus on sharing understanding of common concepts such as patient-centredness, compassion and empathy. Team members can discuss how compassion may be demonstrated and what may lead to a lack of compassion by individuals or indeed the team. Some health professionals may not have considered the nature of compassion before. The underlying emotion of compassion, as expressed through compassionate care in the practice setting, is not easily defined and put into words.[21] Team members may share how they express compassion through a simple gesture such as a smile, an appropriate touch, or even silence.[22]

Conclusion

Team-based care may be compassionate care but teams and wider collaborations need to consider their values and those of their patients. Continuity is important with patients being aware of who is responsible for their ongoing managements. Values can be discussed and teamwork enhanced through interprofessional learning.

References

1. National Institute for Health and Care Excellence. *Patient Experience in Adult NHS Services* (Quality Statement 31). London: NICE, 2012, www.nice.org.uk/guidance/QS15 [accessed 11 May 2015].

2. Smith S, Nicol KM, Devereux J, Cornbleet MA. Encounters with doctors: quantity and quality. *Palliative Medicine* 1999; **13(3)**: 217–23.
3. Manidis M, Slade D, McGregor J, *et al*. *Emergency Communication: report for Prince of Wales Hospital.* Sydney: UTS, 2009.
4. Katzenbach JR, Smith DK. *The Wisdom of Teams: creating the high-performance organization*. Boston: Harvard Business School Press, 1993.
5. Lown BA, Rosen J, Marttila J. An agenda for improving compassionate care: a survey shows about half of patients say such care is missing. *Health Affairs* 2011; **30(9)**: 1772–8.
6. Dawson JF, Yan X, West MA. *Positive and Negative Effects of Team Working in Healthcare: real and pseudo-teams and their impact on safety*. Birmingham: Aston University, 2007.
7. Towle A, Godolphin W, Richardson A. *Competencies for Informed Shared Decision Making (ISDM). Report on interviews with physicians, patients and patient educators and focus group meetings with patients.* Vancouver: University of British Columbia, 1997.
8. Thistlethwaite JE. *Values-Based Interprofessional Collaborative Practice*. Cambridge: Cambridge University Press, 2012.
9. Sackett DL, Rosenberg WM, Muir Gray JA, *et al*. Evidence-based medicine: what it is and what it isn't. *British Medical Journal* 1996; **312(7023)**: 71–2.
10. Thornton T. Tacit knowledge as the unifying factor in evidence-based medicine and clinical judgement. *Philosophy, Ethics and Humanities in Medicine* 2006; **1(1)**: E2.
11. Thomas M, Burt M, Parkes J. The emergence of evidence-based practice. In: J McCarthy, P Rose (eds). *Values-Based Health and Social Care: beyond evidence-based practice*. London: Sage, 2010, pp. 3–24.
12. Royal College of General Practitioners. *The RCGP Curriculum: introduction and user guide*. London: RCGP, 2012, www.rcgp.org.uk/~/media/Files/GP-training-and-exams/Curriculum-2012/RCGP-Curriculum-Introduction-and-User-Guide-2012.ashx [accessed 11 May 2015].
13. World Health Organization. *Framework for Action on Interprofessional Education and Collaborative Practice.* Geneva: WHO, 2010.
14. Canadian Interprofessional Health Collaborative. *A National Interprofessional Competency Framework*. Vancouver: CIHC, 2010, www.cihc.ca/files/CIHC_IPCompetencies_Feb1210.pdf [accessed 11 May 2015].
15. Centre for the Advancement of Interprofessional Education. Defining IPE. London: CAIPE, 2002, http://caipe.org.uk/about-us/defining-ipe/ [accessed 11 May 2015].
16. Freeth D, Hammick M, Reeves S, *et al*. *Effective Interprofessional Education: development, delivery and evaluation*. Oxford: Blackwell Publishing, 2005.
17. Edmondson A. Psychological safety and learning behavior on work teams. *Administrative Science Quarterly* 1999; **44(2)**: 350–83.
18. Argote L, Gruenfeld D, Naquin C. Group learning in organizations. In: M Turner (ed). *Groups at Work: advances in theory and research*. New York: Erlbaum, 2001, pp. 369–411.
19. Elwyn G, Greenhalgh T, Macfarlane F. *Groups. A guide to small group work in healthcare, management and research*. Abingdon: Radcliffe Medical Press, 2001.
20. Kessel M, Kratzner J, Schultz C. Psychological safety, knowledge sharing, and creative performance in healthcare teams. *Creativity and Innovation Management* 2012; **21(2)**: 127–243.
21. Davin L, Thistlethwaite JE. Editorial. Compassion: wherefore are though? *International Journal of Practice-Based Learning* 2014; **2(1)**: 122–6.
22. Dewar B, Pullin S, Tocheris R. Valuing compassion through definition and measurement. *Nursing Management* 2011; **17(9)**: 32–7.

Chapter 13

Revalidation and compassion, continuity and caring

Alastair Blake and Nigel Sparrow

Revalidation – what is it and what is its aim?

Revalidation is the process by which licensed doctors are required to demonstrate to the General Medical Council (GMC) that they are up to date and fit to practise.[1] It applies to all licensed doctors in the UK, in all specialties, at all stages of training, working in both the NHS and private practice. By introducing revalidation, the UK is the first country in the world to have a system of compulsory relicensure of doctors.[2] The UK is the first country to have a compulsory country-wide system for this. The Maintenance of Certification process in the US is organised at state level and so is variable across the country and voluntary.

The aim of revalidation is to improve the care patients receive from doctors and to give them confidence that their doctor meets the professional standards required of them.[1] In this way, revalidation is an important national policy mechanism for improving quality of care.

What is the process of revalidation?

The process of revalidation involves four key steps.[3] First, all doctors are required to have an annual appraisal. During this appraisal the doctor will show to the appraiser that he or she is up to date and fit to practise across the whole scope of his or her role as a doctor in a given specialty. These appraisals are performed by an appraiser organised by the doctor's 'designated body'. All doctors have a prescribed connection to a designated body, which in the case of GPs is often their NHS England Area Team.

Second, doctors have to maintain a portfolio of supporting information which illustrates that they meet the principles and values set out in *Good Medical Practice*,[4] as well as fulfilling the guidance for their specialty. In the case of GPs, this guidance was developed by the Royal College of General Practitioners (RCGP), and involves six components: continuing professional development (CPD), annual quality improvement activity, significant events and quality improvement/clinical audit work, colleague feedback, patient feedback and formal complaints.[5]

Third, every five years the doctor's 'responsible officer' will recommend that the GMC revalidates the doctor if he or she is up to date and fit to practise. This decision will be based upon the outcomes of the doctor's appraisals and other clinical governance information. In this way, the process of revalidation has two component parts: continuous monitoring and episodic relicensing.

Finally, once the GMC receives this recommendation from the responsible officer and it completes other checks, it will reissue the doctor's licence to practise, hence completing the revalidation process.

A SHORT HISTORY OF REVALIDATION

Revalidation was introduced against a long history of increasing desire for a more rigorous way of ensuring doctors remained fit to practise. The era of passive patient trust is rightly long behind us. High-profile examples of poor practice at Alder Hey Children's Hospital and Bristol Royal Infirmary highlighted the potential disconnect between the expectations of the public and that of doctors – undermining the credibility of relying on individuals' sense of 'professionalism' as a means of quality assurance. Compounded with this, the rise of evidence-based medicine and nationally set targets helped to clarify and publicise expected standards of clinical care that had previously lain in the realm of professional judgement. The rise of the debate about a 'new professionalism' for doctors made it clear that a new approach to ensuring the competency of doctors would be needed.[2,6]

In 1975, the Merrison Committee[7] recommended periodic tests of competency for all doctors. These were declared impractical by the Alment Committee a year later.[8] Early changes that paved the way for revalidation began in 1999 when the Department of Health signposted the introduction of compulsory appraisal,[9] which became a contractual obligation for GPs in the 2004 GP Contract. Following this, the GMC incorporated revalidation and appraisal into the 2006 version of *Good Medical Practice*,[4] which was then followed by the introduction of the licence to practise in 2009.[10] The importance of the licence is that it introduced a distinction between holding registration with the GMC and being fit and legally permitted to practise. Once this dissociation was made, doctors could remain registered with or without renewing their licence to practise. In the words of Sir Donald Irvine, former President of the GMC:[11]

> [The licence], hitherto granted on completion of basic medical education, would cease to be a once and for all indicator of professional competence. Instead it would become a continuously updated, evidence-based statement of all doctors' current fitness to practise in their chosen field, renewed every five years.

Revalidation was formally announced by the Secretary of State for Health, Rt Hon Jeremy Hunt, in December 2012. As of 31 October 2014, 71,072 doctors have been revalidated, and the majority of doctors in the country will have gone through the process by December 2016.

How does revalidation relate to 'cum scientia caritas'?

Caritas: compassion for patients at the heart of revalidation

Revalidation is an inherently compassionate endeavour for both our patients and colleagues. It encourages us to reflect on the quality of the care we deliver and the changing nature of the doctor–patient relationship. As individual practitioners, by collecting patient feedback (a mandatory component of revalidation) we consider how effectively we are meeting our patients' needs, in delivering person-centred, compassionate care. This feedback is essential as only patients can truly judge how well they felt they were treated. And more widely as a profession, revalidation encourages us to reflect on how we advocate for patients and safeguard them from poor-quality care at a systems level – working with them as partners, not as paternalists.

It is not just compassion for patients that makes revalidation a laudable endeavour. The process encourages us to be compassionate with our colleagues too – in helping them develop and improve their practice through giving and receiving feedback. Improving and formalising the role of peer feedback in front-line medicine is valuable on two levels. First, for the individual concerned, seeking constructive criticism and challenge from colleagues can hold a mirror up to our practice and reveal our blind spots to us – the 'unknown unknowns' about our practice that we wouldn't otherwise recognise. Second, if feedback is used properly it is integral to building a 'learning organisation', where feedback is viewed as a gift, and safety and organisational performance is improved.[12] The role of revalidation in encouraging this transition towards a learning organisation is all the more important given the way feedback was often historically used in medical education. If revalidation can also help us challenge working cultures – from the historic picture of one where doctors were seen as the unchallengeable 'master apprentices'[6] to that of a multidisciplinary team of life-long learners who work together as a 'pitcrew'[13] then it will be a valuable intervention for clinicians, organisations, systems and ultimately patients.

Scientia: knowledge and revalidation

The practice of clinical medicine has changed dramatically in the last 20 years, nowhere more so than primary care. Conditions that were once managed predominantly by secondary care consultants are increasingly in the realm of day-to-day general practice. As health service redesign places an increasing emphasis on shifting the locus of care towards the community, patients who were traditionally looked after in in-patient settings may now be managed in the community under the care of GPs overseeing a 'Virtual Ward'.[14] Furthermore, as the horizons of what is possible in the field of medicine expand, the amount of knowledge GPs are expected to retain increases correspondingly. It is estimated that a century ago a physician could expect to know everything in the field of medicine,[15] an aspiration now rendered impossible by the growth rate in medical knowledge – it is currently estimated that medical knowledge doubles every 3.5 years.[16]

It is against this backdrop of this 'information revolution' that revalidation has particular pertinence – if we are to deliver compassionate care for our patients as highlighted by '*Cum scientia caritas*', clinicians need to remain abreast of current knowledge. It is precisely because this task is getting harder and harder to assure ourselves of that the need for revalidation grows. In the face of such a challenge, revalidation is surely the professionally responsible thing to do, to ensure we continue to deliver high-quality care for patients – reflecting our professional duty as doctors.

However, although the volume of information and the necessity for doctors to keep abreast of it have increased, the barriers to accessing it have dramatically lowered. This has opened up two important phenomena in the practice of clinical medicine. First, medical knowledge – historically the exclusive privilege of doctors – is increasingly accessible by patients who are now better informed, and sometimes more knowledgeable about their condition than the doctor treating them. Second, the use of computerised clinical decision aids is growing quickly – helping doctors utilise the latest information about a condition or treatment during a consultation that they may not have previously known. The era of Google being an 'accurate diagnostician' is upon us.[17]

Inherent in this extraordinary boom in the quantity of information, and the simultaneous drop in the threshold for accessing it, is there a challenge to the very heart of what it means to be 'up to date'? Do we admit that it is impossible for the twenty-first-century clinician to know everything about his or her chosen field? In this context is it appropriate to shift our focus from the edification of information retention towards assessing practitioners' values and behaviours around learning and using it? After all, facts are of little use unless they are meaningfully applied in an appropriate context. GPs as 'expert generalists' are trained in managing the important interfaces of health and illness as well as certainty and uncertainty. In so doing, they demonstrate this critical distinction between 'information' and 'knowledge'. Although anyone may be able to retain medical facts, the expert clinician adds value through his or her combination of these facts with experience of context and an understanding of risk to create a *knowledgeable* solution to a patient's problem.

The College has already made a significant step towards this in its approach to continuous professional development (CPD). CPD credits are an integral part of the revalidation process, and they can be accrued by undertaking formal learning, but crucially in reflecting on this learning[18] – an important way of demonstrating the requisite values and behaviours towards knowledge. In this respect, revalidation is not just about showing what you know, but about demonstrating one's approach to bringing the vast quantities of medical knowledge to bear for the benefit of patients.

How has the College shaped the revalidation agenda?

This book celebrates how compassion lies at the heart of the College and its members. The strength of this dedication to compassion can be easily seen through the College's efforts in supporting the introduction of revalidation and its support to members going through the process.

In 1998, the RCGP and the other royal colleges were asked by the GMC to lead on developing specialty-specific standards for revalidation. The RCGP, working with the

General Practitioners Committee of the British Medical Association and the GMC, produced *Good Medical Practice for General Practitioners*.[19] This was a vital step in defining standards for revalidation. The College also wrote a core document called *Criteria, Standards and Evidence for Revalidation of General Practitioners*,[20] first published in 2000, which developed into the current *RCGP Guide to the Revalidation of General Practitioners*.[5] The College supported the GMC throughout the early consultations on revalidation, and developed the specialty-specific guidance for general practice.[21] This guidance contextualises revalidation for the primary care setting, and describes how GPs should meet the requirements for revalidation. Furthermore, as the planning for the second cycle of revalidation begins in 2015/16, the College will be updating this guidance and will continue to work with the GMC to ensure the process is appropriate for GPs.

The College also has a track record of setting standards and striving to improve the quality of care provided by GPs. This started with *What Sort of Doctor?*[22] and *Fellowship by Assessment*[23] and then *Membership by Assessment of Performance*.[24] Since 1968 the MRCGP has been the licensing examination for GPs.[25] Therefore it intuitively follows that any process of relicensure should include the standards set in the MRCGP curriculum.

Thinking about the future – how will revalidation evolve?

The first cycle of revalidation has been a success in many ways. Its mere introduction is noteworthy for its uniqueness – the UK is the only country to have a national system of relicensure internationally. However, its future evolution faces some significant challenges, particularly around how revalidation will evolve to meet its ultimate aspiration – a way of ensuring that delivering optimal care for patients becomes a 'professional obligation, not an aspiration without commitment'.[11] The first cycle of revalidation was developed with a sense of combining principles with pragmatism. The opportunity now is to learn from the experience of the first cycle and enhance the system of revalidation to demonstrate robustly that doctors have the knowledge, skills and competencies to deliver safe, effective and compassionate care.

Although logic tells us that revalidation is a compassionate endeavour for both patients and our colleagues (see above), the challenge of *demonstrating* improvements in compassionate care for patients as a result of revalidation remains. It is therefore intuitive that the process could develop a greater focus on patient experience outcomes in order to demonstrate this improvement in compassionate care.

Although getting 40 patient feedback surveys is a useful starting place for evaluating a doctor's performance, over five years of practice this would reflect a very small percentage of a typical clinician's patient interactions. Future iterations of revalidation should seek to increase the quantity and quality of feedback to give a better reflection of a doctor's practice. New technological approaches will help this aspiration become a reality, with websites such as iWantGreatCare.org already providing a platform for patients to leave feedback independently about the quality of their doctor.[26]

And with this increase in the volume of data we have about a clinician's performance, so must the sophistication of our analysis increase. As we discussed above, more information does not necessarily equate to more knowledge or wisdom – it is critical that information is synthesised in a meaningful way. Nowhere is this more important that in the context of negative feedback. With the importance of patient feedback being given more weight in clinical appraisal and revalidation comes the hazard of unjust negative comments being used to the detriment of a doctor's career progression and morale. For example, a complaint or piece of negative feedback may not be based in fact, or may blame a clinician for issues beyond his or her control. Any system we use must be compassionate to both patients and also our colleagues by reconciling freedom of expression with fairness and justice.

A further challenge for increasing the amount of data we have to make assessments about a doctor's fitness to practise is the phenomenon of 'feedback fatigue'. If the burden of giving and receiving feedback is high, then there is a risk that the quality of each piece is low, which could undermine the integrity and utility of the whole appraisal process. This could apply to patients who could become inundated with feedback requests for all the health and care professionals they interact with (often on a daily basis), as well as colleagues, who may have to give feedback about junior doctors, fellow GPs and other multidisciplinary team members. Thus, the feedback mechanisms we develop in future must be robust enough not to be abused while remaining light-touch, honest and meaningful.

If we opine that revalidation improves the quality of care patients receive then we should hope to demonstrate this with improvements in clinical outcomes. This presents an even greater challenge than measuring improved patient satisfaction. However, it is something many patients would legitimately wish to know – after all, one of the first questions any patient asks him or herself is 'Will this doctor help me get better?' This remains a challenge on several fronts. First, it is difficult robustly to link a patient outcome with the actions of an individual clinician in many specialties – particularly internal medicine and general practice. This linkage is easier to make in surgical specialties, which explains why much of the current work on publishing clinical outcomes is focused on this area.[27] As a result, there is a widespread culture of uneasiness within the profession of publishing outcomes data, which remains a challenge to its incorporation into the revalidation process.

Finally, revalidation must win over its critics and confront the cynicism of some front-line staff who view the process as a tick-box exercise rather than the opportunity to encourage excellence for which it was designed. In these pressured times in the NHS, bureaucratic processes, no matter how important, are often framed negatively.[2] We have an opportunity as we move towards a second cycle of revalidation to improve the quality of patient care, protect the public from unacceptable doctors and promote the values of high-quality, patient-centred care provided by doctors with the knowledge, skills and competencies evidenced through revalidation.

Despite these challenges, revalidation will continue to develop as an important tool for assuring the country of the quality of its compassionate, knowledgeable doctors. Ultimately 'compassionate treatment' is in the eye of the beholder and the only way we can know how compassionate we are is by asking our patients and colleagues as we do through the revalidation process.

References

1. General Medical Council. An introduction to revalidation. 2015. www.gmc-uk.org/doctors/revalidation/9627.asp [accessed 2 February 2015].
2. Nath V, Seale B, Kaur M. *Medical Revalidation: from compliance to commitment*. London: King's Fund, 2014.
3. General Medical Council. How revalidation works. 2015. www.gmc-uk.org/doctors/revalidation/9612.asp [accessed 2 February 2015].
4. General Medical Council. *Good Medical Practice*. Manchester: GMC, 2013.
5. Royal College of General Practitioners. *The RCGP Guide to the Revalidation of General Practitioners*. London: RCGP, 2014.
6. Christmas S, Millward L. *New Medical Professionalism: a scoping report for the Health Foundation*. London: Health Foundation, 2011.
7. Merrison A. Report of the Merrison Committee. *Proceedings of the Royal Society of Medicine* 1975; **68(12)**: 763.
8. Alment SA. *Report of the Committee of Enquiry Set up for the Medical Profession in the United Kingdom 'Competence to Practise'*. London: Committee of Enquiry, 1976.
9. Department of Health. *Supporting Doctors, Protecting Patients*. London: DH, 1999.
10. General Medical Council. *Licence to Practise: guidance for doctors*. Manchester: GMC, 2009, www.gmc-uk.org/6a___Annex_B___Licences_to_Practise__Consultation_Report_and_Approval_of_Draft_Guidance_for_Doctors.pdf_25400190.pdf [accessed 2 February 2015].
11. Irvine D. *Patients, Their Doctors and the Politics of Medical Professionalism* (American Osler Society, John P. McGovern Award Lectureship). Oxford: Picker Institute Europe, 2014.
12. Birleson P. Building a learning organisation in a child and adolescent mental health service. *Australian Health Review* 1998; **21(3)**: 223–40.
13. Gawande A. Cowboys and pit crews. *The New Yorker*, 26 May 2011, www.newyorker.com/news/news-desk/cowboys-and-pit-crews [accessed 14 May 2015].
14. Lewis G, Georghiou T, Steventon A, *et al*. *Impact of 'Virtual Wards' on Hospital Use: a research study using propensity matched controls and a cost analysis*. Southampton: NIHR, 2013.
15. Gillam M, Feied C, Handler J, *et al*. The healthcare singularity and the age of semantic medicine. In: T Hey, S Tansley, K Tolle (eds). *The Fourth Paradigm: data-intensive scientific discovery*. Redmond, WA: Microsoft, 2009, pp. 57–64.
16. Densen P. Challenges and opportunities facing medical education. *Transactions of the American Clinical and Climatological Association* 2011; **122**: 48–58.
17. Tang H, Ng JHK. Googling for a diagnosis – use of Google as a diagnostic aid: internet based study. *British Medical Journal* 2006; **333(7579)**: 1143–5.
18. Royal College of General Practitioners. *RCGP Guide to the Credit-Based System for CPD*. London: RCGP, 2013, www.rcgp.org.uk/professional-development/~/media/Files/Revalidation-and-CPD/CPD%20Credits%20and%20Appraisal/CPD%20creditsAug13%20v30%20FINAL.ashx [accessed 14 May 2015].
19. Royal College of General Practitioners. *Good Medical Practice for General Practitioners*. London: RCGP, 2008, www.rcgp.org.uk/~/media/Files/Revalidation-and-CPD/CPD%20Credits%20and%20Appraisal/GoodMedicalPracticeforGPsJuly2008ashx.ashx [accessed 14 May 2015].
20. Royal College of General Practitioners. *Criteria, Standards and Evidence for Revalidation of General Practitioners*. London: RCGP, 2000.
21. Royal College of General Practitioners. *Supporting Information for Appraisal and Revalidation: guidance for general practitioners*. London: RCGP, 2014, www.rcgp.org.uk/revalidation-and-cpd/~/media/Files/Revalidation-and-CPD/Revalidation/Guidance-for-GPs/2-RCGP-Supporting-information-for-appraisal-and-revalidation-for-GPs.ashx [accessed 5 August 2015].
22. Royal College of General Practitioners. *What Sort of Doctor?* London: RCGP, 1985.
23. Royal College of General Practitioners. *Fellowship by Assessment*. London: RCGP, 1990.

24. Royal College of General Practitioners. *Membership by Assessment of Performance. The MAP handbook: written guidance for candidates and assessors*. London: RCGP, 1999.
25. Walker J. *History of the MRCGP Examination* (RCGP Occasional Paper 46). London: RCGP, 1990.
26. iWantGreatCare, www.iwantgreatcare.org [accessed 2 February 2015].
27. NHS Choices. My NHS consultant outcome data. www.nhs.uk/service-search/performance/Consultants#view-the-data [accessed 30 January 2015].

Chapter 14

Compassion – and the need for energy-dependent preservation

Clive Weston

Being invited to contribute some thoughts on compassion is flattering. It might suggest that, as a physician and clinical teacher, I am a paragon of compassionate care, or that, as a clinical academic, I possess a deep understanding of the relevant literature. However, having accepted the invitation, I face unpalatable truths. First, although I aspire to practise 'compassionately', and encourage others in my hospital-based team to do so, I cannot readily describe the characteristics of such practice. Second, if I am providing such care this neither protects me from feelings of fallibility and uncertainty, nor my patients from the effects of their illnesses and of my errors. Compassionate care may not always be the best, at least with respect to 'hard' outcomes.

I asked some university colleagues for advice. One simply replied, 'Read Broyard and Shakespeare.' Another sent me a research paper on empathy in clinical practice in which the authors claimed to measure and then link *compassion satisfaction*, *compassion fatigue*, *empathetic concern*, *perspective taking*, *altruism*, *burnout*, *secondary traumatic stress*, *personal distress* and *alexithymia* in over 7000 doctors. I borrowed a book that considered the neuroscience underlying the doctor–patient relationship. [Apparently there are two neural systems activated when experiencing empathy which differ from that activated during compassion – the latter encompasses the medial frontal cortex, the subgenual frontal cortex, the inferior frontal cortex and the midbrain.]

Out of my depth in this philosophy and science, I have chosen to craft a personal reflection – a series of musings. It is written from a position of ordinariness rather than expertise, from the perspective of a '50-something' hospital consultant who, despite plentiful distractions and frustrations, is still doing what most of us do: speaking with and examining patients; formulating and explaining diagnoses; suggesting and supervising treatments; caring for and about people. Additionally, I have responsibility for the clinical and educational supervision of postgraduate doctors *in training*, and for engaging medical students in considering the traditions of their future practice. This requires a discussion about the nature of that tradition and its guiding values. Where does compassion fit in?

Compassion as a value

I note that the General Medical Council (GMC) publication *Good Medical Practice*[1] – which describes what is expected of all registered doctors – makes explicit a requirement to respect the privacy and dignity of patients, to be honest and trustworthy, and to act within the law and with integrity, but does not mention compassion at all. Perhaps the medical regulator recognises that such a human disposition is beyond its remit. [As an aside, I believe that it is reasonable to consider compassion to be a human quality (though the object of compassion may not necessarily be human – there is a literature on compassion fatigue in vets!).] In any case the anonymous authors of *Good Medical Practice* do not define the achievement of integrity as acting in accordance with a deeply held and enduring belief in the primacy of compassion.

The NHS Constitution for England does make this plain. Compassion is one of the four values that 'should underpin everything it [the NHS] does'. The accompanying paragraph that suggests how this value might manifest itself is refreshingly free of the usual managerial or governmental jargon, and serves as a useful starting point for discussing compassionate care:[2]

> we provide and respond with humanity and kindness to each person's pain, distress, anxiety or need. We search for the things we can do, however small, to give comfort and relieve suffering. We find time for patients, their families and carers as well as those we work alongside. We do not wait to be asked, because we care.

So important are these core values that a values-based recruitment system for selection into the healthcare professions has been encouraged. By extension, this would seek to exclude those who do not possess (or cannot exhibit) the required level of compassion.

Selecting for compassion

This fact is not lost on applicants to our medical schools whose personal statements now are liberally sprinkled with the word 'compassion' (second only to 'leadership' it seems), either as an attribute they claim to possess or a positive quality they have observed while on 'work experience'. During a recent interview, one of the more able applicants, a graduate-entrant, presented me with a sensible framework upon which they placed, and distinguished, sympathy, empathy and compassion. Sympathy they described as a feeling of regret or pity for another (e.g. 'I'm sorry to hear about your mother') and empathy as a belief or assertion that one understands another's situation (e.g. 'You must be so proud of your son'). Compassion is empathy with respect to the suffering of another (e.g. 'That must hurt a lot'), coupled with a motivation to make that suffering more bearable (e.g. 'How can I help you?'). Under the circumstances this was a remarkable conclusion. It resembles the definition proposed by the Canadian psychiatrist Harvey Chochinov – 'a deep awareness of the suffering of another coupled with the wish to relieve it'.[3]

For compassion to exist there must be suffering. Without suffering there can be no compassion. In the presence of suffering, compassion is the purest expression of caring.

Unfortunately we had no time to discuss whether compassion could exist if the intention to help was not converted into some action. Does it require more than an acknowledgement of, or bearing witness to, a patient's suffering? Must the patient recognise that his or her suffering is acknowledged? Can it be present unless both carer and patient *feel* it? Are comforting words enough or must there be helpful acts? To what degree is compassion an intuitive disposition? When and how does it develop? Is it predetermined? Can it be taught? Can it be measured? [I should state here, to avoid later disappointment, that I don't provide the answers to these questions in this piece.]

In any case, I was intrigued by how ready (perhaps I should say, *prepared*) were most applicants to discuss their concepts of compassion – far more willing and more articulate, I thought, than those medical students now on the wards, or the teams of doctors and nurses with whom I work. An attempt to begin a similar conversation with these latter would, oddly, require courage on my part, would risk embarrassment all round, and might be greeted with, at best, surprise or, worse, indifference, even hostility. Therefore, what feels appropriate in the context of the selection interview feels less so in clinical practice, where, arguably, the importance of discussing values is more immediately significant.

Atrophy of compassion

Why should this be? One could be cynical and say that at interview the applicant – then still more likely to *be* a patient than *see* a patient – has little else to talk about than warm abstract constructs, and the mandatory ethical dilemma. They lack the knowledge to debate the practicalities of medical practice. So they are adept at 'talking the talk' before they have 'walked the walk'.

Of course there is another more worrying explanation, and one that gives the lie to the drive for values-based recruitment, namely the frequently reported atrophy of compassion and empathy that occurs during medical (and nursing) education.

In the university, the assessment of newly acquired factual knowledge and technical skills squeeze out considerations of more human aspects of the professional practice of medicine. Students quickly become strategic learners, prioritising whatever will help them both to pass summative examinations and to succeed in the increasingly competitive process of acquiring a Foundation Programme rotation. Thinking about human aspects of caring becomes a distraction from 'things that really matter'.

On clinical placements, where there should be ample opportunities to observe examples of good care, they are also exposed to all the stresses of modern 'health care', with its dominant managerial or industrial discourse – far removed from the warm articulation of NHS values quoted above. The doctor joins a 'workforce' with an emphasis on targets, throughput, time management, pathways, (co)production and rates of occupancy. That recent high-profile reports have blamed this culture for contributing to failures of care matters little if the response to these problems is simply to regulate for even more caution (via the 'patient safety' agenda) and for increased candour. Doing no harm, and admitting when we come close to doing so, are laudable, but there is no guarantee that a clinician who bases his or her practice on these principles alone will be compassionate – cautious and careful, certainly, but not necessarily full of care and compassion.

One of our graduate-entry students, faced with the incongruence of their university-based Professional Practice study days with the 'real world' of the hospital ward, wrote plaintively, 'How can I become the sort of doctor my medical school wants me to be, and still be an efficient doctor?' Efficiency or empathy; competence or compassion – fortunately the choice is not so stark.

Compassion is a moral mode of practice. As such it can be encouraged but not regulated. Organisations (more accurately, those people who lead organisations) cannot enforce it. They can only voice their belief in the importance of a compassionate approach, promote discussion, reward examples of compassionate care, and, through their own actions, express and enact compassion for staff within the organisation. Medical schools, deaneries and trusts/health boards that treat their staff or students harshly, and with apparent lack of care, should not be surprised when the distressed students and clinicians treat their patients with similar disdain. Distress forces one to focus upon oneself (to reduce one's own suffering) rather than upon others.

We cannot *produce* compassionate doctors and nurses as if we were mass-producing to a standard specification. Rather, we can recognise, appreciate, applaud and nurture compassion within individual clinicians – compassion for their patients, their colleagues and (if it is possible, for) themselves. And we can ourselves attempt to practise compassionately. We should not look on our 'supply' of compassion as finite, to be hoarded or used frugally for fear of it being exhausted. To borrow a metaphor used by Michael Sandel in his 2009 Reith Lectures, compassion is muscle – the more it is exercised the more it grows, the more well-defined it becomes, the stronger it gets.[4]

Active transport

Cells maintain their integrity by the active transport of molecules against a concentration gradient. This continuous process of restoration or replenishment is energy-dependent. It does not happen passively.

When an idealistic novice, doctor or student, is placed amongst hardened professionals, in a clinical setting that is characterised by high concentrations of cynicism, self-interest and resentment, their enthusiastic naïvety and compassion becomes diluted. As if by osmosis, the cynicism and fatigue that they experience around them permeates inside. Despite William Osler's prescription for equanimity, 'not to expect too much of the people amongst whom you dwell', disappointment (and conformity) sets in. If they cannot easily effect a substantial change in their new environment, how might they preserve their 'potential difference' with respect to that environment? What might enable them to maintain high levels of compassion when around them it is in short supply?

One option might be to become more impermeable, less impressionable, less readily affected by others. Yet this would be counterproductive. Simply developing a 'thicker skin', although rendering the clinician more impervious to external influences, would also increase his or her detachment from, and insensitivity to, the suffering of others. This is unlikely to encourage the clinician to feel and act compassionately.

Maintenance of personal integrity is energy-dependent. In order to restore and replenish the clinician's faith in the value of compassion and his or her disposition to feel and act compassionately, a form of 'active transport' is required. Effort is needed. Much of this effort comes from within, through personal strength of character, yet [and here the metaphor of the isolated cell begins to fall down] there are external factors that might provide the required energy.

Encouraging compassion

Those of us who espouse compassion would hope to provide good examples of compassionate practice to junior colleagues. However, unassuming role modelling of compassion is ineffective if juniors fail to recognise it (after all, its external demonstration may be subtle – an understanding look, a soothing voice or a gentle touch) or to understand what underlies our actions. Simply imitating a senior's idiosyncrasies without developing a personal disposition to ease suffering is a hollow and probably transient victory. So compassion needs to be brought to the surface – to be talked about, pointed out and celebrated. This holds true both with respect to the practices of established clinicians, and to those of their learner colleagues. I have taken to mentioning compassion in the innumerable ePortfolio and 360 degree appraisals that require completion, e.g. 'You were demonstrating compassion when you decided to…'. I suppose that I am really saying, 'Look, it [compassion] exists, and you may not have realised it, but you have it.' If nothing else it shows that this matters to me, and hopefully gives my colleagues encouragement.

Earlier I suggested that my colleagues would resent a discussion about compassion. On reflection, this is not fair. The majority, although reticent to initiate one, are quite able, eager even, to enter into debate, once they realise that it is permissible to do so. I once spent an hour at the end of the day with a team of doctors discussing Chochinov's A, B, C and D of dignity-conserving care.[3] We were inspired each to perform, and report on, 'one small act of kindness' on the ward round the next day. One of the team even noted all the opportunities to do so that were taken or missed the following morning.

Consideration of compassion can be more opportunistic. I will often conclude an observation of an undergraduate clerking by asking the student to reflect on his or her emotional response to the patient, e.g. 'How did she make you feel. Did you warm to her?' The underlying message is that patients do, and should, affect us emotionally, and it is disingenuous to say otherwise. This can lead on to a discussion about the provision of compassionate care to those who we do not like, or who appear 'undeserving'.

More direct are the questions, 'In what way is this person suffering? How can we reduce that suffering?' In the context of this chapter these are very obvious, but when posed in a busy assessment unit they appear strange. The initial response from the junior doctor is often to reiterate the clinical diagnosis (e.g. chronic pulmonary disease) and the medical management (e.g. nebulisers and steroids). From this we can discuss whether the effective and efficient exercise of clinical skills and knowledge (e.g. getting all the blood forms done, putting in a cannula and prescribing fluid) are in themselves an expression of compassion or whether something more is needed. Being compassionate does not release us from a professional obligation to use our knowledge and skills wisely but it does require the exercise of human (i.e. non-medical) capabilities.

Next I wish to point to the importance of words – about which Iona Heath has written so well.[5] There are some words that appear to have been 'tippexed-out' of normal medical conversation, including kindness, kinship, generosity, helpfulness, gratitude and forgiveness. Restoring these words to dialogues within medical teams has an interesting effect. It shifts the focus from the important activities of diagnosis and treatment of diseases to the needs of the patient and the relationships between doctors and patients.

Returning to my earlier observation that compassionate care does not guarantee the best outcomes, I also realise that not every patient is like Anatole Broyard, who, although not wishing the doctor to share his suffering, entreated his physician to 'grope for my spirit as well as my prostate'.[6] Proud and private patients do not crave pity, and some do not wish to form any connection with their medical attendant – preferring a more business-like transaction; but most still appreciate kindness, as well as the best that modern medical science can offer.

Finally, for the past few years, at Christmas time, I have resisted the temptation to buy the obligatory bottle of wine or voucher from M&S as gifts for members of junior staff. Instead I have given books. These are neither books on cardiology nor those that aid preparation for professional examinations. Rather I give books that say more than I can about suffering, caring and compassion. They are largely non-fiction and include academic explorations of the practice of medicine, reminiscences of practising clinicians, and patients' (or carers') stories. [A list of such books is included as a bibliography.] I hope to provoke my colleagues to consider what it is we are trying to do as doctors, how we can gain fulfilment in our work, the effect illness has on the lives of people, and the effect that doctors may have on the ill and the healthy.

Many years ago William Osler, who famously promoted 'the Art of Detachment', stated that it is more important to know what sort of a patient has a disease than what sort of disease a patient has.[7] Scientific medicine has increasingly, and with remarkable results, concentrated on diagnosing the disease. Compassionate care, through an awareness of the suffering of another person and of our kinship with him or her, brings us back to the patient.

References

1. General Medical Council. *Good Medical Practice*. Manchester: GMC, 2013, www.gmc-uk.org/Good_medical_practice___English_0414.pdf_51527435.pdf [accessed 3 June 2015].
2. NHS England. *The NHS Constitution: the NHS belongs to us all*. London: DH, 2013, www.gov.uk/government/uploads/system/uploads/attachment_data/file/170656/NHS_Constitution.pdf [accessed 3 June 2015].
3. Chochinov H. Dignity and the essence of medicine: the A, B, C, and D of dignity conserving care. *British Medical Journal* 2007; **335(7612)**: 184–7.
4. Sandel M. The Reith Lectures 2009. A new citizenship. Lecture 1: markets and morals. Transmitted 9 June 2009, BBC Radio 4. Transcript available at: http://downloads.bbc.co.uk/rmhttp/radio4/transcripts/20090609_thereithlectures_marketsandmorals.rtf [accessed 18 June 2015].
5. Heath I. Words are all we have. *British Medical Journal* 2011; DOI: 10.1136/bmj.d7166.

6. Broyard A. Doctor talk to me. *New York Times Magazine*, 26 August 1990, www.nytimes.com/1990/08/26/magazine/doctor-talk-to-me.html?pagewanted=1 [accessed 18 June 2015].
7. Osler W. Teacher and student. In: *Aequanimitas: with other addresses to medical students, nurses and practitioners of medicine* (2nd edn). Philadelphia: Blakiston's Son & Co., 1910, pp. 21–43, https://archive.org/stream/aequanimitaswit04oslegoog#page/n8/mode/2up [accessed 18 June 2015].

Bibliography

- Ballatt J, Campling P. *Intelligent Kindness: reforming the culture of healthcare*. London: RCPsych Publications, 2011.
- Broyard A. *Intoxicated by My Illness: and other writings on life and death*. New York: Ballantine Books, 1992.
- Cassell E. *The Nature of Suffering and the Goals of Medicine* (2nd edn). Oxford: Oxford University Press, 2003.
- Coutts M. *The Iceberg: a memoir*. London: Atlantic Books, 2014.
- Fish D. *Refocusing Postgraduate Medical Education: from the technical to the moral mode of practice*. Gloucester: Aneumi Publications, 2012.
- Frank A. *The Renewal of Generosity: illness, medicine and how to live*. Chicago: University of Chicago Press, 2005.
- Gwande A. *Complications. A surgeon's notes on an imperfect science*. London: Profile Books Ltd, 2003.
- Marsh H. *Do No Harm. Stories of life, death and brain surgery*. London: Weidenfeld & Nicolson, 2014.
- Montgomery K. *How Doctors Think: clinical judgment and the practice of medicine*. Oxford: Oxford University Press, 2005.
- Morrison B. *And When Did You Last See Your Father?* London: Granta Publications, 1993.

Addendum

A respected friend (who remains anonymous) had sight of the final draft of this chapter and provided a fairly uncompromising critique. Her interpretation was that my musing relegated compassion to just another item on the prescription chart with which doctors should 'dose their patients'. And that I suggested that prescribing it is exhausting, hard work, prone to cause burnout (in clinicians), is impossible to teach, measure or assess, and doesn't change 'hard outcomes'. She was saddened to find no mention of the compassion that we have for ourselves and the compassion that we receive from others – 'Compassion is like the sun,' she wrote, 'it just shines.'

Part III

Compassion and the clinician

Chapter 15

Cum scientia caritas – compassion with knowledge

Simon Gregory

Introduction

The founders of the Royal College of General Practitioners (RCGP) chose a motto of succinct wisdom. The order of the correct translation of the Latin is key. That compassion is foremost and guides and shapes the application of knowledge. Recent scandals and negative press would have us believe that compassion is lacking in the NHS, perhaps in the health and care systems. These awful events must be addressed but also should be seen in context.

The NHS is acknowledged by the Commonwealth Fund as the best healthcare system in the world. It is a brilliant system within which unacceptable, awful things have happened. Amongst these are instances where compassion has been found to be lacking. This is unacceptable.

The problem

We cannot escape the evidence that there have been unacceptably low levels of care with significant shortfallings. The Health Service Ombudsman for England in a report into the care of ten elderly people stated, 'These accounts present a picture of NHS provision that is failing to respond to the needs of older people with care and compassion.'[1]

The events at Mid Staffordshire Hospital are now well known but the patient stories listed in the report of the first inquiry make hard yet essential reading. Each narrative is heartbreaking including people buzzing for help with no help coming and stories of frail people left to soil themselves and then left in that state.[2] Sadly these are not isolated instances, with other instances such as those at Winterbourne View,[3] NHS Lanarkshire, Vale of Leven,[4] Princess of Wales Hospital, Bridgend, and Neath Port Talbot Hospital, Abertawe Bro Morgannwg (ABMU).

Many of these problems are due to the working environment, which is meant to be a caring environment. The second inquiry into Mid Staffordshire found many deep systemic problems across the system.[5] It is not within the scope of this chapter to revisit the entire inquiry and its recommendations. But of pertinence to a chapter considering compassion is that the culture of the trust was not conducive to providing good care for patients or providing a supportive working environment for staff; problems included bullying and low morale. The culture and context within which professionals work is undoubtedly a factor.

Fatigue?

In addition to the culture and context, which is the environment, the state of the individual is also a factor. The changing demographic of an ageing population surviving previously fatal events or conditions, and typically with multiple co-morbidities, combines with changing societal expectation and therefore ever increasing demand. Thus needs (to which we might add wants) continue to outstrip provision, and this pressure is absorbed by those who work in the health service working ever harder. These pressures put strain on the system but also on the individuals who work in that system. Although not justifying poor care that is lacking in basic compassion, it is clear that sometimes doctors (and others) are exhausted. Sometimes we are simply too busy to demonstrate that we care.

People not targets

The medical professions have been complicit in the seismic shift from a professional, person-centred model of care to a target culture, whether it be the mode of implementation of the Emergency Department four-hour wait that leads to patients being moved before they are ready (a manifestation of the implementation) or the insipid effect of the Quality and Outcomes Framework (QOF) on the doctor–patient consultation.

The QOF was well intentioned and sought to improve the quality of care and the application of research to practice. But along the way the essence of general practice has been harmed. Targets are based on single disease studies or 'best practice' but GPs work in the context of our patients' world. GPs deal with patients' ideas, concerns and expectations. They deal with complex multi-system disease in the patient's context shaped by uncertainty. Do GPs now serve the needs of the patient or do they serve the computer in the corner reminding them of the required targets?

Compassion overwhelmed

It is at the level of the individual that compassion has really been squeezed. Whether it be a severely understaffed hospital ward on which the nurses and healthcare support workers cannot respond to requests for help or a general practice that cannot recruit and cannot afford the locums, and just cannot cope.

The GP specialty registrar covering a hospital at night, with no time to respond to the request for help, or the GP running an hour late with a waiting room that is heaving – they are overwhelmed.

Sir Mike Richards of the Care Quality Commission summed this up:[6]

> people sometimes ask, is compassionate care a thing of the past? Absolutely not, it's very much alive and well. But where individuals are under such strain, usually due to staffing levels, compassion can be overwhelmed.

This is also true of general practice where workloads have doubled in ten years and GPs are overwhelmed.

Towards solutions

But just as 93% of care is delivered in primary and community care yet people refer to hospitals so we should not allow standards of care to be defined by these dire examples, while still stating clearly that they are unacceptable. The vast majority of patient care episodes (contacts) in the NHS are with caregivers who are caring and compassionate. But how do we address those situations where compassion is lacking and how do we support doctors and others to give compassionate care throughout their daily and professional lives? These scandals give us an opportunity to reconsider how we support those that care.

Values

GPs as caregivers, professionals and often as educators are guided by many value sets: whether it is their personal values, the Hippocratic Oath, its more modern manifestations, *Good Medical Practice*[7] or *Good Medical Practice for General Practitioners*.[8] It might be said that the Hippocratic Oath did not entirely put patients first but the others clearly do. Patients and their needs are at the heart of all that we do. The needs are our purpose. The values by which we work are well covered in the NHS Constitution. This outlines six core values:[9]

- respect and dignity
- commitment to quality care
- compassion
- improving lives
- working together for patients
- everyone counts.

These values guide our practice and compassion is at their heart. But what do we do with these values? Do we recruit medical students solely on A-level grades or do their values matter also? And, if they do, how do we assess these?

Then in careers as doctors do we assess and value the manifestation of values such as in specialty recruitment or in annual appraisals? Do we as individuals even state and test our own value set? Perhaps if values were more explicit we might be better protected from the dehumanising influence of the box-ticking measurement culture.

HUMANISM IN MEDICINE

Professor Lynn Getz of Trondheim, Norway, galvanised the 2011 RCGP Conference with her exposition of humanism in medicine. She defined this as

> an enlightened solidarity with the patient as a living, culturally situated human being.

She encouraged us to consider this as including trust, belonging and nourishment, respect, care, honour and pride. The core of humanism in medicine is about acknowledging the soul. Humanistic medicine attempts to connect with patients through empathy and compassion. This approach will help to ameliorate the worst aspects of the current decay to the minimum data set.

THE HUMANITIES IN MEDICINE

But how do we foster such humanism? Perhaps it is through the application of the arts to medicine, to our lives and those of our patients? Perhaps the focus of medicine has become too much on the scientific basis of medicine rather than the art of being a physician. But more than that the arts, the humanities as they are so well named can support us in developing and continuing as physicians who understand and empathise with the human condition.

In Iona Heath's foreword to John Salinsky's excellent book on medicine and literature she says that:[10]

> patients come to doctors to give an account of experience and sensations that they have found troubling or difficult. They must find words to communicate distress and the listening doctor must find words to signal that he or she has at least partly understood. Novelists use words in ways which show they have understood parts of the experience of all of us.

This is true of so much of the humanities. Does not Simon Russell Beale's portrayal of King Lear as suffering from Lewy body dementia challenge our response to dementia? Whereas Robin Williams's soliloquy in a professional tribunal in *Patch Adams* is a fabulous reminder of our purpose:[11]

> at what point in history did a doctor become more than a trusted and learned friend who visited and treated the ill?

His challenge of indifference is a challenge to each of us.

Similarly literature can both support compassionate practice such as in Cronin's *The Citadel*,[12] or challenge the dehumanising nature of medicine such as in Samuel Shem's captivatingly awful portrayal of junior doctors in *The House of God*,[13] which should surely scream at us that this is WRONG, and also should challenge the use of black humour, a trap into which many of us fall.

In the arts we have amazing resources that focus on the human condition and which can stimulate us to understand our fellow man, and meet with them in their deepest and darkest moments. If we are to really understand, empathise with, support and treat with compassion those that we seek to serve then we should embrace the arts.

Compassionate resilience

Much of the focus of medical education has been on the acquisition and application of scientific knowledge. Such knowledge and how to access information are vital but they need to be placed in a humane context if care is to be compassionate and based on the needs of the individual patient in his or her time of need. The profession now needs to build into curricula and training ways of vocalising and accepting the emotional cost, and supporting people through the highs and lows rather than inoculating them to suffering. We need to support the development of compassionate resilience.

Summary

There have been too many examples of poor care, lacking in compassion. Thankfully these are few compared with the many examples of excellent, compassionate, empathic, person-centred care but that does not justify them and they are totally unacceptable. But with a focus on people not targets, on humanism and learning through the humanities and with professionalism at the fore, we can ensure that patients come first and that compassionate care is at the heart of all that we do.

'*Cum scientia caritas.*'

References

1. Health Service Commissioner for England. *Care and Compassion? Report of the Health Service Ombudsman on ten investigations into NHS care of older people*. London: TSO, 2011, www.ombudsman.org.uk/care-and-compassion [accessed 18 May 2015].
2. Francis R. *Independent Inquiry into Care Provided by Mid Staffordshire NHS Foundation Trust January 2005–March 2009*. London: TSO, 2010, http://webarchive.nationalarchives.gov.uk/20130107105354/http:/www.dh.gov.uk/en/Publicationsandstatistics/Publications/PublicationsPolicyAndGuidance/DH_113018 [accessed 18 May 2015].
3. Bubb S. *Winterbourne View: time for change. Transforming the commissioning of services for people with learning disabilities and/or autism*. Leeds: NHS England, 2014, www.england.nhs.uk/wp-content/uploads/2014/11/transforming-commissioning-services.pdf [accessed 15 June 2015].
4. The Vale of Leven Hospital Inquiry, www.valeoflevenhospitalinquiry.org [accessed 15 June 2015].
5. Francis R. *Report of the Mid Staffordshire NHS Foundation Trust Public Inquiry*. London: TSO, 2013, www.midstaffspublicinquiry.com/report [accessed 18 May 2015].
6. Hospital 'worry wards' put patients in danger. *The Times*, 7 March 2014, www.thetimes.co.uk/tto/health/news/article4025598.ece [accessed 18 May 2015].
7. General Medical Council. *Good Medical Practice*. Manchester: GMC, 2013.
8. Royal College of General Practitioners. *Good Medical Practice for General Practitioners*. London: RCGP, 2008, www.rcgp.org.uk/~/media/Files/Revalidation-and-CPD/CPD%20Credits%20and%20Appraisal/GoodMedicalPracticeforGPsJuly2008ashx.ashx [accessed 14 May 2015].

9. Department of Health. *The Handbook to the NHS Constitution*. London: DH, 2013, www.nhs.uk/choiceintheNHS/Rightsandpledges/NHSConstitution/Documents/2013/handbook-to-the-nhs-constitution.pdf [accessed 18 May 2015].
10. Heath I. Introduction. In: J Salinsky. *Medicine and Literature: the doctor's companion to the classics*. Abingdon: Radcliffe Medical Press, 2004, pp. v–vi.
11. *Patch Adams*, 1998. Directed by Tom Shadyac. USA: Universal Pictures.
12. Cronin AJ. *The Citadel*. London: Victor Gollancz, 1937.
13. Shem S. *House of God*. New York, NY: Dell Publishing, 1978.

RESOURCES AND FURTHER READING

- Bailey J. *From Ward to Whitehall: the disaster at Mid-Staffs*. Stafford: Cure the NHS, 2012.

Arts and humanities resources

Literature

General

J Salinsky. *Medicine and Literature: the doctor's companion to the classics*.
T Greenhalgh, Hurwitz B. *Narrative Based Medicine*.

Specific

AJ Cronin. *The Citadel* – ethical practice and perhaps the NHS.
Samuel Shem. *The House of God* – dehumanisation.
Aleksandr Solzhenitsyn. *Cancer Ward* – moral responsibility and suffering.
Life after a mastectomy. Veronique Mistiaen – say no more.

Arts

General

E Powley, R Higson. *The Arts in Medical Education: a practical guide*.

Specific

Poetry
Larkin P. *The Old Fools* – ageing.
Larkin P. *This Be the Verse* – emotional damage.

Opera
La bohème – the impact of suffering, tuberculosis.
Madame Butterfly – the effect of suicide.

Cinema

General

M Alexander, P Lenahan, A Pavlov. *Cinemeducation*.

Specific

Shadowlands – suffering and pain.
Marvin's Room – compassion in practice.

Chapter 16

Bringing compassion to the homeless

Catherine Hall and Eleanor Wilman

In his foreword to the standards of the Faculty for Homeless and Inclusion Health, Aidan Halligan says:

> The way we treat the most vulnerable and damaged is a basic test of our civilisation.[1]

Accepting that homeless people are both vulnerable and damaged is a sign of a certain level of compassion in our view.

It is also well known that, clinically speaking, homeless people are a group particularly in need of care. Unfortunately they are the group least likely to be able to access health care. If we are agreed that they are particularly deserving of compassion and that they are particularly in need of health care, why do they find it so difficult to access compassionate health care?

Tri-morbidity

> Homelessness is an independent risk factor for premature mortality and is associated with extremes of deprivation and multi-morbidity. There is a growing understanding, supported by international research, that chronic homelessness is an associated marker for tri-morbidity, complex health needs and premature death. Tri-morbidity is the combination of physical ill health with mental ill health and drug or alcohol misuse.[1]

Homeless people, as a group, are significantly sicker than the housed population of equivalent age. Homeless people are prone, among other things, to skin, soft tissue and circulatory problems from long periods of standing or walking, poorly fitting or damp shoes, and lack of access to clean clothes or washing/drying facilities. In addition, they are susceptible to vitamin deficiencies, sequelae of drug and alcohol misuse, injecting behaviour, respiratory infections including TB, and mental illness including psychotic illness and depression with risk of self-harm and suicide.

The homeless are significantly over-represented in A&E attendances and emergency admissions, and stay in hospital three times as long. Despite this, their outcomes are worse than that of the housed population, with a much lower average age of death with high morbidity and reduced quality of life, partly because they struggle to access the ongoing care that they need.

A Department of Health consultation for mental health in 2010 stated that homeless people are 40 times less likely to be registered with a GP, making referrals to specialist services difficult or impossible.[2] The phenomenon whereby the group in the greatest need are least able to access care (know as the 'inverse care law'[3]) is one that must be addressed.

A compassionate approach is essential to understand the complex issues involved and so to provide services in such a way that this particularly vulnerable group is able and willing to access them.

There is a clear need to improve how we engage with homeless patients, as a health service in general and as primary care providers specifically. It is imperative that we act with compassion not only in our individual interactions with homeless patients but also when designing and implementing our care systems and practices. Specialist primary care services for homeless people are a way of addressing some barriers.

These specialist services will, through experience, find the best way of providing compassionate care to their particular population. Specialist services cannot provide the whole solution though. They will, by their nature, exclude rural areas and smaller towns. In addition specialist homeless services must focus their resources on the most vulnerable period in the lives of this group. Many of the factors making these patients so in need of care and so relatively restricted in accessing it will persist even when they are housed and ready to access mainstream services. These mainstream services will need ways of addressing this.

The Standards of the Faculty of Inclusion Health take the expertise and experience of those working with excluded groups (including homeless people, travellers and vulnerable migrants) to provide a framework for *all* services providing care to this group, not just specialist services. The standards rightly place compassion at the forefront, both for moral and pragmatic reasons:[1]

> Our primary purpose is to re-affirm the fundamental rights of all people to be treated with dignity, compassion and respect. But an increasing body of evidence provides an additional driver for change. At the sharp end of health inequalities, homelessness and other expressions of social exclusion are associated with extremely high health care costs coupled with appalling outcomes – we have to be able to do better than this.

These standards are freely available and provide a much more detailed framework than that presented here.[1]

HARD TO REACH OR EASY TO IGNORE? COMPASSION IN SYSTEMS AND PRACTICES

Received wisdom had it that homeless people do not prioritise their health to the same extent as the housed population. This has some face validity. Such immediate concerns as lack of shelter, clothing, food and money for transport, as well as drug dependence, could easily, we would think, overshadow concerns about health problems, especially chronic illness.

> *Qualitative research has shown that homeless people do prioritise their health and are keen to access healthcare where they perceive it is available to them.*[4]

The very factors once seen as distracting homeless people from their health can act as barriers to receiving health care. Deciding where to register with a GP and physically getting there can be a problem when there is no stable geographical base and very limited or no money for transport.

The necessity of finding a place to sleep that night, some food for the day and access to some money (negotiating the ever more complicated benefits system) can make it difficult to structure a day so as to attend appointments (and structure and time-keeping become all but impossible when drug and alcohol dependence or mental illness are added to the picture).

All of the above has led to homeless people being classed as a 'hard to reach' group in terms of healthcare provision. Although this is often said with the best of intentions, this language can seem to leave the responsibility with the patient. They are causing difficulties for the system.

> *It is they who fail to access health care rather than we who fail to provide it.*

It has been suggested that, on the contrary, homeless people are in fact 'easy to ignore'.

Whatever the terminology, it is important that we accept responsibility for addressing the barriers that exist so that homeless people are able to access the primary care that they need.

As well as being a practical barrier to those with very chaotic lives, strict or inflexible structures can be an emotional barrier to those who have previously experienced authority in a negative or damaging way. Many homeless people have experienced complex trauma in childhood or earlier adulthood including neglect and abuse, and many have spent time in care and/or in prison.

These people can perceive strict appointment times, complicated pathways for getting appointments or the 'gatekeeper receptionist' as threatening and choose to stay away. Some specialist homeless services have tackled this by offering 'drop-in' clinics for homeless patients with flexible access to doctors, nurses, support workers and drug therapists. Others have 'care navigators' to help homeless patients to organise and attend appointments.

'Suspicion, indifference and hostility' or 'dignity and respect' – compassion in individual interactions

> For many disadvantaged groups, clinical encounters and contact with service providers is still too often characterised by suspicion, indifference and occasionally, hostility, rather than dignity and respect. … [ideally] generosity, kindness, and compassion combine with a passionate commitment to professional quality to become the defining characteristics of health services for homeless and multiply disadvantaged people.[1]

Although it is, thankfully, uncommon to hear healthcare workers reporting that they feel hostility or suspicion towards homeless people in general, it remains the case that many find it difficult to show compassion in individual encounters with homeless people. Part of the problem may be their inability to fit into our existing systems, as discussed above. When we have developed a structure to try to control a spiralling workload it can be easy to act defensively when someone challenges this or is unable to work within it. Feeling defensive is not an ideal base from which to show compassion.

Personality disorder

Another issue is the link between homelessness and personality disorder. Because individuals with personality disorder are more likely to suffer from drug and alcohol problems, and suffer adverse life events including housing problems and long-term unemployment,[5] it follows that personality disorder is over-represented in the homeless population. Developing compassionate therapeutic relationships with patients with personality disorder is certainly challenging. Some behaviour can be difficult or manipulative and those with personality disorder have been described as 'the patients psychiatrists dislike'.[5]

The National Institute of Mental Health England (NIMHE) found that many otherwise compassionate clinicians found the nature of interactions with personality-disordered individuals so difficult that they were reluctant even to get involved.[5] Specific training around personality disorder (e.g. that provided by groups such as Emergence) can improve the skills and confidence of staff to interact with patients with personality disorder. Sometimes this challenging behaviour can manifest as aggression or violence and this presents particular difficulties for even the most compassionate of approaches.

This behaviour may have its roots in childhood trauma, in current environments or relationships – for example in prison or hostel environments where shouting or threatening may be the best way to get needs met – or may be due to the effects of drugs, alcohol, pain, hunger or frustration with life.

What impact these factors have on personal responsibility for behaviour and mitigating or defending aggressive or violent behaviour is an interesting area of moral philosophy that is outside the scope of this chapter. This aside, we do collectively have a responsibility to provide good health care even to violent or aggressive people and understanding the factors underlying this behaviour may help us to deal with it more effectively.

Emphasis must be on the safety of staff and other patients, but strict 'zero tolerance' policies are unlikely to be helpful either to patients or to staff. It is important to have a clear threshold for behaviour that would be unsafe in a particular service and a policy for what is done when behaviour becomes unsafe – often involving the police and violent patient schemes. Beneath this threshold, though, honest discussions and challenging of inappropriate behaviour – rather than immediate rejection of the patient because of his or her behaviour – form a valuable part of the treatment of vulnerable people, equipping them to have better relationships and to move forwards in society.

Compassion and integrated care

The importance of integrating services for homeless people has been widely emphasised.[1,6] This is important in ensuring that homeless people are able to access all the services they need and recognises the particular problems they may have with navigating complex systems and attending appointments.

In addition to this, integrated care has an important role in the relationship that a homeless person will have with healthcare providers. People who have been socially excluded may, even more so that other non-homeless people, perceive rejection when they encounter rigidly ring-fenced services. It is of course true that a primary care service cannot be all things to all people and there is a need to control increasing workload and mission drift.

> *But to be told 'We don't offer that service, you need to go somewhere else' is to be told yet again 'You don't belong here, you are asking the wrong things, you are the wrong person'.*

Specialist services tackle this by hosting some additional services in the same building, and building partnerships with other relevant services to enable a more positive and streamlined signposting approach, with or without support workers or care navigators to help facilitate this.

Compassion and continuity of care

Continuity of care is important when caring for homeless people. Obviously it would be ideal for patients to be able to see the same practitioner at every consultation but it is in the nature of these chaotic and emotionally challenging services that many staff – doctors in particular – choose to work part time, often combining with work in mainstream practice.

Multidisciplinary team working with a case management approach can address this problem. This allows patients to feel comfortable that, whichever member of the team they see, their care is progressing in a coherent direction. This approach is vital when 'holding' the most vulnerable patients to prevent them from slipping through the net. An example of this is the emergence nationwide of 'Pathway'[7] services that provide hospital in-reach from primary care to streamline the pathway from hospital admission, through discharge, back to the community.

Specialist and mainstream services

Most large cities now have specialist primary care services for homeless people, many providing integrated drug and alcohol, mental health and housing support services as well as having clinical staff with a special interest in and experience of the specific health problems of homeless people.

Specialist services have a key role in people's lives when they are at their most vulnerable, insecurely housed or in the grip of addiction, but many of their behaviours won't change quickly even when these problems have been resolved. Mainstream services need to be flexible in their approach to accommodate some of these behaviours, which will be ongoing. Specialist services will aim to equip vulnerable people to be able to access mainstream services as their situation improves, but mainstream services also need to be supported to be ready for them.

Conclusion

Homeless people need more health care but find it harder to get it.

The healthcare system needs to accommodate them and individuals need to be able to deal compassionately with challenging behaviour to create and maintain therapeutic relationships while keeping themselves safe and well. Wherever possible primary care services need to work in conjunction with other services – including the third sector – to provide integrated care.

Extra effort and resources will be required to achieve this, adding to the already significant pressure on general practice, but it would be hoped that managing to provide effective primary care for this vulnerable group will greatly improve their health and wellbeing – preventing some of the health complexity, morbidity and mortality down the line.

If we can manage to provide compassionate care for the most disenfranchised in society we are in a better position to get it right for everyone.

References

1. Hewlett N (ed.). *Standards for Commissioners and Service Providers*. Version 2.0. London: Faculty for Homeless and Inclusion Health, 2013, www.pathway.org.uk/publications/faculty-for-homeless-and-inclusion-health-publications/ [accessed 19 May 2015].
2. Rees S. *Mental Ill Health in the Adult Single Homeless Population: a review of the literature*. London: Crisis, 2009, www.crisis.org.uk/data/files/publications/MentalHealthReview.pdf [accessed 6 August 2015].
3. Hart JT. The inverse care law. *Lancet* 1971; **1(7696)**: 405–12.

4. Wright NMJ, Tompkins CN, Jones L. Exploring risk perception and behaviour of homeless injecting drug users diagnosed with hepatitis C. *Health and Social Care in the Community* 2005; **13(1)**: 75–83.
5. Department of Health. *Personality Disorder: no longer a diagnosis of exclusion*. Leeds: National Institute for Mental Health in England, 2003.
6. Wright N. Drug use and housing issues. In: N Wright, C Gerada, L Sheard (eds). *RCGP Guide to the Management of Substance Misuse in Primary Care* (2nd edn). London: RCGP, 2013, pp. 397–406.
7. Pathway, www.pathway.org.uk/.

CHAPTER 17

CONDUCTING THE PRESCRIBING ORCHESTRA

Complexity, continuity and care

Arnold Zermansky

What could be simpler? You have an illness. You swallow a pill. The illness gets better.

Paul Ehrlich, the German physician and biochemist credited with being the father of antibiotics, dreamed of the 'magic bullet' ['*magische Kugel*'] that would target the disease without harming the patient.[1] In so many fields of therapeutics we have achieved his dream. We can address a specific disorder with a molecule that restores physiology or reverses pathology.

Paradoxically, because our drugs are now so effective, the management of their use has become more important. Their potency also increases the risk that they may cause harm. Many more medicines are taken long term, thereby lengthening exposure. And (as we shall see) polypharmacy increases the risk of adverse reactions and interactions. The fact that many more people survive into their eighties and nineties is at least partly due to the effectiveness of their drugs. Conversely, their older physiology, with mental and physical frailty and less efficient drug clearance by liver and kidneys, increases the risk of harm. In each of three very large studies (with remarkable consistency!), 6.5% of acute hospital admissions were caused by a medication problem.[2–4] Of these, half were aged 65 and over.

Not only are more medicines prescribed. There are also many more prescribers. Hospital specialists, nurses, pharmacists, dentists, podiatrists, alternative medicine practitioners, health food shops, internet suppliers: there can be a vast orchestra of prescribers and dispensers for each patient. This makes for a very complex therapeutic score, in which each of these players may only see their own bit part.

More people take medicines – 43% of the population take at least one regular medicine. Seventy-seven per cent of items prescribed are repeats. Older people nearly always take multiple drugs – the average number of repeats per patient aged 80–89 is 7.1.[5]

The risk of a direct adverse effect obviously increases geometrically with the number of drugs taken. But the potential for drug interaction rises *exponentially* because each drug might interact with each of the other drugs and vice versa. Thus a patient on two drugs has the potential for two interactions. If on three drugs there are six possibilities of interaction; if on four, 12 possibilities; if on five, 20 possibilities, etc.[i]

Fortunately not all pairs of drugs interact and not all interactions are harmful. Some are beneficial. But the arithmetic of the possibility of interaction is staggering when many elderly patients take as many as ten or more drugs (90 possibilities). And this is not the end of the matter, because drugs can also interact with foods (e.g. grapefruit and statins), alcohol and even sunlight. They can also interact in larger groups, such as when three or more drugs share either a biochemical pathway or act on the same system, adding together their sedative, hypotensive or gastric irritant effect.

Preventive drugs cause harm more often than benefit. This is because the proportion of patients experiencing an adverse effect to a medicine is generally given as between 5% and 10%. Although drugs given for acute problems (e.g. antibiotics, analgesics) benefit around a third of patients in a short time, most preventive drugs (such as hypotensives, statins and aspirin) benefit a very small percentage of patients in any year. Benefits accumulate slowly over several years, and even then the numbers are relatively small. The overwhelming majority of people who take these drugs derive no benefit at all. They are the ones who were never destined to have a cardiovascular event. Even those who *do* benefit will never know. The best outcome the patient can hope to experience is that nothing happens. Indeed, it is an article of faith, albeit statistically justifiable faith, to continue to take them. Which is probably one of the reasons why compliance is a problem and real outcomes are never quite as good as those in clinical trials.

This is all very depressing – enough to induce a state of therapeutic nihilism in every thinking prescriber. But preventive therapeutics has taken off in a big way because it works. People live longer, healthier lives. However unpleasant and frequent the adverse effects of treatment, they are manageable and mostly reversible by stopping or changing treatment. But this is only so if we choose our patients and drugs carefully and maintain a vigilant approach to their continuing care.

The task is simply stated. Ensure the patient is likely to benefit from the medicine. Choose a medicine that is effective, safe, economical and acceptable to the patient. Start the medicine. Watch for adverse effects and monitor therapeutic effect (if appropriate). And when it is no longer needed, stop it ... because a medicine that does no good can only be doing harm.

There are a number of reasons why reality sees to it that this process is not as simple as it seems.

Initiation of the medicine

We have become better at initiating medicines. Guidelines help identify patients and propose the most appropriate treatment. The much-derided Quality and Outcomes

i The formula for calculating this potential number of drug interactions is $x^\star(x-1)$, when x is the number of drugs taken.

Framework (QOF) incentivises general practices to identify and treat at-risk patients.[ii] IT systems support QOF and they allow us to think of the health of our populations but also to flag up patients opportunistically. And after two decades of cost-centred but also quality-oriented pharmaceutical advisers, who have identified the most cost-effective drugs, we tend to choose our drugs from a fairly narrow and uniform palette that are both effective and safe as well as good value. So far, so good.

Premeditated and involuntary non-compliance

Consumerism has turned non-compliance into an art form. And, like much modern art, it is not always easy to identify or interpret. Frankly, our therapeutic virtuosity does not always impress patients. They have become more discerning. They have a view. And if they didn't have one to start with, their neighbour, the *Daily Mail*, the drug information leaflet and the internet will help them form one. But respect for their doctor may mean that they would not dream of challenging him or her directly. They just choose which tablets to take, and which not to take. Non-compliance is not new, but *premeditated non-compliance* as a dimension of patient choice has become endemic. The more you look, the more you find. The National Institute for Health and Care Excellence (NICE) suggests that between a third and a half of repeat medicines are not taken as recommended.[6]

Involuntary non-compliance, on the other hand, is better recognised. The development of monitored dosage systems (such as Dosette boxes), timers and reminder apps on mobile phones has probably reduced its prevalence, though the frequency of complicated multi-drug regimens, especially in the elderly and confused, is an exacerbating factor. And even the best system can be undermined by frequent changes in drug regimens, necessitating pharmacists to re-package the Dosette box.

Patients are more likely to follow a treatment if they understand what it is for and how it will help. So a clear explanation of the benefit to be gained and what to expect is helpful. Some prescribers indicate on their prescription (and therefore label) what a medicine is for, thereby reinforcing the message.

Non-compliance is sometimes appropriate and a considered response to circumstances. It makes good sense to consider whether the patient was right to stop the pills or alter the regimen.

Is it working? Is it hurting? The early review

If you put a new medicine straight on to the repeat file and arrange to review the patient in (say) six months, you are making two major assumptions. These are that the medicine is effective and is causing no problems. Neither assumption is necessarily valid, especially the latter. You really must see the patient sufficiently soon to identify

ii Those who criticise QOF, generally because they haughtily believe it undermines the professionalism of GPs, fail to recognise how far it changed the very nature of general practice. Before QOF, good practices followed up patients with chronic diseases and some used systems to identify defaulters and those who were hard to get. QOF brought the great majority of GPs up to the level of the few. General practice is no longer just about what happens to walk though the door; it is also about optimising the long-term care of those with chronic disease.

any problems, which may also include non-compliance. Not all adverse effects are obvious to the patient. You need to ask about them, and that means knowing potential adverse effects. Who would ever imagine their eye drops are the cause of their cold feet?[iii]

Some adverse effects are transient, such as muscular aches after starting levothyroxine, but the patient may stop the pills because of them. Some therapeutic effects are slow in onset, such as that of antidepressants … the patient may need encouragement to hang on in there a little longer.

Supply of medicines

No one designing a health service from scratch would propose that an elderly patient visit the doctor's every month, come back two days later for a piece of paper, take this down the street (or sometimes across town), deposit it at the chemist's shop and return later to collect the pills. The patient has completed between five and seven journeys in spite of the weather and any disability, and will have to repeat the process in another month. Pharmacist delivery systems are helpful and electronic prescribing/dispensing may short-circuit this pantomime. But leaving it to the pharmacist to request the prescriptions each month assumes that the pharmacist knows the patient's supply situation. Some do. Some just reorder the lot. So, if you wonder why the patient has a whole cupboard full of lactulose. …

The process of preparing, issuing and controlling repeat prescriptions is protocol led, 'technology supported' and delegated to receptionists. The work is complex and surprisingly 'creative', but less hazardous than might be imagined because of their pragmatic skill and knowledge.[7]

Should patients be restricted to one month's supply of medicines? After all, there are a few who can't be trusted with even a week's supply. But doubling the prescribing interval halves the workload for patient, receptionist and prescriber. The cost in wasted medicines is negligible in this context. What about three months supply? Or six months? There is a balance to be struck and it may make sense to have a bespoke prescribing interval.

How is it for you?

Reviewing how the patient is doing is a chore of general practice. We are not good at it, perhaps for temperamental reasons, perhaps because of more pressing priorities, and most of us realise this. There is an important question as to whether the GP is the most appropriate person to conduct it. There is now much evidence that clinical pharmacists can conduct the task effectively, but for the time being there are not enough of them around in primary care for it to be the norm.[8]

Review is partly about evaluating response to treatment, but also looking for harms and risk. *Patients change; their illnesses change; therapeutics changes.* Each of these dimensions needs to be considered.

iii This is a recognised adverse effect of beta-blocker eye drops.

A 55 year-old man whose epilepsy has been well controlled for years became unsteady on his feet and requested a visit. As I came into his living room he got up to greet me ... and his trousers fell down. He had a transient but severe gastroenteritis and had lost nearly a stone in weight. He had stayed on the same dose of antiepileptic medicine, but his weight loss meant that his effective dose had increased, causing toxicity. A reduction in his antiepileptic dose resolved the problem.

A retired professor thought his inability to do the crossword was a facet of his age. He went away for the weekend and forgot his blood pressure pills. He felt he had reawakened from twilight sleep. A switch of pills allowed control of his blood pressure without fogging his brain. He could do the crossword again.

Patients grow older, they get fatter or thinner, they mature, become pregnant or lactate, they develop other illnesses, they take varying quantities of alcohol or recreational drugs, they change occupation or level of physical or mental activity. Their renal or liver function may also change. Any or all of these might affect their treatment.

Illnesses often progress, but sometimes improve or resolve. It is often appropriate to increase, reduce or stop treatment.

Therapeutics and the evidence basis for it seem to alter almost daily. So last year's drug list may need a radical rethink. Older people's drug lists can be archaeological, containing fossilised evidence of historic prescribing fashions. This may be the result of an almost unspoken collusion between patient and prescriber not to disturb an established drug regimen. People get attached to their medicines, even when they can't remember why they take them.[9] But therapeutic momentum is as much the result of prescriber reluctance to change. And there is good precedence for this reluctance. Over 40 years ago Marinker described the 'peaceful' repeat prescription as one that the GP disturbs at his and the patient's peril.[10] Marinker was really talking about the psychological dimension of the repeat prescription, but the pharmacological dimension can be just as unpredictable.

The trouble with changing (or stopping) medication is that you never know quite what will happen. So the prescriber is committed to review the patient afterwards to make sure the change has not harmed the patient. Then a review becomes two consultations rather than one. Does it really matter if the patient stays on the omeprazole or amitriptyline? Do I really want to increase the dose of antihypertensive when the systolic BP is 144? Best leave well alone?

The conductor

Therapeutics has always been central to general practice, even in the days when remedies were often foul-tasting placebos. As the science has become cleverer, the potential benefits are hugely greater, but so are the hazards. The GP may not always be the initiator of all the patient's medicines, but he or she is the only person who has simultaneous access to and understanding of the patient, the drug list and the clinical record. Other players, including non-doctor prescribers, may be involved with the patient's medicines, but no one else can see the whole picture. We therefore cannot and must not withdraw from the central role as the conductor of the therapeutic orchestra. It is a big task. But there is no one else. If our knowledge and skills are not up to it, we need to improve them. If our systems are suboptimal, we must develop them. If we haven't the time, we must delegate roles, and a clinical pharmacist to lead the orchestra should be the norm. But the baton must reside with the GP.

It is simplistic to dismiss prescribing as an important but essentially technical component of care. We have seen how listening to the narrative, observing the broad picture, perceiving the patient's perspective and following the outcome are as vital in prescribing as in all other dimensions of personal care. Humanity, both in our patients and in ourselves, permeates the science of prescribing, in its problems, in its solutions. Engagement, empathy, collaboration and continuity are central:

> To write prescriptions is easy, but to come to an understanding with people is hard.
> (Franz Kafka)[11]

References

1. Bosch F, Rosich L. The contributions of Paul Ehrlich to pharmacology: a tribute on the occasion of the centenary of his Nobel Prize. *Pharmacology* 2008; **82(3)**: 171–9.
2. Howard R, Avery A, Howard P, Partridge M. Investigation into the reasons for preventable drug related admissions to a medical admissions unit: observational study. *Quality and Safety in Health Care* 2003; **12(4)**: 280–5.
3. Pirmohamed M, James S, Meakin S, *et al.* Adverse drug reactions as cause of admission to hospital: prospective analysis of 18 820 patients. *British Medical Journal* 2004; **329(7456)**: 15–19.
4. Bates DW, Cullen DJ, Laird N, *et al.* Incidence of adverse drug events and potential adverse drug events. Implications for prevention. ADE Prevention Study Group. *Journal of the American Medical Association* 1995; **274(1)**: 29–34.
5. Petty DR, Zermansky AG, Alldred DP. The scale of repeat prescribing – time for an update. *BMC Health Services Research* 2014; DOI: 10.1186/472-6963-14-76.
6. National Insititute for Health and Clinical Excellence. *Medicines Adherence* (Clinical Guideline 76). London: NICE, 2009, www.nice.org.uk/guidance/cg76/resources/guidance-medicines-adherence-pdf [accessed 19 May 2015].
7. Swinglehurst D, Greenhalgh T, Russell J, Myall M. Receptionist input to quality and safety in repeat prescribing in UK general practice: ethnographic case study. *British Medical Journal* 2011; DOI: 10.1136/bmj.d6788.
8. Zermansky AG, Silcock J. Is medication review by primary-care pharmacists for older people cost effective? *Pharmacoeconomics* 2009; **27(1)**: 11–24.
9. Dickinson R, Knapp P, House AO, *et al.* Long-term prescribing of antidepressants in the older population: a qualitative study. *British Journal of General Practice* 2010; DOI: 10.3399/bjgp10X483913.
10. Marinker M. Peace. In: M Balint (ed.). *Treatment or Diagnosis: a study of repeat prescriptions in general practice*. London: Tavistock/Lippincott, 1970, pp. 77–101.
11. Kafka F. A country doctor. In: NN Glatzer (ed.). *The Penguin Complete Short Stories of Franz Kafka*. London: Penguin, 1983, pp. 220–5.

Chapter 18

Compassion in primary care nursing

Kirsty Millard

Introduction

General practice nursing is an evolving role. It has developed over the last 25 years from qualified nurses who took blood samples and dressed wounds to our modern practice nurses who can prescribe drugs, perform minor surgery, manage chronic diseases and sit on Clinical Commissioning Group boards. In practice nursing, many nurses are advancing their roles. Rather than a conscious effort it appears that many practice nurses develop slowly over many years without much structure or thought to their development.

In primary care there appears to be two main areas of work for advanced nurses. First-contact or minor-illness work is now often led by a nurse with the back-up of a GP for more complex cases. The management of long-term conditions is a massive and continually growing area of development for the nursing team in primary care. In both of these areas nurses can work autonomously. It's the author's experience that many advanced nurse practitioners (ANPs) in primary care have the back-up and support of a team of healthcare professionals including GPs. So although much of their work will be autonomous for some cases, they will be seeking advice from other healthcare practitioners (HCPs) in order to manage the patient. The doctors may only look at one presenting problem whereas the ANPs are skilled at considering all factors that impact on care. ANPs also carry out more health promotion work within their consultations.

Many of the original practice nurse roles are now performed by healthcare assistants (HCAs). There are no standards or regulation for HCAs and their roles have developed to encompass many of the traditional nursing roles such as suture removal, phlebotomy and health checks. Concerns remain about the standards of an unregulated workforce and recently the RCGP has developed standards for HCA training and competency assessment in primary care.

The current situation

In primary care there are three main drivers for change. These are demand for appointments, chronic disease and the ageing population. The development of preventive drugs such as statins provided a clearly defined opportunity to improve health promotion but a workforce was needed to provide this care and monitoring. At the other end of the spectrum the incidence of chronic disease is rising.

Total deaths from chronic obstructive pulmonary disease (COPD) are projected to increase by more than 30% in the next ten years without interventions to cut risks, particularly exposure to tobacco smoke.[1] COPD is the fifth biggest killer in the UK. COPD is the only major cause of death whose incidence is on the increase and is expected to be the third leading cause of death worldwide by 2020 (exceeded only by heart disease and stroke). An estimated 3 million people have COPD in the UK, although approximately 900,000 (1.5% of the population) are diagnosed.

This presents a huge area of development for the whole team in primary care. These figures show how urgently the NHS needs to address smoking cessation and screening for COPD, which is just one disease area. Hence a skill mix of nursing is apparent across most primary care settings. It is individual and based on many factors including availability of applicants for vacant posts. Trained practice nurses are rare and over 25% in our area are over 55. This is another factor in the rapid recruitment of HCAs in primary care.

Advanced nurses in primary care

So let us consider the advanced nursing role within primary care. Benner points to the whole nursing process from novice to expert[2] and McGee focuses on meeting the needs of patients in whatever setting these arise.[3] Many of the descriptions of advancing practice hold a core set of expectations that an advanced nurse practitioner will possess. These include being a leader, expert clinician, collaborator, role model, policy developer, patient advocate, researcher, educator and innovator. In November 2010 the Department of Health released a position statement for advanced level nursing.[4] This document acknowledged two levels of nursing: basic and advanced. It pointed to advanced nurses being clinically based but with specific notes regarding improvement of public health. This goes some way to clarifying the current confused position of advancing nursing but it does not point to an educational level or suggest that ANPs should hold any specific educational qualifications.

This again leaves a difficult decision for nurses working at this level. For many the extension of their role has developed slowly with no specific plan, just responding to needs within their area. This leads to nurses working within limited areas of the core expectations for advanced practitioners. For example, a nurse who can fit a chest drain isn't necessarily a policy developer, leader or role model. It may just be a skill needed in her work area. Regulation of the advanced nursing role would develop such extra skills within the framework of a higher-education programme. This may lead to development of wider policy to promote the advancing nursing role and enhance patient care further. For many nurses working in primary care they often work across all the levels due to the small nature of many primary care providers.

Day-to-day compassion in practice

The word compassion has over recent years become the latest buzz word. It is often used in a negative way to describe what is lacking in nursing care. So what is compassion in primary care nursing and how does this differ? As I prepared to write this chapter, I reflected on my compassion in my day-to-day role. I confess it is not something I think very much about. I did reflect upon it today at work while I held a bucket for a patient with a leaking wound that leaked 600 ml of fluid everywhere. I stood holding the bucket in one hand and the patient's hand in my other hand. I felt so sorry for him. This would mean a readmission for a tired and weak patient who just wanted it all to go away. So I did the typical nurse care of holding his hand and telling him it would all be fine, and I would see him when he came home and look forward to seeing him then.

> *Compassion – a kindness that cannot be taught, but can be shown every day.*

Did I hold his hand and reassure him as a conscious effort to be compassionate? No, not at all. I am thinking about my actions now but I didn't give it a thought at the time. I just wanted him to feel better, although I couldn't 'cure' him because he needed my secondary care colleagues for that. I was driven to try to help by an intuitive empathetic response. Isn't that what makes nurses? An intuitive holistic approach to everyone. A kindness that cannot be taught, but can be shown every day. The best skill we have as nurses is kindness. Even in the most desperate situation a few kind words or actions are noticed as much as a surgeon's skill or a key diagnosis. The patients don't forget the good nurses!

> *Even in the most desperate situation a few kind words or actions are noticed as much as a surgeon's skill or a key diagnosis.*

It is easy to be compassionate for someone in trouble like that, but what about the less clear-cut situations? The morbidly obese patient with huge complications such as diabetes and ulceration who can't or won't consider support to lose weight. How much harder is it to be compassionate when the situation drags on and the nurses feel impotent to make a difference? When we look at the Francis Report[5] and significant events at Winterbourne[6] we see overstretched staff becoming numb to the needs of their patients. In primary care we see our 'heartsink' patients for ten minutes. It is much harder to show compassion when you have a whole eight-hour shift and a ten-day stretch of those shifts to deal with the same patient.

When I consider the Francis Report and Winterbourne, and the other reports that have reflected so badly upon the NHS, I do wonder about leadership and role models, and caring for the carers. Where are the leaders who are reporting upwards on key issues? Who is caring for the tired nursing teams? This is an issue in primary care as many nurses are working alone and drowning in a sea of ageing patients and long-term conditions. If the nurses are tired it is so much harder to consider our patients' needs. As the practice nurse development lead for Solihull CCG I spend a great deal of time offering supportive care to my nursing teams across the patch. This work is unseen and its great value often unmeasured.

So let us consider the unhappy patient. Many long surgeries bring this to my mind. Imagine I am running late, very late. My morning is overrunning due to a worried parent whose young child has had a significant asthma attack and been in hospital. The mother needs education and reassurance to empower her to care for her son's asthma. I have also seen another woman, who is struggling to come to terms following a recent termination of pregnancy. Both appointments have run well over the booked ten-minute slots allocated. I am now running 30 minutes late and my heart sinks when I look at my next patient.

You can appreciate that they are angry and are unable to understand why I am running late, despite my best attempts to explain without breaking patient confidentiality. This person accuses me of being unprofessional, and, out of their ten-minute slot, I spend six or seven minutes listening and trying to explain and apologise for my lateness. The patient is a poor attendee, they have two long-term conditions and other lifestyle issues. It is impossible to build a rapport but as a patient they need my help and I am trying to consider this as we plough through a disease check in a few minutes of tense dialogue. As a nurse or a doctor when we are tired and struggling with a huge workload, angry patients come high up the list of people who are hard to care for. However, these patients are often the people who need our help most and by trying to see past the anger we must endeavour to offer high-quality equitable care while recognising that each patient has a choice of when and where, and from whom, to receive their care. The NHS response to trying to improve compassion across nursing is the 6Cs. It is sad that we need reminding of this.

The 6Cs for practice nursing encourage us to take action to improve the six areas (Care, Compassion, Courage, Competence, Communication and Commitment).[7] The Department of Health urges us to embed these core functions into daily professional life and to consider the obstacles to doing so. In primary care we are lucky as we have a longstanding, dedicated nursing workforce who have all these factors embedded into their lives. Primary care may be struggling in many other ways, such as with ageing workforces and increased demand, and with issues around working for small employers and a lack of structure. However, despite this, we have been showing the 6Cs for the last 25 years and I am sure we will continue to do so.

The 6Cs for nursing: Care, Compassion, Courage, Competence, Communication and Commitment.

The challenges for nurses working at advanced level are common across all specialties. The lack of a clear and all-encompassing definition of advanced practice is a problem. If the role cannot be defined by the nurses themselves and their clinical teams then the public will also be unable to perceive it.

There are many positives about working in primary care. It is easier to be compassionate towards people you know. After five years in a small practice many individuals and families are already known to me. Today's current trend of huge practices takes away that luxury for both the patient and the nursing teams. Its unmeasured value has been floundering in a sea of audit and outcome measures.

> *Compassion – its unmeasured value has been floundering in a sea of audit and outcome measures.*

The reverse can also be true. The task of dealing with angry and unhappy patients cannot be given to someone else if you are the only nurse. Struggles to overcome this take time and effort on both sides.

CONCLUSION

Nursing in primary care is a privilege. We are fortunate enough to be able to develop long-term relationships with our patients. Over the next few years we will see many experienced practice nurses retire and new nurses begin their careers in primary care. We must strive to ensure we always are compassionate even in the most difficult times. We need to invest time in caring for our primary care teams to allow them to develop and expand the services they can offer to their patients. We must be mindful, though, that in order to face the workload challenges ahead we must respond to the needs of our primary care teams by valuing the work they do and recognising the huge impact this work has, both on individuals and communities.

REFERENCES

1. World Health Organization. Global Health Observatory (GHO) data: United Kingdom. www.who.int/gho/countries/gbr/en/ [accessed 30 June 2015].
2. Benner P. *From Novice to Expert*. Menlo Park, CA: Addison-Wesley, 1984.
3. McGee P. *Advanced Practice in Nursing and the Allied Health Professionals* (3rd edn). Oxford: Blackwell Publishing Ltd, 2009.
4. Department of Health. *Advanced Level Nursing: a position statement.* Leeds: DH, 2010, www.gov.uk/government/publications/advanced-level-nursing-a-position-statement [accessed 7 May 2015].
5. Francis R. *Report of the Mid Staffordshire NHS Foundation Trust Public Inquiry*. London: TSO, 2013, www.midstaffspublicinquiry.com/report [accessed 7 May 2015].
6. Department of Health. *Transforming Care: a national response to Winterbourne View Hospital.* London: DH, 2012, www.gov.uk/government/uploads/system/uploads/attachment_data/file/213215/final-report.pdf [accessed 7 May 2015].
7. Department of Health. *Compassion in Practice: nursing, midwifery and care staff. Our vision and strategy*. Leeds: DH, 2012, www.england.nhs.uk/nursingvision/ [accessed 7 May 2015].

Chapter 19

Post-conflict symptoms

A challenge for military GPs

Rich Withnall

Introduction

The core curriculum statement produced by the Royal College of General Practitioners (RCGP) highlights that general practice is an extremely challenging patient-centred discipline. Each consultation is unique but the RCGP motto '*Cum scientia caritas*' (science with compassion) provides a laudatory overarching philosophy. In his 1971 James Mackenzie Lecture, Dr D.L. Crombie, a GP in Birmingham and then Director of the Birmingham Research Unit, highlighted how compassion is complex and extends beyond the pure scientific methods that logically link identifiable causes with effects. Today, Birmingham is the home of the Ministry of Defence's (MOD) Royal Centre for Defence Medicine and the Academic Department of Military General Practice. As members and fellows of the RCGP, GPs working within the Defence Medical Services (DMS) are also charged to deliver science with compassion, even when the fog of war clouds the link between cause and effect.

The role of the MOD is: 'to deliver security for the people of the UK and Overseas territories by defending them, including against terrorism, and to act as a force for good by strengthening international peace and security'.[1] For as long as governments send the UK Armed Forces into harm's way, the DMS will be amongst the MOD's most important assets. The versatility of DMS GPs enables them to support the UK government's policies at home and overseas throughout the full spectrum of military tasks. The DMS GP cadre includes: military GPs (all commissioned medical officers); civilian medical practitioners (CMPs) employed by the MOD who provide essential clinical and educational continuity; and increasingly reservists. All DMS GPs are vocationally trained and undertake the same licensing processes as NHS GPs.

In recent years, DMS GPs' efforts have been focused upon supporting the International Security Assistance Forces (ISAF) in Afghanistan and Iraq. Concurrently, however, they have also contributed to: standing strategic responsibilities, such as defending the Falkland Islands; North Atlantic Treaty Organization (NATO) operations; peace support activities; UK Special Forces missions; anti-piracy initiatives around the Horn of Africa; and counter-narcotic operations in the Caribbean. In collaboration with international governmental and non-governmental organisations, DMS GPs also provide humanitarian assistance whenever and wherever the need arises. Examples include after the 2004 tsunami, the 2005 Kashmir earthquake, the 2007 flooding in Central Africa, and more recently as part of the UK response to the Ebola outbreak in West Africa. Due to the diverse healthcare needs of the patients they support, DMS GPs' scope of work routinely includes pre-hospital emergency care, occupational medicine, environmental medicine, tropical medicine, sports and exercise medicine, and community mental health.

Mental health issues in NHS general practice

Mental illness is the leading cause of disability worldwide. In the UK, 20% of the total burden of disease is attributed to mental illness compared with 17.2% for cardiovascular disease and 15.5% for cancers.[2] Approximately 11 million people of working age in the UK experience mental health problems and about 5.5 million have a common mental disorder.[3] Nearly one-third of NHS GP consultations include a mental health component, and mental health problems occupy one-third of an NHS GP's time.[4] This chapter will describe how military GPs have long faced similar challenges.

Mental health issues in military general practice

The UK Armed Forces are amongst the most operationally experienced in the world. From the perspective of potential adverse mental health outcomes, though, this is not necessarily a good thing. Psychological distress is associated with duration of deployment.[5] The pace and frequency of military operations may lower morale, place strain on relationships and adversely impact upon the health of service personnel and their families.[6] DMS GPs are often the first port of call in such storms. Together with their wider multidisciplinary teams, DMS GPs are key to mitigating such risks by delivering high-quality care to military personnel on and off the battlefield, and support to registered families at home.

Post-conflict stress syndromes

A particular challenge for military GPs is the lack of consistency in the onset and nature of post-conflict symptoms. There remain wide variations in the symptoms experienced, even amongst individuals serving within the same military formation in the same place at the same time. The form of post-conflict syndromes, the terms used to describe them, and the explanations offered by military GPs have long been influenced by advances in medical science, changes in the nature of warfare and underlying cultural factors at the time of each conflict.[7]

Historical accounts describe military 'operational stress' under many different concepts and labels, including: a debility syndrome; a somatic syndrome; and a neuropsychiatric syndrome.

Debility syndrome

Debility syndrome was the most prevalent post-conflict disorder in the nineteenth and early twentieth centuries. Throughout the Crimean War (1853–6) and the Indian Mutiny (1857), soldiers commonly presented with symptoms including general fatigue, rheumatic pains and weakness for which military doctors were unable to find convincing explanations. Soldiers with fatigue continued to experience symptoms even after receiving a pension, confirming the belief at the time that debility syndrome was a physical disorder.[8] In the First (1880–1) and Second Boer Wars (1899–1902), the commonest presentations were fatigue, difficulty completing tasks, shortness of breath and weakness. Rapid heart rate, tremor, headache, dizziness, pains in the joints, difficulty sleeping, changes in weight and anxiety were prevalent too, leading some military doctors to believe their patients were experiencing a 'disordered action of the heart'.[9]

Somatic syndrome

The somatic syndrome is most associated with the First World War (1914–18) when soldiers in the trenches experienced unrelenting artillery bombardment. 'Shell shock' is perhaps the best-known term, but somatic presentations were also referred to as 'war neurosis', 'Da Costa's syndrome' or 'battle fatigue'. Thousands of soldiers were labelled with, and treated for, 'shell shock', which encompassed a range of physical and psychological symptoms, including: headache; memory impairment; slow reaction times or 'paralyses'; dream-like dissociative states manifest as the 'thousand-yard stare'; indecision; nausea; behavioural changes, including difficulty in controlling mood reactions such as anger; and depression.

Bespoke hospitals for 'shell-shocked' UK soldiers were established, including Craiglockhart War Hospital in Edinburgh. Although the Craiglockhart story has captured the public imagination, largely because of its two most famous patients, Siegfried Sassoon and Wilfred Owen, its patient numbers were low and very few received analytically influenced psychotherapy. Far more typical was the emergence of large, tended hospital encampments in France capable of handling several thousand cases at a time whose treatments were brusque and brief.[10] Soldiers were usually categorised as 'wounded' if a shell-blast was thought to have caused their symptoms. If not, individuals were classified as 'sick' or 'unfit for military service'. Many were regarded as cowards. Some, albeit a small number, were executed for desertion.[11] Only a small number of those executed were clearly suffering from 'shell shock'. One of these, Private Harry Farr, became a test case that led to posthumous pardons for all those executed during the First World War.[12] Nevertheless, as late as 1922, the Southborough Report (War Office Committee of Enquiry into 'Shell Shock') still opined that 'shell shock' was largely a failure of morale, leadership, discipline and selection. Far from ushering in more contemporary approaches to GP-led community mental health care, the First World War ended with a restatement of Victorian and Edwardian concepts of character.[10]

One hundred years on, 'shell shock' still occupies a central place in the popular memory of the First World War, and stands as a powerful emblem of the suffering of war.[13]

Neuropsychiatric syndrome

It was not until the Second World War (1939–45) that mental breakdown was accepted as a consequence of prolonged exposure to intolerable levels of stress. It became recognised that no matter how well selected, trained or led, even the best could eventually break down.

During the Second World War the most prominent presenting complaints following exposure to operational stress were chest pain, shortage of breath, tiredness and dizziness. Military doctors attributed these to 'effort syndrome', 'psychoneurosis', 'combat exhaustion', 'combat stress reaction' or 'combat operational stress'. Soldiers also presented in epidemic numbers with acute anxiety and gastrointestinal symptoms. Again, sufferers commonly faced accusations of cowardice and malingering. Famously, General Patton once slapped a soldier suffering from a post-conflict syndrome calling him a 'gutless bastard'.[14] It is sometimes forgotten this incident cost General Patton his command until he was reinstated in time for D-Day.

The Falklands Conflict

In 2002, the South Atlantic Medal Association claimed that more UK servicemen who served in the Falklands Conflict (1982) had committed suicide than were killed in action there. In 2013, a study confirmed 95 Falklands veterans had taken their own lives since 1982 compared with 255 killed in battle. Nevertheless, any suicide directly linked to service in the UK Armed Forces is too many, and several small studies have demonstrated poorer mental health outcomes among those who served in the Falklands.[15,16] The presence of the symptoms was associated with intensity of combat experience and the retrospective report of emotional difficulties in the initial period on return from the conflict.[17]

Gulf War syndrome

As the fighting only lasted 100 hours and there were minimal UK casualties, acute combat stress reactions were not prevalent during the 1990–1 Gulf War. By the end of the twentieth century, though, UK Armed Forces personnel involved in the 1990–1 Gulf War were more likely to present to their military GP with headache, depression, anxiety and ill-defined, subjective symptoms, including fatigue, pain, low mood, concentration difficulties, memory problems and general malaise.[18]

It is unclear where the phrase 'Gulf War syndrome' originated. Despite a modest increase in patients presenting with multiple physical symptoms,[19] no evidence of any unique 'Gulf War syndrome' has been found.[20–22] UK personnel exposed to combat in the Gulf are twice as likely to report symptoms suggestive of post-traumatic stress disorder (PTSD) and alcohol misuse,[23] but the actual numbers remain low. Most Gulf veterans, even those with more physical symptoms, do not have mental health disorders.[24]

Afghanistan

Since the '9/11' attack on the World Trade Center in New York on 11 September 2001, counterinsurgency (COIN) operations have become the cornerstone of international military effort against global terrorism. COIN activities are complex and expose military personnel to unfamiliar stressors.[25] Although modern reconfigurations have reduced the size of the UK Armed Forces and the risk of large-scale casualties, long-term ill health has not fallen.[11] Military GPs now recognise that, just like war fighting, COIN operations and even peacekeeping activities can also lead to psychological trauma and potential adverse mental health outcomes.

Portrayals of the UK's involvement in Afghanistan have made 'operational stress' almost synonymous with PTSD. In reality, UK Armed Forces personnel most commonly present to their military GPs with symptoms suggestive of common mental disorders (such as anxiety, panic attacks and depression) (19.7%) and alcohol misuse (13.0%). The prevalence of probable PTSD remains low (4.0%). Many UK Armed Forces personnel have served in Afghanistan several times. There is no association with number of deployments and mental health issues, but reporting of probable PTSD does increase with time after return to the UK.[26] With the correct degree of support from their DMS GPs, peers and military leaders, individuals affected by operational stress may recover swiftly.

The future

Serving in the Armed Forces is inherently stressful, and military personnel are at risk of developing adverse psychological outcomes.[7] Debate continues as to whether the development of post-conflict symptoms represents a normal or an abnormal process.[27] Post-conflict syndromes may simply represent normal responses to the physical and psychological challenges of war.[9] Some men, especially male officers, report more desirable effects of military service (e.g. mastery, self-esteem and coping skills) than undesirable ones, but both the positive and negative effects of military service increase linearly with combat exposure.[28,29]

Despite their heightened presentations inferring poorer health, analyses of death certificates demonstrate that patients with post-conflict syndromes, past and present, have neither different causes of death nor die any younger than their unaffected contemporaries.[30,31] If morbidity patterns since the Boer War persist in the future wars that 'should be expected',[32] adverse mental health outcomes after exposure to operational stress are likely to continue.

Conclusion

The recognition and treatment of post-conflict syndromes have improved greatly in recent years now government-funded screening programmes are available to UK military veterans.[18] Nevertheless, newer forms of psychological injury may be less predictable, less well understood and harder to manage.[11] For as long as the UK Armed Forces are sent into harm's way, DMS GPs and their multidisciplinary teams are likely to remain 'on the front line' of post-conflict symptoms. When surrounded by the fog of war, DMS GPs can take solace in the philosophy of '*Cum scientia caritas*' and Dr D.L. Crombie's wise words. Science, compassion and patient-centredness are equally applicable on the battlefield and in the consulting room.

References

1. Ministry of Defence. *Delivering Security in a Changing World*. Norwich: TSO, 2003.
2. World Health Organization. *The World Health Report 2004: changing history*. Geneva: WHO, 2004, www.who.int/whr/2004/en/ [accessed 21 May 2015].
3. Royal College of Psychiatrists. *No Health Without Public Mental Health: the case for action* (Position Statement PS4/2010). London: RCPsych, 2010, www.rcpsych.ac.uk/pdf/Position%20Statement%204%20website.pdf [accessed 12 June 2015].
4. Jenkins R, McCulloch A, Friedli L, Parker C. *Developing a National Mental Health Policy* (Maudsley Monograph 43). Hove: The Psychology Press, 2002.
5. Dolan CA, Adler A. Military hardiness as a buffer of psychological health on return from deployment. *Military Medicine* 2006; **171(2)**: 93–8.
6. Adams G, Durand D, Doris B, *et al*. Direct and indirect effects of operational tempo on outcomes for soldiers and spouses. *Military Psychology* 2005; **17(3)**: 229–46.
7. Jones E, Hodgins-Vermaas R, McCartney H, *et al*. Post-combat syndromes from the Boer war to the Gulf war: a cluster analysis of their nature and attribution. *British Medical Journal* 2002; **324(7333)**: 321–4.
8. Jones E, Wessely S. Case of chronic fatigue syndrome after Crimean war and Indian mutiny. *British Medical Journal* 1999; **319(7225)**: 1645–7.
9. Jones E, Wessely S. Hearts, guts and minds: somatisation in the military from 1900. *Journal of Psychosomatic Research* 2004; **56(4)**: 425–9.
10. Jones E, Wessely S. 'Forward psychiatry' in the military: its origins and effectiveness. *Journal of Traumatic Stress* 2003; **16(4)**: 411–19.
11. Linden SC, Hess V, Jones E. The neurological manifestations of trauma: lessons from World War I. *European Archives of Psychiatry and Clinical Neuroscience* 2012; **262(3)**: 253–64.
12. Wessely S. Risk, psychiatry and the military. *British Journal of Psychiatry* 2005; **186(6)**: 459–66.
13. Loughran T. Shell shock, trauma, and the First World War: the making of a diagnosis and its histories. *Journal of the History of Medicine and Allied Sciences* 2012; **67(1)**: 94–119.
14. Atkinson R. *The Day of Battle: the war in Sicily and Italy 1943–1944*. New York: Henry Holt & Co., 2007.
15. Iversen A, Dyson C, Smith N, *et al*. 'Goodbye and good luck': the mental health needs and treatment experiences of British ex-service personnel. *British Journal of Psychiatry* 2005; **186**: 480–6.
16. Orner R, Lynch T, Seed P. Long-term traumatic stress reactions in British Falklands War veterans. *British Journal of Clinical Psychology* 1993; **32**: 457–9.
17. O'Brien LS, Hughes SJ. Symptoms of post-traumatic stress disorder in Falklands veterans five years after the conflict. *British Journal of Psychiatry* 1991; **159**: 135–41.
18. Bale A, Lee H. An observational study on diagnoses of 3,233 Gulf veterans (Op Granby 1990–91) who attended the Ministry of Defence's Medical Assessment Programme 1993–2004. *Journal of the Royal Navy Medical Service* 2005; **91(2)**: 99–111.
19. Hotopf M, Hull L, Fear NT, *et al*. The health of UK military personnel who deployed to the 2003 Iraq war: a cohort study. *Lancet* 2006; **367(9524)**: 1731–41.
20. Cherry N, Creed F, Silman A, *et al*. Health and exposures of United Kingdom Gulf War veterans. Part 2: The relationship of health to exposure. *Occupational and Environmental Medicine* 2001; **58(5)**: 299–306.
21. Everitt B, Ismail K, David AS, Wessely S. Searching for a Gulf War syndrome using cluster analysis. *Psychological Medicine* 2002; **32(8)**: 1371–8.

22. Simmons R, Maconochie N, Doyle P. Self-reported ill health in male UK Gulf War veterans: a retrospective cohort study. *BMC Public Health* 2004; **4**: 27.
23. Stimpson NJ, Thomas HV, Weightman AL, *et al*. Psychiatric disorder in veterans of the Persian Gulf War of 1991. Systematic review. *British Journal of Psychiatry* 2003; **182**: 391–403.
24. Ismail K, Kent K, Brugha T, *et al*. The mental health of UK Gulf war veterans: phase 2 of a two phase cohort study. *British Medical Journal* 2002; **325(7364)**: 576.
25. Applewhite L, Keller N, Borah A. Mental health care use by soldiers conducting counterinsurgency operations. *Military Medicine* 2012; **177(5)**: 501–6.
26. Fear NT, Jones M, Murphy D, *et al*. What are the consequences of deployment to Iraq and Afghanistan on the mental health of the UK armed forces? A cohort study. *Lancet* 2010; **375(9728)**: 1783–97.
27. Auxéméry Y. The Gulf War Syndrome twenty years on. *L'Encéphale* 2013; **39(5)**: 332–8.
28. Aldwin CM, Levenson MR, Spiro A 3rd. Vulnerability and resilience to combat exposure: can stress have lifelong effects? *Psychology and Aging* 1994; **9(1)**: 34–44.
29. Maclean A. The privileges of rank: the peacetime draft and later-life attainment. *Armed Forces Society* 2008; **34(4)**: 682–713.
30. Wooley CF. Where are the diseases of yesteryear? DaCosta's syndrome, soldiers heart, the effort syndrome, neurocirculatory asthenia – and the mitral valve prolapse syndrome. *Circulation* 1976; **53(5)**: 749–51.
31. Kang HK, Bullman TA. Mortality among US veterans of the Persian Gulf War: 7-year follow-up. *American Journal of Epidemiology* 2001; **154(5)**: 399–405.
32. Gray C. *Another Bloody Century: future warfare*. London: Phoenix, 2006.

CHAPTER 20

COMPASSIONATE SUICIDE PREVENTION

Alys Cole-King

> People don't always remember what you say or even what you do, but they always remember how you made them feel.
>
> (Maya Angelou)

SETTING THE SCENE

> It's 3 a.m. and your patient is at home, wide awake and being tormented by suicidal thoughts. What is likely to stop them ending their life, and make them seek help? A complex, lengthy risk assessment they underwent earlier that day, or the support of a skilled, compassionate and trusted GP with whom they agreed a simple safety plan?[1]

Every year approximately 6000 people in the UK die by suicide. This is three times the number of deaths from road traffic accidents. Although only 25% of those who die by suicide are known to specialist mental health services, the majority of the remaining 75% will be in contact with front-line services including with primary care.[2] This chapter highlights the importance of compassion when assessing and responding to patients in primary care who are experiencing suicidal thoughts.

Undertaking a suicide risk assessment is potentially life saving, but the clinical encounter is completely dependent on what the patient chooses to reveal or keep hidden. In making a 'diagnosis' of suicide risk, we rely on our patient to trust us with the often painful and difficult disclosure of their suicidal thoughts. The importance of such disclosure cannot be underestimated; indeed it can itself be a protective factor.[3,4] A compassionate approach is by far the most useful interaction to engage positively with a patient. Healthcare professionals who are empathetic and compassionate encourage increased disclosure by patients about their concerns, symptoms and behaviour, and are ultimately more effective at delivering care.[5]

Conversely, negative reactions from professionals can lead to patients feeling that the clinician is hostile, unsympathetic and uncaring, putting the therapeutic relationship at risk.[6] Negative reactions to self-harming behaviour among healthcare professionals are common, and typically result from the professional's belief in his or her own helplessness about making a difference.[7] Patients often have well-tuned 'radar', which can detect a clinician's level of interest. This kind of reaction is detrimental to a patient's immediate safety and recovery. Meanwhile compassionate care must also be competent care. The establishment of a therapeutic alliance and trusting relationship between clinician and patient must be matched by a comprehensive and skilled risk assessment and response.

Compassionate suicide prevention

When undertaking an assessment of a patient experiencing suicidal thoughts and feelings, compassion is as important as the technical skill of a clinical mental state examination. It is the quality of the therapeutic relationship that makes it possible for the patient to disclose suicidal thoughts. Given that our understanding of the exact mechanism of how suicidal thoughts and feelings progress to suicide attempts and suicidal behaviour it is proposed that the only safe response is to adopt a 'suicide mitigation' approach.[3] Suicide mitigation starts from the assumption that suicidal thoughts need to be taken seriously and met with compassion and understanding on every occasion. For the many suicidal individuals who are ambivalent about their wish to die, a compassionate interaction with another person can be the tipping point back to safety, providing the fragile difference between succumbing and enabling the patient to resist acting on their suicidal thoughts. Every contact with a suicidal patient represents an opportunity to intervene and prevent that person from going on to die by suicide. Small acts of compassion that last minutes may be remembered for a lifetime.

Compassion is not just about warmth, kindness and gentleness; it evolved from the capacity for caring required in the infant–parent relationship and is hard-wired into our brains. Today compassion is commonly defined as 'A sensitivity to the distress of self and others with a commitment to try to do something about it.' It entails awareness, attention and motivation.[8]

Gilbert suggests that human capacities for compassion depend upon six essential qualities and attributes:[8]

- *motivation* – compassion requires the motivation to be caring, supportive and helpful
- *sensitivity* – a capacity to sensitivity and open attention, to be able to notice when others are needing help and not 'turning a blind eye' or using denial or finding justification to avoid engaging with suffering
- *sympathy* – the emotional ability to be moved by distress in others
- *distress tolerance* – the ability to tolerate difficult emotions and situations both in ourselves and others. This is an essential component of compassion. People who feel overwhelmed by another's distress may turn away from it or try to deny or

minimise it. Alternatively they can act as 'rescuers' wanting to turn off distress as fast as possible because it is distressing to them

- *empathy* – the ability to understand and emotionally recognise the feelings, motivations and intents of another. Empathy allows us to make sense of our feelings and those of others, and to be able to predict the effects of a behaviour on others
- *non-judgement* – compassion involves being non-judgemental and non-condemning. Feeling angry or frustrated about a situation beyond our control makes us vulnerable to burnout and becoming demoralised, thus interfering with our capacity to be compassionate.

Risk assessment should be viewed as a therapeutic intervention with the potential to save lives, rather than an information-gathering exercise. Instead of focusing on simply quantifying and characterising risk, the emphasis should be on identifying the patient's needs and empowering them to accept help, reducing their distress and maximising their protective factors. Compassionate engagement with the patient can help identify reasons for living and instil hope. This should be accompanied by the co-creation of an immediate safety plan that includes a comprehensive array of support and a longer-term risk mitigation plan.

The compassionate risk mitigation approach emphasises the degree of ambivalence felt by many suicidal individuals. It also challenges the common perception that it is not possible for someone without specialist psychiatric knowledge and training to help a suicidal individual resist his or her suicidal thoughts. Increasing hopefulness, resilience and reasons for living have been shown to reduce suicide rates.[9] The question practitioners should be asking is: 'What can be done to prevent this person ending their life today … this week … this month?'

Potential barriers to a compassionate risk assessment

A patient contemplating suicide, or one who has tried to take his or her life, will at the very least be experiencing personal distress that needs respectful consideration. Failure to treat these patients with understanding and compassion is likely to have a detrimental impact on their mental state.[10] Therefore, clinicians should routinely ask patients with depression or emotional distress about thoughts of suicide, self-harm and suicidal behaviour.[3,4,10] Assessment of suicide risk requires a biopsychosocial assessment of the patient, including details of his or her suicidal thoughts, intent, plans, personal demographic factors and a comprehensive mental state examination. Everyone who has had or is having suicidal thoughts should have a robust safety plan.[11] Useful resources and further reading are included at the end of this chapter. GPs are also encouraged to seek training as they would for basic and advanced life support.

Undertaking a suicide risk assessment is a potentially life-saving clinical encounter and the assessor is dependent on what the patient chooses to tell or not tell him or her. In the quest to develop the 'perfect' suicide risk assessment scale, researchers may have overlooked the importance of compassion and a therapeutic relationship during the assessment. A good rapport and therapeutic relationship is essential to the quality of the information underpinning an assessment. A therapeutic alliance between suicidal patients and their GP can be a protective factor against suicide.[11]

Even when the underlying disorder prompting suicidal thoughts has a primarily biological aetiology, psychosocial interventions can help. The key to a compassionate suicide mitigation approach is the emphasis on collaboration rather than direction. Meanwhile the way in which professionals assess suicide risk is influenced by their knowledge of and attitude towards suicide and self-harm. If professionals are afraid to discuss suicidal thoughts due to lack of confidence or competence, or a fear of triggering a suicidal episode, then an opportunity to intervene will be lost. We will not increase the risk of someone ending their life simply by asking them if they are having suicidal thoughts, but, unfortunately, suicidal thoughts are often not inquired about during clinical assessments in primary care and even in specialist mental health services. Studies of people who died by suicide show that they were often not asked about their suicidal thoughts when they were assessed by professionals. All suicidal thoughts, however 'minor', require a response and that response needs to be proportional and timely.

The importance of a thorough assessment is also backed up by the latest research from the National Confidential Inquiry. Researchers studied case notes of patients known to services who had died by suicide within a week of their last assessment and found that 14% had an inadequate mental state assessment, 26% had an inadequate risk formulation and 38% had an inadequate risk 'management plan'.[12]

Solutions to facilitate a compassionate approach

A variety of unconscious factors may be at work to explain why many health professionals fail to elicit suicidal thoughts in patients.[13] How clinicians assess this risk is likely to be influenced by their knowledge of and attitude towards suicide and self-harm.[1] One of the main reasons for not identifying suicide risk could be a lack of the necessary knowledge and skills, including an inaccurate belief that suicide is not preventable, coupled with a fear of being expected to manage suicide risk once it is acknowledged.[1] Fear, stigma and lack of confidence all contribute to not asking about suicidal thoughts, therefore a sophisticated organisational approach that explicitly recognises and overcomes these barriers is required.

Connecting with People is an innovative approach that follows a values-based commissioning style by ensuring that the training is based on patient and carer perspectives, clinical expertise and knowledge derived from scientific evidence.[14] Connecting with People also emphasises the importance of a strategic approach that includes organisational culture change. The development of this approach was informed by extensive consultations, including with academics, practitioners, managers, expert suicide prevention voluntary organisations and people with lived experience as patients and carers. *It is vital to understand and tackle* the psychological and institutional barriers to and opportunities for compassionate practice, and to create nurturing environments that support and engage GPs, validate the particular stresses of their work, respect their capabilities and make provision for the need for reflection and self-care strategies.

The more information the GP and primary care team have about a patient's suicidal thoughts, the greater the chance to intervene appropriately, helping the patient to resist acting on those thoughts. This chapter has outlined the crucial role of compassion in suicide mitigation, but there is also no substitute for developing suicide awareness and response skills, ideally through appropriate training. As well as learning necessary skills, clinicians will be more able to manage real-life scenarios (see further resources for suggested training courses).

Compassion should run like a thread through everything we do, not be seen as an optional add-on. Suicide and self-harm cause significant emotional distress, mortality and morbidity. Health professionals working in primary care who experience the death of one or more of their patients by suicide are often severely affected, particularly when the death occurs after major efforts to intervene have been made. Most of us choosing medicine as a profession do so with the intention of being compassionate towards our patients, and indeed to our colleagues. But the long hours, intense workloads and range of institutional pressures can cause cynicism and burnout. There is a need to create clinical environments where compassion can flourish and to enhance self-compassion, resilience and resourcefulness in primary care. Given that distress tolerance is a major aspect of compassion it is vital that clinicians have good peer support and supervision when treating patients experiencing suicidal thoughts who have complex needs, and who may therefore place significant emotional demands on healthcare professionals.

Suicide is not an inevitable outcome of suicidal thoughts. The most robust assessment and response involves combining excellent clinical governance with a compassionate and collaborative approach. Primary care is at the front line of suicide prevention and every contact with a suicidal patient presents an opportunity to intervene and help save his or her life.

> Compassion may not be rocket science … but it is rocket fuel.
>
> (Dr Chris Manning)

References

1. Cole-King A, Lepping P. Personal view: will the new government change our approach to risk? *British Medical Journal* 2010; DOI: 10.1136/bmj.
2. Luoma JB, Martin CE, Pearson JL. Contact with mental health and primary care providers before suicide: a review of the evidence. *American Journal of Psychiatry* 2002; **159(6)**: 909–16.
3. Cole-King A, Lepping P. Suicide mitigation: time for a more realistic approach. *British Journal of General Practice* 2010; **60(570)**: 3–4.
4. Cole-King A, Green G, Peake-Jones G, Gask L. The assessment and management of patients with suicidal thoughts in primary care: an introduction to the concept and practicalities of suicide mitigation. *InnovAiT* 2011; **4(5)**: 288–95.
5. Larson EB, Yao Y. Clinical empathy as emotional labour in the patient-physician relationship. *Journal of the American Medical Association* 2005; **293(9)**: 1100–6.
6. Thompson AR, Powis J, Carradice A. Community psychiatric nurses' experience of working with people who engage in deliberate self-harm. *International Journal of Mental Health Nursing* 2008; **17(3)**: 153–61.
7. Taylor TL, Hawton K, Fortune S, Kapur N. Attitudes towards clinical services among people who self-harm: systematic review. *British Journal of Psychiatry* 2009; **194(2)**: 104–10.

8. Gilbert P. Introducing compassion-focused therapy. *Advances in Psychiatric Treatment* 2009; **15(3)**: 199–208.
9. McLean J, Maxwell M, Platt S, *et al*. *Risk and Protective Factors for Suicide and Suicidal Behaviour: a literature review*. Edinburgh: Scottish Government, 2008, www.gov.scot/resource/doc/251539/0073687.pdf [accessed 26 May 2015].
10. Hawton K, van Heeringen K. Suicide. *Lancet* 2009; **373(9672)**: 1372–81.
11. Cole-King A, Walton I, Gask L, *et al*. *Suicide Mitigation in Primary Care* [factsheet]. London: RCGP, RCPsych, 2012, www.rcgp.org.uk/clinical-and-research/clinical-resources/~/media/Files/CIRC/Mental%20Health%20-%202014/RCGP-Suicide-Mitigation-In-Primary-Care-Factsheet-December-2014.ashx [accessed 17 June 2015].
12. Centre for Mental Health and Safety. National Confidential Inquiry into Suicide and Homicide by People with Mental Illness, www.bbmh.manchester.ac.uk/cmhr/research/centreforsuicideprevention/nci [accessed 26 May 2015].
13. Cole-King A, Jenkins PL. A prospective study of psychiatric patients who attempt deliberate self harm. Proceedings of winter meeting of Royal College of Psychiatrists, Cardiff, January 1997.
14. Connecting with People. www.connectingwithpeople.org/resources [accessed 26 May 2015].

Useful resources

- Connecting with People has useful resources including the Royal College of General Practitioners/Royal College of Psychiatrists *Suicide Mitigation in Primary Care* factsheet. www.connectingwithpeople.org/resources [accessed 26 May 2015].
- Connecting with People. Staying safe if you're not sure life's worth living – practical, compassionate advice and many useful links for people in distress including *U Can Cope*, *Feeling Overwhelmed: helping you stay safe* and *Feeling on the Edge: helping you get through it*. www.connectingwithpeople.org/StayingSafe [accessed 26 May 2015].
- Henden J. *Preventing Suicide: the solution focused approach*. Chichester: John Wiley & Sons, 2008, pp. 141–3.
- Royal College of General Practitioners. Suicide prevention e-learning course. www.elearning.rcgp.org.uk/suicideprevention [accessed 26 May 2015].

Nationally available suicide prevention training

Suitable for GPs and primary care practitioners

- Charlie Waller Memorial Trust – mental health and wellbeing training for practice nurses (including e-learning) and for GPs (preventing medical error and clinical risk). Half-day training courses. www.cwmt.org.uk/.
- Connecting with People – bite-sized suicide and self-harm mitigation training. Clinical tools provide a robust clinical governance framework designed to enhance quality, consistency and documentation of assessment triage and safety plans. Two-hour modules build confidence and ability to respond safely and compassionately to patients at risk of suicide. An app is used to integrate records easily and securely with NHS IT systems.

Suitable for non-clinical staff

- ASIST – two-day course suitable for non-clinical staff. Also offers three-hour introduction. www.livingworks.net.
- One-day Understanding Suicide Intervention training: (City & Guilds accredited). www.suicidesaferlondon.org.uk/.
- Samaritans. www.samaritans.org/your-community/workplace-staff-training.

Part IV

The future

CHAPTER 21

SCHOLARSHIP

The missing link between *scientia* and *caritas*?

Joanne Reeve

The College motto – science with compassion – sums up one of the greatest challenges of professional practice in the twenty-first century. Our scientific knowledge and understanding of human suffering grows at an ever expanding rate. The challenge for us is to make best use of that knowledge to understand and address the problems and needs of each individual who walks in to our consulting room. *Cum scientia caritas* defines our profession by our capacity to *combine* medical scientific understanding with our knowledge of this person to reach an individually tailored[1] decision about how to care.[2] The reason why this matters was brought home to me, as ever, by a patient.

ANN'S STORY

Let me introduce you to Ann, a woman in her fifties who was dying of breast cancer. Ann was a participant in a research study I was involved in that explored experiences of distress in people living with terminal cancer.[3] During a long interview, Ann spent much time talking about the work needed to juggle her family roles as mother and grandmother, to keep the usual daily tasks ticking over, as well as dealing with her illness and medical care. One sentence in her story stood out for me:

> The [doctors] do listen, but they don't always think it's something they need to take note of.

Ann talked about receiving great personal care from empathic health professionals who were able to see beyond her cancer. Staff recognised the nature and breadth of her whole experience, providing practical help with the work of living and dying with cancer – support for symptom management, as well as financial, personal, emotional and spiritual problems. But Ann also described how that recognition didn't translate into personalised cancer care – where decisions about her medical treatment were explicitly tailored to reflect her personal circumstances.[3] Medical decisions were instead based on disease-focused evidence of prognosis, benefit and risk.

Ann was expected to 'fit' the evidence (e.g. with regard to continuing palliative chemotherapy), rather than becoming part of a beyond-protocol medical decision. She spoke of how that left her feeling 'trapped on a conveyor belt' – caught in a depersonalised system of medical care that made her feel upset, anxious and lacking control. We know a lot about the burden that illness can create for individuals. Ann spoke of an additional burden that came not from her illness, but from the services that were trying to help her. Ann described receiving empathic care, but not personalised – individually tailored – *medical* care. The medical practitioners were apparently unable to bring together the *caritas* and *scientia* – to integrate the understanding of illness offered by both perspectives in order to best support their patient.

Not a new problem

Ann was describing recent experiences of health care. But Donald Crombie, Director of the (then) RCGP Birmingham Research Unit, recognised similar challenges in his 1972 James Mackenzie Lecture, entitled '*Cum scientia caritas*'.[4] He proposed that medical practice requires the use of two forms of knowledge. One, which he called isomorphic knowledge, is the objective scientific knowledge derived from the natural sciences and their study of disease aetiology and management. But, he argued, a large part of the clinical problem-solving activities of doctors cannot be described in biomedical scientific terms. The doctor must also use what Crombie called amorphous knowledge. This includes the extra knowledge needed to deal with clinical problems that extend beyond a biomedical description. But it also refers to the skills of the practitioner to *apply* biomedical knowledge in the context of a patient's individual problems. Crombie's expressed concerns were that too much emphasis was being placed in medical education and practice on acquiring a body of scientific knowledge, at the risk of neglecting the development and acquisition of 'the other form'.

Since then, these debates have been shaped by growing concerns about whether and how it is possible for a generalist practitioner to keep up to date with the amount of new scientific knowledge.[5] We have seen a proliferation of guidelines, summaries, decision aids and other developments aimed at helping practitioners.[6] But, in turn, we now see disquiet over the contribution of these new knowledge management approaches in exacerbating problems[7–9] of overdiagnosis and treatment burden.[10,11] The evidence-based medicine (EBM) movement[12,13] was originally described as a tool to support the critical professional judgement of best fit in applying medical knowledge to the individual. However, the way it has been applied and used in practice has arguably exacerbated Crombie's concerns.[4] Although the College motto, Crombie's discussion, and the original descriptions of EBM argue the need to recognise the synergy derived from scientific and professional knowledge, the current reality has been a separation of the two. GPs express misgivings that an overemphasis on science, or at least the scientific knowledge that lies at the top of the evidence hierarchy, diminishes capacity for compassion within practice.[14] Is *scientia* overwhelming *caritas*?

Yet I would suggest that this position reflects an incomplete understanding of science; it is compounded by an overemphasis on the product rather than the process of science and research. I will argue why I feel that scientific process – notably scholarship – is the missing link that allows us to enhance compassion in modern, scientific-grounded, clinical practice. Based on which I will suggest some priorities for the future direction of professional practice.

Compassion is important but not sufficient for clinical practice

> Compassion (our usual translation of *caritas*) is the emotion felt in response to others' suffering, which in turn motivates a desire to help.[15]

It is the emphasis on action that characterises the work of the compassionate practitioner. Recent headlines have called for a need to restore compassion in health care, and enhance compassion within professional practice.[16] We know that empathy – the capacity to recognise and understand the emotions (suffering) experienced by others[17] – is associated with patient enablement, satisfaction, lower anxiety and stress, and better patient outcomes.[18,19] Yet it is perhaps the link between empathy and *action* – what we do in response to recognition of suffering – that helps us understand the observed links between empathy and outcomes. A response to suffering – in other words, compassion – is important, but not in itself sufficient when it comes to meetings the needs of individuals. *How* we respond matters too, as is evident from Ann's story.

A hierarchy of knowledge

The clinicians in Ann's case clearly demonstrated empathy, and indeed compassion. They were drawn to act to help her, for example, in dealing with the financial consequences of her illness. Ann's clinicians were able to gather and utilise information about her wider biopsychosocial circumstances. Where problems arose was in the failure to integrate that wider knowledge with the scientific knowledge about disease prognosis and treatment impact in order to make an individually tailored decision about medical need and intervention.

We can only speculate about the physicians' reasoning in Ann's case, but other work has highlighted physicians' difficulties in going beyond a protocol-defined model of best medical care in making decisions for individual patients.[14] GPs use a range of knowledge in the consultation in order to meet their patients' needs.[20] But the use of knowledge in practice is increasingly shaped by the way that the EBM movement has been applied in practice – notably in the development of what Harrison described as Scientific Bureaucratic Medicine (SBM) (see Box 21.1, overleaf).[5,6] EBM created a hierarchy of knowledge. SBM created a framework of quality standards based on adherence to application of that hierarchy into practice. The combination perhaps explains why it feels like *scientia* is overwhelming *caritas*.

Box 21.1: Describing EBM and SBM[2]

The EBM movement defines best evidence (or knowledge) as that derived from empirical observations of defined disease within populations. It is undertaken by scientific method, and provides objective knowledge including quantitative estimates of the certainty of that knowledge.[21] Professional knowledge and skills are still needed in the 'conscientious, explicit and judicious application of best evidence in making decisions about the care of individual patients',[13] and in interpreting whether scientific evidence can and should be applied to individual patients (just as Crombie described).

The system of SBM[5,6] describes the extension of these ideas into managed healthcare systems. The introduction of clinical governance saw quality systems of care described as those that set clear standards, outlined how to meet those goals, and monitored adherence.[22] Like EBM, SBM regards the primary source of valid knowledge about the effectiveness of medicine as that based on objective research, conducted by experts and judged by its proximity to 'truth', rather than the opinion of professionals.[2] However, it is in the use of this knowledge that EBM and SBM differ. EBM acknowledges the legitimacy of professional judgement in the interpretation and application of this knowledge: in deciding when and where to apply research findings to guide decision making in the assessment and management of patients. By contrast, SBM hands the responsibility for interpreting and judging this externally derived knowledge to external knowledge management experts. Contending that working clinicians 'don't have the time to discover and collate the information themselves',[5,6] SBM creates a role for external experts to distil findings for professionals into algorithms for action in the form of diagnostic tools, decision aids and clinical guidelines. Management systems can then be designed to support consistent implementation of tools. SBM is a model that supports organisational needs for consistency and predictability in health care (over the variability/uncertainty of professional practice). Responsibility for decision making shifts from the individual professional to systems or protocols; trust in individual professionals is replaced by confidence in (quality) systems.[5] The result is a 'technical bypass' of professional decision making.[23]

The hierarchy of knowledge described within the EBM movement privileges a narrow view of what is scientific knowledge over all other forms of knowledge. Experimental method and meta-synthesis of the results are valued over, for example, the wealth of research from the social sciences, which focuses on individual experience, as well as the personal experiential knowledge of both the patient and the professional. Although clinicians may still seek to use these other sources of knowledge, a failure to adequately describe the 'judicious use'[23] of knowledge has contributed to an over-reliance on scientific knowledge to inform clinical decision making. Clinicians are left feeling uncertain about what counts as 'credible evidence'[24] and therefore find it difficult to defend clinical reasoning based on other forms of knowledge.[19,24] The translation of EBM into systems of health care defining quality standards and processes (SBM – see Box 21.1) supports organisational needs for efficiency and reduced uncertainty, but has contributed to a further split between science and compassion, and a further deviation away from the College motto.

Best knowledge

However, the assumption that scientific knowledge is 'better' than other forms is based on a set of assumptions about the nature of knowledge: the assumptions of scientific realism.[25] Scientific realism states that scientific practices are the best ways to produce knowledge of the 'real' world that exists external to our perceptions of it.[25] Scientific method purports to offer certainty and objectivity, both of which are used to justify its dominance within the hierarchy of knowledge informing medical practice and policy. This assumption – that scientific method offers the best knowledge – is so prevalent within modern Western health care that it often goes uncontested.[26]

However, sociologists studying the construction of knowledge within societies highlight that all knowledge is shaped by societal forces and reflects the value systems of the dominant group rather than representing a certain or absolute 'truth'.[27,28] The rules that distinguish 'genuine knowledge' from 'mere thought' reflect value structures, and hence power structures, within a given society.[28] Assumptions that the scientific knowledge which underpins medicine is 'homogeneous, culture-independent and founded on objective observation and experimentation',[29] representing value-free statements of truth, need critical reflection because scientists who purport to discover objective truth are trained to think and 'see reality' within their given 'thought-style'.[29]

Scientists create theories and test them experimentally, but all within the constraints (assumptions) of a given model of the world. These models within which they explore the world are influenced by religious, economic, political and other social factors. Medical 'facts' should therefore be seen as a socially constructed view of reality rather than the 'objective labels' for 'real' natural phenomena that they purport to be.[30] Viewing medical knowledge from the perspective of the sociology of knowledge questions the dominance of biomedical or scientific accounts (or 'knowledge') of illness. We have long witnessed debates about the benefits and harms of the social construction of mental health diagnosis such as depression.[31] We now see extension of those debates into physical health problems too.[32]

The critique does not reject medical knowledge, but simply requires us to take a more thoughtful stance in understanding a 'hierarchy' of knowledge. Knowledge needs to be understood, critiqued and used from an understanding of the full range of processes by which it was constructed.[33] This includes a consideration of whether those methods are appropriate/best for the purpose for which they are constructed and to be used.

Going beyond scientific knowledge to understanding scientific process

In her recent critique of EBM, Trish Greenhalgh, Professor of Primary Care Health Sciences at the University of Oxford, also calls for a refocus on combining evidence *with* professional expertise so that individuals can receive optimal treatment.[34] She highlights a need to rethink both the scientific output required for individualised care, and supporting expert judgement. In 1972, Crombie acknowledged the importance of judgement but stated that it involved 'procedures which have not yet been made explicit'.[4] My current work exploring barriers to the practice of generalist expertise suggests that this is still the case. Practitioners lack language to describe what they refer to as 'intuitive practice' or 'gut instinct': a form of practice that they value, but feel they cannot defend in a world of SBM.[14] It is in tackling these issues of credible judgement, in order that professionals can combine science with compassion, that I propose scientific process – scholarship – has much to offer our professional practice.

Defending interpretive practice – the role of scholarship

Defending interpretations or judgements of knowledge is the 'bread and butter' of scientific research practice. Not unlike clinical professional practice, for many years the process underpinning these judgements was opaque – viewed as the art of professional academic practice, learnt through apprenticeship with other scholars. However, this way of working has been transformed in recent decades – with clearer description of the scientific method of interpretation that supports trustworthiness of the output.[2,33,35] Scientists have had long experience of establishing and demonstrating the trustworthiness of interpretive practice.[2]

Understanding the nature and credibility of knowledge and evidence is the first part of the application of evidence to practice.[24] So it is this aspect of science and research – of *scientia* – which I propose as the element that can help enhance *caritas*. Scholarship describes the principles and practice used by scholars to make their claims about the world as valid and trustworthy as possible. I have translated one such model (based on Maxwell[35]) into an approach that could be used to support judgement of the trustworthiness of clinical practice,[2] and so described a new consultation model based on these principles.[36] I am now engaged in work with GPs, trainers, trainees and academics to examine whether this approach can indeed enhance generalist practice.[37]

Professionals need scientific *method*, rather than just outputs, if they are to transparently, safely and best put into practice what I have described as Interpretive Medicine:[2] the critical, thoughtful, professional use of a range of knowledge in the dynamic shared exploration and interpretation of illness experience. Translating these aspects of scientific process, of scholarship, into the clinical context potentially offers professionals a language to articulate phronesis,[38] intuitive practice[4,14] and the use of amorphous knowledge,[4] and so build trust and trustworthiness by exposing them to critical reflection and external scrutiny.

Future implications

I have described a shift in viewing science (*scientia*) as an output (knowledge to be implemented) to a process that can be used in the critical interpretation of need and professional practice. *It supports a new view of professionalism – from a focus on what you know, to looking at how you use what you know.* We still need science and research to offer us new knowledge – to build the basic scientific understanding of the core principles of our discipline – of empathy,[39] continuity[40] and generalism.[33] But we also need scientific method to enhance our professional practice. Enhanced training in scholarship may help improve quality and confidence in individually tailored care,[14] and so support a professional reconnection with *caritas*.

We need to enhance scholarship training at all stages of the general practice career – from undergraduate to established practitioner. We need to raise the profile and understanding of academic work in professional practice as well as building the academic workforce to continue to provide the necessary scientific underpinnings for our discipline.

The Society for Academic Primary Care (www.sapc.ac.uk) is working closely with the Royal College of General Practitioners, the National Institute for Health Research's School for Primary Care Research (www.spcr.nihr.ac.uk) and others to do just that. By exploring mechanisms for curriculum review, enhanced training and developing new career options, we aim to ensure that science is understood and used as a means to an end, not the end in itself, in professional practice.

Conclusion

I have argued that, to live up to our motto, the future of professional practice needs a strengthening of scholarship and academic practice. Instead of knowledge management systems bridging the worlds of science and vocational practice, we need to bring together – blur the boundaries between[41] – research and practice. In this way, we can reconnect with our motto, *Cum scientia caritas.*

References

1. Tinetti ME, Fried T. The end of the disease era. *American Journal of Medicine* 2004; **116(3)**: 179–85.
2. Reeve J. *Interpretive Medicine: supporting generalism in a changing primary care world* (RCGP Occasional Paper 88). London: RCGP, 2010.
3. Reeve J, Lynch T, Lloyd-Williams M, Payne S. From personal challenge to technical fix: the risks of depersonalised care. *Health and Social Care in the Community* 2012; **20(2)**: 145–54.
4. Crombie DL. *Cum scientia caritas.* The James Mackenzie Lecture. *Journal of the Royal College of General Practitioners* 1972; **22**: 7–17.
5. Harrison S. New Labour, modernisation and the medical labour process. *Journal of Social Policy* 2002; **31(2)**: 465–85.
6. Harrison S, Moran M, Wood B. Policy emergence and policy convergence: the case of 'scientific-bureaucratic medicine' in the United States and United Kingdom. *British Journal of Politics and International Relations* 2002; **4**: 1–24.
7. Moynihan R, Henry D, Moons KGM. Using evidence to combat overdiagnosis and overtreatment: evaluating treatments, tests, and disease definitions in the time of too much. *PLoS Medicine* 2014; DOI: 10.1371/journal.pmed.1001655.
8. Martin SA, Boucher M, Wright JM, Saini V. Mild hypertension in people at low risk. *British Medical Journal* 2014; DOI: 10.1136/bmj.g5432.
9. Moynihan RN, Cooke GP, Doust JA, *et al.* Expanding disease definitions in guidelines and expert panel ties to industry: a cross-sectional study of common conditions in the United States. *PLoS Medicine* 2013; DOI: 10.1371/journal.pmed.1001500.
10. May C, Eten D, Boehmer K, *et al.* Rethinking the patient: using Burden of Treatment Theory to understand the changing dynamics of illness. *BMC Health Services Research* 2014; **14**: 281.
11. May C, Montori V, Mair F. We need minimally disruptive medicine. *British Medical Journal* 2009; DOI: http://dx.doi.org/10.1136/bmj.b2803.

12. Wyer PC, Silva SA. Where is the wisdom? 1 – a conceptual history of evidence based medicine. *Journal of Evaluation in Clinical Practice* 2009; **15(6)**: 891–8.
13. Sackett DL, Rosenberg WM, Muir Gray JA, *et al.* Evidence based medicine: what it is and what it isn't. *British Medical Journal* 1996; **312(7023)**: 71–2.
14. Reeve J, Dowrick C, Freeman G, *et al.* 2013. Examining the practice of generalist expertise: a qualitative study identifying constraints and solutions. *Journal of the Royal Society of Medicine Short Reports* 2013; DOI: 10.1177/2042533313510155.
15. http://en.wikipedia.org/wiki/Compassion.
16. NHS England. *Compassion in Practice: one year on*. Leeds: NHS, 2013, www.england.nhs.uk/wp-content/uploads/2013/11/comp-pract-1yr-on.pdf [accessed 26 May 2016].
17. Oxford English Dictionary. www.oed.com/view/Entry/61284?redirectedFrom=empathy#eid.
18. Derksen F, Bensing J, Lagro-Janssen A. Effectiveness of empathy in general practice. *British Journal of General Practice* 2013; DOI: 10.3399/bjgp13X660814.
19. Mercer S, Jani BD, Maxwell M, *et al.* Patient enablement requires physician empathy: a cross-sectional study of general practice consultations in areas of high and low socioeconomic deprivation in Scotland. *BMC Family Practice* 2012; **13**: 6.
20. Robinson P, Heywood P. What do GPs need to know? The use of knowledge in general practice consultations. *British Journal of General Practice* 2000; **50(450)**: 56–9.
21. National Institute of Clinical Excellence. Hierarchy of evidence and grading of recommendations. *Thorax* 2004; **59(Suppl 1)**: i13–i14.
22. Department of Health. *A First Class Service: quality in the new NHS*. London: TSO, 1998, http://webarchive.nationalarchives.gov.uk/+/www.dh.gov.uk/en/publicationsandstatistics/publications/publicationspolicyandguidance/dh_4006902 [accessed 26 May 2015].
23. Reeve J, Blakeman T, Freeman GK, *et al.* Generalist solutions to complex problems: generating practice-based evidence – the example of managing multi-morbidity. *BMC Family Practice* 2013; DOI: 10.1186/1471-2296-14-112.
24. Jones M, Higgs J. Will evidence-based practice take the reasoning out of practice? In: J Higgs, M Jones (eds). *Clinical Reasoning in the Health Professions*. Oxford: Butterworth-Heinemann, 2000, pp. 307–15.
25. Potter G. *The Philosophy of Social Science*. Harlow, Essex: Pearson Education, 2000.
26. Seale C, Pattison S, Davey, Swale C. *Medical Knowledge: doubt and certainty*. Buckingham: Open University Press, 1994.
27. Berger P, Luckmann T. *The Social Construction of Reality: a treatise in the sociology of knowledge*. London: Penguin, 1966.
28. Dant T. *Knowledge, Ideology and Discourse: a sociological perspective*. London: Routledge, 1991.
29. Lowy I. Ludwik Fleck on the social construction of medical knowledge. *Sociology of Health and Illness* 1988; **10(2)**: 133–55.
30. White K. The sociology of health and illness. *Current Sociology* 1991; **39**: 1–124.
31. Horwitz AV. Creating an age of depression: the social construction and consequences of the major depression diagnosis. *Society and Mental Health* 2011; **1(1)**: 41–54.
32. Yudkin JS, Montori VM. The epidemic of pre-diabetes: the medicine and the politics. *British Medical Journal* 2014; DOI: 10.1136/bmj.g4485.
33. Doucet A, Mauthner N. Knowing responsibly: linking ethics, research practice and epistemology. In: M Mauthner, M Birch, J Jessop, T Miller (eds). *Ethics in Qualitative Research*. London: Sage, 2002, pp. 123–45.
34. Greenhalgh T, Howick J, Maskrey N; Evidence Based Medicine Renaissance Group. Evidence-based medicine: a movement in crisis? *British Medical Journal* 2014; DOI: 10.1136/bmj.g3725.
35. Maxwell J. Understanding and validity in qualitative research. In: A Huberman, M Miles (eds). *The Qualitative Researcher's Companion*. Thousand Oaks, CA: Sage, 2002, pp. 37–64.
36. Reeve J. Supporting expert generalist practice: the SAGE consultation model. *British Journal of General Practice* 2015; **65(633)**: 207–8.

37. School for Advancing Generalist Expertise. www.primarycarehub.org.uk/sage [accessed 26 May 2015].
38. Hilton S. Education and the changing face of medical professionalism: from priest to mountain guide? *British Journal of General Practice* 2008; **58(550)**: 353–61.
39. Consultation and Relational Empathy, www.caremeasure.org/.
40. Freeman J, Hughes J. *Continuity of Care and the Patient Experience*. London: King's Fund, 2010, www.kingsfund.org.uk/sites/files/kf/field/field_document/continuity-care-patient-experience-gp-inquiry-research-paper-mar11.pdf [accessed 26 May 2015].
41. Evans S, Scarbrough H. Supporting knowledge translation through collaborative translational research initiatives: 'bridging' versus 'blurring' boundary-spanning approaches in the UK CLAHRC initiative. *Social Science and Medicine* 2014; **106**: 119–27.

Chapter 22

Compassionate care

Building resilience in GPs by exploring self-compassion

Jenny Bennison

Take the shame away and put the joy back in!

Compassion and caring are usually seen as outward-looking qualities, 'patient-facing' in the current jargon, but it is important to remember that we ourselves as health professionals need to be taken care of as well. One aspect of this lies in the habit of honesty, sharing and looking out for one another, but another, more difficult but arguably much more important, is the concept of self-care and self-compassion, and in this short chapter I will address these ideas and how they can relate to health and resilience as we go through our careers.

Compassion can be seen as a hard-to-reach ideal for many GPs, beset as we are in the UK by rising patient expectation, the constraints of time, and demands that feel as if they are beyond our control (the Quality and Outcomes Framework is but one). Sometimes compassion can be felt as an individual rather than a collective demand, one uttered in a peremptory, almost aggressive way, which can add to the burden of potential failure to which many GPs, as natural perfectionists, are prone. Compassion too can sometimes focus on suffering and death, rather than more positive areas such as creativity and learning together.

Ballatt and Campling in their book *Intelligent Kindness* propose the term 'kindness' as a more approachable concept;[1] the derivation is from *kin*, as in kinship, and the recognition of kinship helps us to realise that 'we are all in this together', making it easier to act with and on behalf of the wider society as we pursue our work in medicine. From this understanding comes a recognition that as well as it being OK to be kind to our colleagues, and to expect kindness from them, it is OK to be kind and understanding to *ourselves*.

Figure 22.1 (overleaf) shows how these understandings can set off a virtuous circle where this connectedness with our colleagues, or *kinship*, gives rise to *kindness*

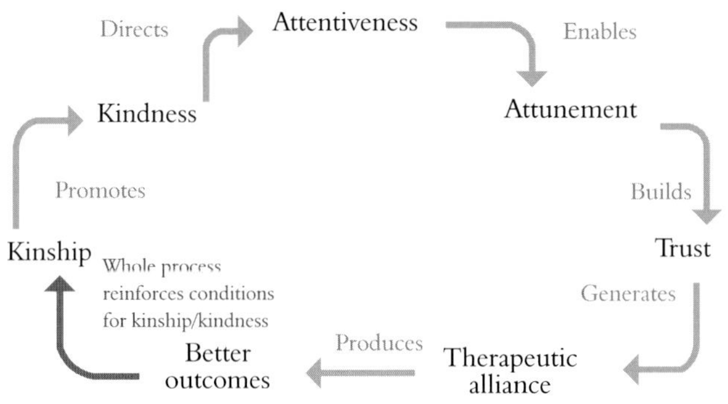

Figure 22.1: The virtuous circle
Source: Ballatt J, Campling P. *Intelligent Kindness: reforming the culture of healthcare.*[1] © John Ballatt and Penelope Campling.

and attentiveness, both with patients and colleagues, which then leads to improved attunement, and builds *trust*. Trust helps to build better alliances, whether these are therapeutic or professional, and outcomes are improved, thus encouraging further kinship and more kindness.

It sounds great, doesn't it? Of course there are plenty of barriers to this working, and we need to be on the lookout for these. Time is often the enemy of attunement: it is so easy to fail to listen and just write out the prescription or the sick certificate when time is short. And trust can be the victim of busy-ness: GPs who are too busy to get to meetings with their colleagues, or to have coffee with the team in the mornings, will bury themselves in ever growing piles of paperwork and can retreat into a suspicious world where they are convinced they are working harder than anyone else.

So how can we try to prevent this, and ensure that individual GPs within the primary care team look after themselves as well as others, and that we all work more kindly within our teams?

Robin Youngson in his book *Time to Care*[2] suggests that there is an element of choice in how one '*decides to be*' each day (see Figure 22.2).[3] And this again has some useful points as to how to build more positive outcomes, but there is a need for a model that looks at the working of the whole team as well as of the individual.

I believe that, at various levels, one can introduce small changes that together can influence the way individuals work together. By building in these small changes, step by step, it might be possible to change the culture of our working worlds so that self-compassion ceases to be a notion that is strange to so many of us.

On a personal level, the one-to-one communications that take place each day can be wearing and difficult, but trying to remind oneself that perfection is not the aim is a useful mantra. The 'good enough' scenario originally proposed by Winnicott works well for parenting,[4] but can equally well be applied in general practice. 'Healthy perfectionism' allows for delegation, human fallibility, and forgiving oneself for small mistakes.[5] A culture of perfectionism and infallibility is unforgiving, and can lead to a 'compulsive triad' of chronic doubt, chronic guilt and an exaggerated sense of responsibility.

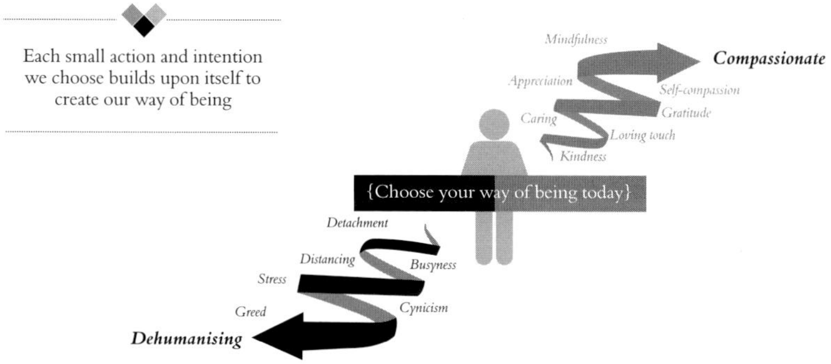

Figure 22.2: Choose your way of being today
Source: Hearts in Healthcare.[3] Copyright © heartsinhealthcare.com.

Being a good enough doctor who can survive a career in medicine requires self-compassion, the ability to accept sometimes that no more can be done. It is not about all-or-nothing thinking, and is distinct from extreme conscientiousness, which is not sustainable and can lead to poor outcomes for both clinicians and their patients.

On a team level, or within our own general practices, kindness and compassion can be kindled by remembering that everyone is working towards a common goal, and if immediate priorities seem to be in conflict it is often worth trying to tease out why this is the case. Role-modelling is really important here:[6,7] if GPs in training see senior colleagues being abrupt with receptionists in front of patients, for example, then this hierarchical behaviour may recur. On the other hand, public expressions of gratitude and appreciation throughout the team go a long way to build healthy relationships, and a climate of encouragement and honesty.

On a wider level, it is often the primary–secondary care 'interface' that is responsible for conflicts at work in primary care. Perhaps better named an abyss sometimes, this interface is fraught with difficulties.

Communication across IT systems that speak different languages is slow and frustrating. And getting it right for our patients – for instance when trying to prescribe for an elderly patient with complex co-morbidities who has been discharged home on new medications on a Friday afternoon – can seem ridiculously difficult. How to build bridges here?

Often a phone call to a real human being at the other end can help us towards a positive outcome, and if the response is not immediately helpful then some sort of personal reminder of the human being at the centre of the story, 'our patient', can be a lever for change. Perhaps joined-up health and social care will make these interactions easier for all of us.

So, I have shown some examples of how our interactions with others at different levels might change, and how these changes could alter the way in which we understand and are understood by colleagues and patients. How then can this translate into more self-compassion and resilience?

Various models address the concept of allowing time for oneself in different ways, but the core idea is the same: unless one looks after oneself, then one is not fit to look after anyone else. Roger Neighbour's famous consultation model talks of housekeeping,[8] and one of Stephen Covey's *Seven Habits of Highly Effective People*, Sharpening the Saw, is about maintaining personal balance and renewing resources, energy and health to create a sustainable long-term, effective lifestyle.[9] Mindfulness techniques, for example as described by Williams and Penman,[10] again encourage personal attention and focus on the present, but perhaps the best fit for GPs today could be compassion-focused therapy (CFT).

CFT is an integrated therapy drawing from social, developmental, evolutionary and Buddhist psychology, as well as neuroscience.[11] Gilbert describes three main affect regulation systems in the human brain, and looks at the way in which they interact.

- The *threat and protection system* detects and deals with threats; evolving from primitive mammalian states this is now often concerned with social threats, and responses may conflict with one another. Strategies that result can cause increased vulnerability to anxiety and depression, low self-esteem and difficulty in achieving goals.
- The *drive system* evolves from animals' need for emotional and motivational systems to steer them towards important rewards and resources. Associated feelings in humans are linked with feeling aroused, or energised, but in depression this system can be toned down.
- The *contentment system* in animals can only come to the fore when they are not under threat, and have sufficient resources. The positive emotions of this state, in humans as well, are characterised by a calm peacefulness, wellbeing and quiescence. Some argue that this state is more difficult to find for those in whom attachment in early life has been limited, as described by Bowlby in 1969.[12]

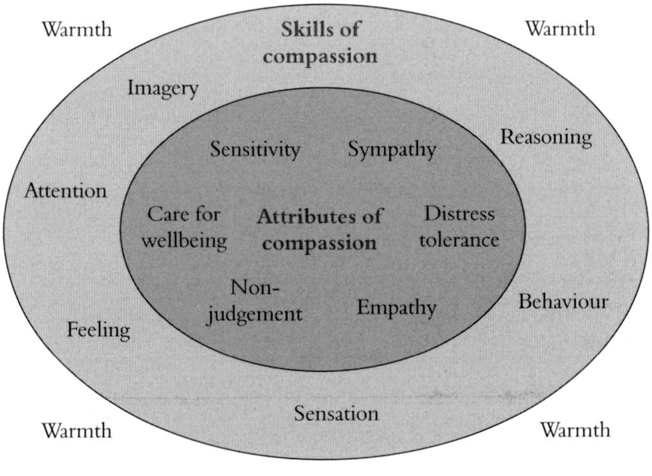

Figure 22.3: Multimodal compassionate mind training
Source: Gilbert P. *The Compassionate Mind: a new approach to life's challenges*. Reprinted with permission from Little, Brown Book Group.[13]
Note: the key aspects and attributes of compassion are shown in the inner ring. The skills training required to develop them are shown in the outer ring.

In CFT, the focus is on development of the contentment system, also known as the social safeness system, and individuals are encouraged to engage with others using the attributes and skills of compassion.

As GPs we are well equipped with the attributes of compassion when we are with our colleagues and clients: we tolerate their distress, feel both sympathy and empathy, avoid judgement (mostly), and care for the wellbeing of others with sensitivity. This is where the '*caritas*' part of '*Cum scientia caritas*', the RCGP motto, is usually seen to be: the caring GP listening actively to patients, picking up on cues, and accompanying them on their medical journey.

Cole-King and Gilbert describe the way in which compassion, as the true desire to help alleviate suffering and move forward with the patient on their journey, requires further skills and also courage.[14] For me, this is the true meaning of '*caritas*' in our motto. Some of us learn these skills as doctors by trial and error, some from role-modelling as part of the hidden curriculum, some from our own mentors or therapists, but many not at all. The three major dimensions of self-compassion as described by Kristin Neff are:[15]

- kindness – the understanding of one's own difficulties, being kind and warm in the face of failure or setbacks rather than harshly judgemental and self-critical
- common humanity – seeing one's experiences as part of the human condition ('we're all in this together'[1]) rather than as personal, isolating and shameful
- mindful acceptance – awareness and acceptance of painful thoughts and feelings, rather than over-identifying with them.

Without exception, these qualities can be directed towards ourselves in order to better understand our working and personal lives, and perhaps to undo some of the barriers to acceptance. For many doctors, the trait of conscientiousness has been praised and developed since schooldays, and extreme conscientiousness is associated with positive rewards and career success. But with increasing stress, associated with high work demands and environmental pressures, the threat and protection system comes into play, and the same conscientious doctor can turn into someone paralysed by anxiety, double-checking everything they do, unable to delegate to others, unable to forgive themselves even the smallest of errors, and blind to their own successes, let alone those of their colleagues.

So, my belief is that if we bring together ideas of kindness and kinship, positive choices and self-compassion, we can help ourselves not only to be better and more compassionate doctors, but also to stay that way for longer. Burnout is a very real threat in today's NHS and finding ways to maintain our own mental health and resilience as GPs should be a very high priority. I think that these concepts of self-kindness should be introduced to medical students, doctors in training, even those working at school to gain entry to medical school.

On the other hand, one could do worse than revisit Maslow's hierarchy of needs,[16] updated for the present day (see Figure 22.4, overleaf).

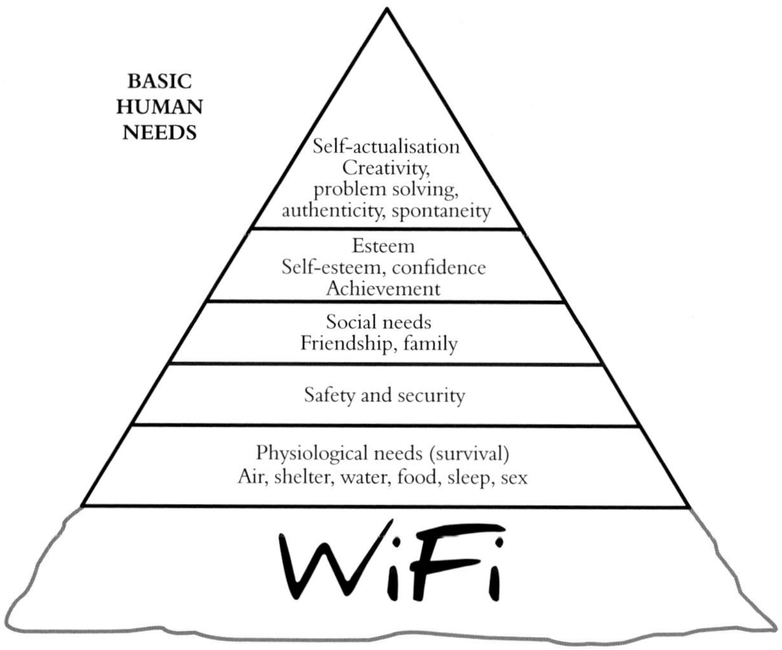

Figure 22.4: Maslow's hierarchy of needs – updated

References

1. Ballatt J, Campling P. *Intelligent Kindness: reforming the culture of healthcare*. London: RCPsych Publications, 2011.
2. Youngson RAJ. *Time to Care: how to love your patients and your job*. Raglan, NZ: Rebelheart Publishers, 2012.
3. Hearts in Healthcare. Restorative learning opportunities. http://heartsinhealthcare.com/learn/ [accessed 30 June 2015].
4. Changing Minds. Donald Winnicott. 2012. http://changingminds.org/disciplines/psychoanalysis/theorists/winnicott.htm [accessed 8 June 2015].
5. Peters M, King J. Perfectionism in doctors. *British Medical Journal* 2012; DOI: 10.1136/bmj.e1674.
6. Lempp H, Seale C. The hidden curriculum in undergraduate medical education: qualitative study of medical students' perceptions of teaching. *British Medical Journal* 2004; **329(7469)**: 770–3.
7. Cruess SR, Cruess RL, Steinert Y. Role modelling – making the most of a powerful teaching strategy. *British Medical Journal* 2008; **336(7646)**: 718–21.
8. Neighbour R. *The Inner Consultation: how to develop an effective and intuitive consulting style*. Abingdon: Radcliffe Publishing, 2005.
9. Covey SR. *The Seven Habits of Highly Effective People: restoring the character ethic*. 1st Fireside edn. New York: Fireside Books, 1990.
10. Williams JMG, Penman D. *Mindfulness: a practical guide to finding peace in a frantic world*. London: Piatkus, 2014.
11. Gilbert P. Introducing compassion-focused therapy. *Advances in Psychiatric Treatment* 2009; **15(3)**: 199–208.
12. Bowlby J. *Volume One of the Attachment and Loss Trilogy: Attachment*. London: Pimlico, 1997.
13. Gilbert P. *The Compassionate Mind: a new approach to life's challenges*. London: Constable & Robinson, 2009.

14. Cole-King A, Gilbert P. Compassionate care: the theory and the reality. *Journal of Holistic Healthcare* 2011; **8(3)**: 29–37.
15. Neff K. Definition of self-compassion. http://self-compassion.org/the-three-elements-of-self-compassion-2/ [accessed 29 June 2015].
16. Abraham Maslow's Hierarchy of Needs and diagrams of Maslow's motivational theory – pyramid diagrams of Maslow's theory. www.businessballs.com/maslow.htm [accessed 8 June 2015].

CHAPTER 23

MINDFULNESS IN MEDICINE

Majid Khan and Dharmachari Padmakumāra

As doctors you'll recognise that we can end our working day in a range of physical and mental states. From exhaustion to effervescence, irritation to elation, we can be blown by winds that see us slump on the sofa in front of the television or take interest in our children's days at school, helping them with their homework and play.

To what extent though do we look at the conditions underlying these states? What happened at work today? I don't mean in a general sense but specifically. Whom did I see and talk to? What did I say and how did I say it? Did I respond to my patients with care and understanding or harshness and irritation? How did I really feel when ignored by a colleague and teased by the practice nurse? Was I hard on myself for turning up late, or did I understand that I too need to hear a soft voice, just as everybody else? To what extent do we creatively examine what we felt, said and did, and evaluate how this conditioned our experience?

Mindfulness in Medicine is the application of simple practices that link our thoughts, attitudes, emotions, feelings and sensations with what we say and do. It is a means therefore of understanding the part *we play* in our experience in surgery. Its application extends from our professional judgement and efficacy to our interpersonal interactions and certainly to our sense of satisfaction and wellbeing at the end of our working day.

MINDFULNESS

'Mindfulness' says Jon Kabat-Zinn, is the deliberate paying of attention, on purpose, non-judgmentally, in the present moment. By paying such deliberate attention to their states of mind, a clinician is able to acknowledge signs and levels of stress,[1] recognise errors (and also hopefully prevent them), refine technical skills, make evidence-based decisions, and clarify values so they can act with compassion.[2]

Once considered by many to be the preserve of Buddhist monks and nuns, mindfulness is increasingly being recognised as a tool we can all apply in all spheres of our life. It is not the preserve even of a meditation retreat with other like-minded professionals: mindfulness can enter our life at any moment, any *present* moment. It is therefore a practice for encountering another's grief, as their lips quiver in shock and grief as they cry about their diagnosis, or when seeing a patient's elation at discovering their first pregnancy. Mindfulness is a practice for *that* patient, addicted to methadone and alcohol, the one accompanied by an aroma that makes your stomach turn.

Mindful medical practice

Mindful medical practice begins therefore with an honest recognition of what is happening in each moment. As indicated this involves the objective elements (what we say, to whom, and so on) but also the internal, subjective ones. In Jon Kabat-Zinn's definition of mindfulness there is also a moral perspective: mindfulness is 'non-judgemental'.[3] If we begin to apply mindfulness in our medical practice we can become aware of what we do that is unhelpful, which creates interpersonal difficulty and also intrapersonal stress and tension. Mindful medical practice is also then the appreciation of the way I feel, of what I think, of what my prejudices are. Embracing what I like as well as what I dislike, it can reveal things I would rather not be aware of, feelings and even needs that we may otherwise have ignored.

The function of mindfulness though is not just about an awareness of unhelpful actions. We have greater opportunity to recognise and celebrate the positive, the creative, the successes in patient treatment, interaction, and the meeting of practice targets. Rooted in a daily meditation practice, preferably conducted morning and evening, the mindful consultation will begin from a place of calm alertness.

Mindfulness and communication

> The single biggest problem in communication is the illusion that it has taken place.
> (George Bernard Shaw)

> Raise your words not your voice, it is rain that grows flowers, not thunder.
> (Mowlana Jalaluddin Rumi)

Imaginative exercise

Think of a time when a communication you had with a patient broke down. Try to choose an example that isn't too emotionally charged, a simple misunderstanding rather than intense conflict. Perhaps you forgot to sign their prescription on time and their medicine arrived a day late. Passing them near the entrance you could see they looked a little annoyed when they came to collect their script. You did not mention it, instead choosing to ignore it and hope that the patient would just likewise overlook it. That you could apologise was a consideration in your mind, but, because you felt awkward, decided not to. Try to imagine yourself into that moment:

How were you feeling? Be honest.

Were you scared? Were you annoyed? Were you indifferent? Were you embarrassed? What thoughts were floating about in your mind?

Was it the patient's fault? Was it your fault? Was it the admin team's fault? Why is the patient annoyed? It was just a simple mistake, which anyone could have made. …

Were there any sensations you can recall in your body? A tightening of the throat? A sinking of the heart? An urgency to avoid eye contact?

Awareness of our states of mind, of the thoughts, emotions, feelings and sensations that make up our experience in any given moment, is central to authentic communication. As doctors, nowhere is this more important perhaps than the consultation room.

In our short imaginative exercise you may have noticed a range of thoughts, feelings and emotions. Perhaps you experienced anger for example? To be aware of anger does not mean to indulge it. Rather, the awareness operates like a pause button and allows a space to open up in which we can make more conscious choices that unhook us from our habitual, often reactive, responses. How does this work?

Well, first of all we recognise what the emotion of anger feels like. We can see that our temperature is raised, we feel 'blushed' as it were, there's heat rising into the chest in particular, a heat that also has a kind of tightness, like a knot. We notice that our fists are slightly clenched, our teeth set tight against each other. Yet, more than this, we note that our whole body has tensed to some degree, as if we've steeled ourselves for a fight, our breathing has become more shallow and rapid, and so on. Not only this, our thoughts have also taken off into a splenetic justification/attack/defence that seems to power our next action. …

Being aware of anger means gently acknowledging 'this is anger'. This whole collection of experiences *is* anger. We consciously accept 'this is anger', we consciously accept that this collection of experiences is what is happening right here, right now, and these comprise what it means to be angry. Far from just an intellectual labelling this conscious acknowledgement is a more complete, *mind full* acceptance that involves head, heart and body.

A middle ground, however slender, has been created. The ground operates between the extremes of indulging ('this guy is really annoying me!') and denying (the inauthentic smile that attempts to conceal a truth my patient and I would rather not be aware of). Mindfulness opens this middle ground, this new vantage point. It is considered liberating because from here we can *choose* how to respond. We can see the consequences of indulgence and denial, and we can choose to avoid them. We can also see the consequences of care, understanding and patience, and we can choose to act in their influence.

Whenever I have communicated with a patient from this perspective I experience a refreshing air of authenticity based on me having emotions as opposed to emotions having me. I suddenly realise that perhaps I do not need to roll my eyes, or raise my voice. I can respond with kindness, care and flexibility, rather than harshness and rigidity. I just might, from this perspective, be able to alter the entire course of a consultation that, I now recognise, need never have broken down in the first place.

Mindfulness and compassion

Even
After
All this time
The Sun never says to the Earth,
'You owe me.'

Look
What happens
With a love like that,
It lights the whole sky.
(Hafiz)

Practical exercise

Consider three of your patients sitting in front of you. The first is someone you always look forward to seeing. You deeply enjoy their company, the way they speak, the way they present themselves, the way they always thank you, even for things you have not done.

The second is someone you have no particular attachment to. You have seen them once, or at most twice, maybe for a pill check. They were in and out of the room as fast as you could sign their prescription.

The final individual is someone you've had some difficulty with. Choose someone with whom your relationship is not too emotionally charged, perhaps someone who always turns up late rather than someone you'd describe as a 'heartsink'.

Find somewhere comfortable to sit that is quiet. Bring your awareness slowly and gently first to the sounds in the room and then to your body. Note any points of tension or relaxation and acknowledge 'this is tension'. Without uttering a word, ask 'How am I feeling right now?' Just acknowledge and be mindful of the tendency to get caught up in distraction.

Now bring, in turn, each individual to mind. Try to rest your awareness in the qualitative feel that each individual evokes. Once again, be aware of the tendency to become entangled in associative thinking and instead rest your awareness as best you can solely into the feelings evoked. What is it about each individual that generates this? Perhaps something they said or did? Has your response to a single incident defined the relationship? Have your responses enhanced the relationship? Have your responses confined the relationship?

What I can notice is that the objective yearning to 'help people' that I raved about at my medical school interview seems to have metamorphosed into the subjective categorisation of people I like, those I don't, and those to whom I am indifferent. When I choose to respond based on my likes and dislikes a pattern develops: I find it easier to be compassionate with the former than I do to the latter, raising the question of whether my compassion is really compassion at all. What would it mean to let go of these value-based categorisations? Could I experience compassion towards *that* patient?

Cum scientia caritas

This all sounds plausible, logical and possible, but where's the catch? Well, although a 3-year-old can understand what mindfulness means, a person of 80 will find it difficult to put into practice. Yes, in spite of my deep-seated desire to show compassion and care to all whom I come across, I cannot help myself: people seem to either make me feel one way or another.

Some patients call me 'bro', some 'Dr Khan'. Some patients *are* more demanding than others. For me, becoming more mindful has meant that I've recognised how I interpret my experience to reinforce an idea I have of the type of person they are, and therefore how I should behave towards them.

Perhaps you recognise yourself in this common tendency. Ask yourself the question: What would it mean to cultivate compassion towards them? How can I wish this little old lady to be free of suffering? How can I wish for her to be happy, to receive respect and kindness? How can I be genuinely sad at hearing of her pain? How can I extend this desire to treat her BP vigorously, for no other reason than because I *care*?

Such reflections shed light on the way I feel towards my patients, and are gently and patiently acknowledged by awareness. This means that resistance, irritation and even disgust are part of the practice of mindfulness just as much as the desire to be compassionate. It does not mean therefore that such thoughts and attitudes are wiped away. This is important. Unacknowledged emotions easily lead to us becoming entangled in trains of associative thought; mindfulness enables disentanglement. We can fully acknowledge our pain and negativity *and* be compassionate. Compassion is volition, a practice, through which we can begin to imagine that there is perhaps nothing 'heartsink' about a 'heartsink' after all.

Mindfulness and death

> I have never seen a certainty about which there is no doubt bear greater resemblance to a doubt about which there is no certainty, than death does.
>
> (Hasan of Basra)

On the final week of the Mindful Medical Practice special study component (SSC) (using the module developed by Epstein *et al.*)[4] at the medical school we look at mindfulness and death.

The course addresses not only the logistical aspects of treating the dying patient but also some of the more emotional elements. We address such questions as whose responsibility the care of the dying is, why it may often not be performed adequately, what this reveals about us as individuals, and also why there is such awkwardness surrounding the management of death.

In a theme that threads through the entire SSC, I remind students again that the essence of mindfulness is always exactly the same: we ask 'What are my thoughts/emotions/feelings/sensations *in this moment*?'

Looking at these in response to the issues surrounding care of the dying, we ask these questions:

- which physician responses are helpful/unhelpful in the care of the dying?
- at what point do we refer to the hospice?
- to what extent do we give false optimism about prognosis? Why?
- is one of the difficulties in the care of the dying the fear evoked by confronting us with the death of ourselves?

We conclude the SSC with a reflective meditation that encounters Heidegger's 'possibility of the absolutely impossible':[5] the death of ourselves. We ask, over a 30-minute period, with ten minutes to each section:

> Since death alone is certain ...
> … and the time of death not certain...
> … what should I do ...?[6]

Our aim is not necessarily to find answers to these questions. It's more important to live the questions, as it were. What does it mean to bring awareness to the felt sense of living with the certainty of my own death? Perhaps we have more in common with *that* patient than I like to think .... maybe compassion is my only sensible option because, at the end of the day, there's really no great difference between me and them after all.

Mindfulness exercise

Find a comfortable place to sit. If you prefer to do this in your own clinic, your doctor's chair perhaps may not be the most sensible option. You will, of course, practise mindfulness in exactly this position, but it will have all kinds of associations in which we can become entangled. To help avoid this you may choose to sit on the examination couch. Indeed, over time you could try sitting in the patient chair(s).

Make note of the time. You may be tempted to undertake this if you have a string of 'did not attends', though this always runs the risk of being suddenly interrupted. I prefer after morning surgery, and before any visits. That way you can let reception know that you need your ten minutes of quiet time.

You might have images of certain postures in association with meditation. Ignore them. If you are able and prefer to do so, sit cross-legged. There's no need for heroics, however. Indeed, there are none. If you try this and it is too uncomfortable then sitting on a chair is fine. Indeed, if you are not familiar with sitting cross-legged it is better to approach this guided by someone with experience. In terms of posture it's essential to adopt what is appropriate for you. Appropriateness is determined by a sense of comfort, support, balance and ease that allows the spine to rise up naturally and without strain. In a chair, have your legs uncrossed placing both feet flat on the ground. You may choose to remove your shoes or not, experimenting to see what works.

Rest your hands either in your lap (if you want to be funky you can place the dorsum of one hand in the palm of the other, and touch the tips of your thumbs together), or on your thighs, face up or down. Again what's important is that your hands or arms aren't held in an uncomfortable way. The length of your arms may mean that it's best to have a cushion on your lap. You're seeking to let the arms hang loosely with the shoulder-blades dropping down the back, as it were.

If you're choosing to keep your eyes open, then try to keep your gaze a few feet in front of you, on some point, rather than allowing the eyes to wander and invite more distraction.

Take note of any points of tension in your shoulders or jaws, and relax them. If it helps, rather than 'relax them', which sounds like something we have to do, just 'let go'.

Take a deep breath, and just notice the body as it breathes. Notice the sounds of the breath, the sensations: the temperature of the air, the rising of the abdomen, the expansion of the lungs. With a sense of extension notice what emotions are taking place and what emotions arise in response.

Note too your thoughts. It is quite easy to get entangled in these thoughts, and indeed in the proliferation thereafter. If you notice this has happened (a moment of mindfulness), then gently redirect your attention to the act of breathing itself. If your experience in any way mirrors mine, you may notice these thoughts arising:

- 'This meditation stuff is easy'
- 'There's nothing to this'
- 'Oh God, I have to visit Mr X again, I'm not sure I've got time for this'
- 'Afternoon surgery starts in three hours and I'm just sitting here'.

If you notice yourself becoming engrossed in these thoughts then again gently and patiently return to the act of breathing.

You may even notice how different patients from the morning's surgery have left a definite energy within you: some pleasant, some perhaps not so. Pay attention to this and be aware of the tendency to become stuck on the feeling or patient. If you do, and you notice (another moment of mindfulness), then gently redirect your attention to this present moment, the feelings/sensations/emotions/thoughts as they are happening *right now.*

It's important to consciously bring the practice to a close. First of all, let go of making any effort whatsoever. Over time our awareness can build and it's important to allow this to flow without any sense of effort or conscious application. If we just start to drift off then of course consciously bring your attention back to what's happening, starting with physical sensations. Even if you do this try to keep this absence of effort alive. Then, after a short period, about one minute of this (in a ten-minute practice), begin to note external sounds, having a sense of letting the practice go, experience yourself in relation to the environment of the consultation room, of its situation in the whole surgery. Recognise that soon you'll be opening your eyes and engaging with fellow staff and patients alike. What does this elicit? Acknowledge this and when appropriate gently begin to move your fingers, your toes, and open your eyes. You have begun to live mindful medical practice.

References

1. Krasner MS, Epstein RM, Beckman H, *et al*. Association of an educational program in mindful communication with burnout, empathy, and attitudes among primary care physicians. *Journal of the American Medical Association* 2009; DOI: 10.1001/jama.2009.1384.
2. Epstein RM. Mindful practice. *Journal of the American Medical Association* 1999; DOI: 10.1001/jama.282.9.833.
3. Kabat-Zinn J. *Full Catastrophe Living: how to cope with stress, pain and illness using mindfulness meditation*. London: Piatkus, 2013.
4. Mindful medical practice. www.urmc.rochester.edu/family-medicine/mindful-practice.aspx?redir=www.mindfulpractice.urmc.edu [accessed 18 June 2015].
5. Heidegger M. *Being and Time*. Trans. J Stambaugh. Albany, NY: State University of New York Press, 1996.
6. Batchelor S. *Buddhism without Beliefs*. New York, NY: Riverhead Books, 1997.

Chapter 24

Continuity of care

Samuel Finnikin

Continuity of care is a defining feature of general practice. Indeed, the Royal College of General Practitioners (RCGP)-endorsed definition of primary care proposed by WONCA Europe specifies 'longitudinal continuity' as one of the key characteristics of general practice.[1] For doctors and patients alike, the concept of longitudinal continuity conjures up images of a lone GP providing cradle-to-grave care to an individual and his or her family. A reliable and dependable guide through the turbulent and traumatic periods of a patient's life with a meaningful understanding of the patient's needs over and above his or her immediate health requirements. Of course, this romantic notion is long gone.

The 2004 General Medical Services (GMS) contract absolved GPs of the responsibility to provide out-of-hours cover, so patients could no longer expect to see a familiar doctor if they needed care in the middle of the night. Furthermore, many GPs choose to pursue interests that take them away from core general practice consulting such as education, research or special interests. This, combined with part-time working, means that many GPs are only available to be seen on two or three days of the week. So we need to reconsider the concept of continuity in the context of modern primary care and question whether it is still relevant to patients and doctors. If continuity is still an important facet of primary care we need to highlight and counter influences that may undermine its prominence in the modern NHS and look at how we can hold on to this traditional bastion of general practice.

Longitudinal continuity

Perhaps as a result of the fact that continuity of care is under threat, there has been considerable academic interest in this area over recent years. Before examining the evidence, it is first important to explore the terminology. As alluded to above, the term 'longitudinal continuity' implies a personal relationship over time. However, continuity has been split into three areas in order to delineate and clarify its meaning.[2] Informational continuity refers to the use of information on past events and personal circumstances to ensure current care is appropriate to each individual. Management continuity describes a consistent and coherent approach to the management of a health condition. Finally, relational continuity is defined as an ongoing relationship between a patient and one or more providers. When it comes to primary care, we are mostly concerned with relational continuity, which is sometimes referred to as interpersonal continuity. Although informational and management continuity are important, they should not be seen as a substitute for relational continuity.[3]

The fundamental question in this discussion is whether continuity is important or not. To address this, we will consider whether continuity affects health outcomes, how doctors and patients feel about the subject, and the potential problems of continuity.

RELATIONAL CONTINUITY

It is generally perceived that continuity of care is a good thing and there is evidence to back up this assertion. Improved continuity of care has been found to be associated with reduced use of out-patient services, fewer hospital admissions and lower healthcare costs,[4–6] all of which are important outcomes when considering a modern healthcare system. Additionally, patient outcomes may also be improved in some clinical areas (such as the management of diabetes or hypertension) by improving continuity of care.[7,8] But these aspects of continuity of care are difficult to quantify, not least because it is problematic to quantify continuity itself. Continuity in primary care is about relationships, and it can be difficult to standardise and measure the quality or impact of a relationship. However, it is easier to ask patients and doctors how they feel about that relationship, and how much they value it, and these data provide an interesting insight into continuity.

In general, there has been found to be a consistent and significant positive relationship between interpersonal continuity of care and patient satisfaction.[9] Seeing the same clinician consistently has a positive influence on the development of relationships in primary care and improves a patient's sense of affiliation.[10] Patients, however, make a distinction between acute problems and more routine issues when considering the importance of continuity. They may prefer to wait longer to see a familiar practitioner if they have a problem causing uncertainty or for a routine check-up, but prefer quick access if the problem is acute.[11] It has also been found that patients would prioritise speed of access over choice of doctor or choice of time if the appointment was for a child or a new health problem.[12] So patients seem to value continuity, but not to the exclusion of all else. There are competing issues of speed of access and acuteness of the problem that may influence how highly patients prioritise continuity.

Of course, caring for patients is about more than just patient satisfaction and measurable outcomes. A GP has an important role to play as a repository of information in order to become an expert in the patient and his or her medical conditions. These are issues that make patients feel safe and secure in the care that they receive from their GP, and they are strongly associated with continuity of care.[13] It is reassuring for patients to know that their doctor is aware of their background, know what is normal for them and notice if anything is different. It is also important that the GP can put all this into a psychosocial context than not only informs the GP's opinions, but also facilitates communication and development of a therapeutic partnership. It is important to note that this relationship involves two people. The views of the patient are, of course, paramount, but it is also interesting to consider continuity from the point of view of the clinician.

When asked about continuity of care, GPs place a high value on the importance of this aspect of their work.[14] Continuity has been found to be especially important to GPs when managing patients with serious or psychosocial issues, as well as for routine checks of chronic diseases.[15] This is perhaps because, in these areas, over the course of a long-term relationship GPs can see the impact that their care has had on the wellbeing and quality of life of their patients and thus derive satisfaction from seeing a positive result from their contribution to the relationship. GPs may also feel that continuity of care allows them to deliver a higher standard of care and benefit patients further through the development of a therapeutic relationship.[16] Moreover, it is easy to see how continuity of care can increase job satisfaction in general practice, as well as professional confidence and identity. Not only do GPs get to see the effects of their therapeutic input, but also they undoubtedly derive satisfaction by the fact that a patient chooses to come back and see him or her (assuming the patient was given the choice). If a patient chooses to see the same GP again it is safe to assume that the patient was content with the care he or she received in previous consultations, and, although it is unspoken, this validation that the GP is doing a good job can only serve to bolster the relationship in a positive way.

So continuity of care has therapeutic benefits and is a positive influence on the doctor–patient relationship. Anything that helps build this relationship has the potential to encourage compassion and promote caring so it is not surprising that continuity is a cornerstone of primary care. But it would be a mistake to think that continuity is only a benevolent principle; there are potential harms associated with continuity as well.

Potential harms from continuity

To illustrate the potential for harm through continuity we would do well to remember the old adage 'familiarity breeds contempt'. In the context of the doctor–patient relationship it is possible to see how the patient's minor complaints over a period of time may add up to a clear picture of something more significant, but, if the GP has been through all these minor issues many times before, he or she may perhaps miss the opportunity to step back and see the whole picture, whereas a fresh take on the presentation achieved by seeing a new doctor may make the problem clear. To put it another way, continuity may make it difficult for a GP to 'see the wood from the trees'.[16]

It is also possible that a particular GP has a knowledge or skills deficit that a colleague may be able to fill, and unless a patient avails him or herself of a second opinion by seeing another doctor, the patient may remain undiagnosed or misdiagnosed. It is easy to make an error in diagnosis early in the course of an illness, but over time the clinical picture may change. If a patient sticks with the same clinician, for the sake of continuity, it is possible that the patient would remain in this 'diagnostic rut' longer than if he or she saw a different doctor. It was identified in the 1950s by Balint that seeing multiple doctors does not necessarily lead to improved diagnostic ability because the problem of 'collusion of anonymity' may come into play.[17]

Continuity may also be detrimental to the doctor's experience. Too much continuity in a doctor's practice may decrease the variety of clinical contacts and reduce his or her exposure to the knowledge and support of colleagues. Moreover, the concept of a 'heartsink' consultation, familiar to many GPs, is not possible without continuity. But, perhaps more importantly, continuity may promote an emotional reliance on a particular clinician. This dependence could place a burden on the GP to always make him or herself available to that patient. However, as it is not possible to always be available, not meeting this perceived obligation, especially in a time of patient need, may produce feelings of failure in the GP that could be damaging to the patient's emotional wellbeing.

Although there are risks associated with dogged pursuit of continuity, in reality these can be mitigated against through individuals having insight into the potential pitfalls and working effectively with colleagues to avoid them. It is obvious how good teamwork and communication between clinicians would reduce the risks described above. So, overall, the benefits of continuity are likely to significantly outweigh the risks, and therefore continuity of care should be something we are striving towards in modern general practice. Unfortunately, however, instead of moving towards improving continuity, there are various forces that are shifting the focus away from this aim.

Access – implications for continuity

The increasing trend towards part-time work has already been mentioned, and the impact this can have on continuity is obvious. Less availability makes continuity more difficult. But another, more subtle influence has been identified as a potential problem.[18] Changes in working patterns in secondary care, partially influenced by the European Working Time Directive, are perhaps producing a generation of doctors who are not gaining experience of having personal responsibility for patients. Problems in secondary care can always be handed on to someone else (the opposite of continuity) and, although the impact of this on care in hospitals will not be explored here, it may be that this culture is permeating through to primary care. Perhaps the most detrimental influence on continuity, however, is the seemingly relentless prioritisation of 'access' over all else.

Access to health care is undoubtedly important. Patients want timely access to their GPs, and delays in access can potentially delay diagnoses and lead to worse outcomes. However, increasing efforts to improve access necessarily lead to a loss of focus on continuity. Patients can't have 24-hour access to the clinician that they usually see who perhaps knows them best. They have to choose between speed of access and clinician of choice. And patients are probably very capable of prioritising between these two aspects of their care if both options are available to them.[10,19] The problem arises when policy-makers create a situation where the options become limited. NHS priorities seem to be more focused on access rather than continuity.[20]

Introducing seven-day-a-week access is only achievable at the expense of continuity. Integrated electronic medical records and good organisational communication may improve informational and management continuity but relational continuity will surely suffer at the hands of improved access.

As GPs, we have to decide how important continuity is to us and our patients. If we value this fundamental facet of primary care then we need to develop systems that preserve and promote it.[18] This may mean looking at different appointment systems or alternative ways for patients to consult with us. It will inevitably mean working closely with colleagues, including reception staff and other clinicians, to foster a team-based approach to continuity. It will also mean listening to our patients and being adaptive to their needs.

Continuity of Care Toolkit

The RCGP has also proposed a number of steps that practices can take to try to tackle this problem in its *Continuity of Care Toolkit*.[21] But for continuity to flourish, it will require policy-makers to realise how much patients value this aspect of their care. While access dominates the political agenda, continuity, and therefore patient care, will suffer. Continuity will always require dedicated, patient-centred, generalist clinicians at its heart, and we are fortunate in the UK that these clinicians already exist in the form of GPs. With the right resources and system support in place, GPs can continue to provide continuity of care to the benefit of patients, the healthcare system and society as a whole.

References

1. Allen J, Gay B, Crebolder H, *et al*. *The European Definition of General Practice/Family Medicine*. Barcelona: WONCA Europe, 2002.
2. Haggerty JL, Reid RJ, Freeman GK, *et al*. Continuity of care: a multidisciplinary review. *British Medical Journal* 2003; **327(7425)**: 1219–21.
3. Guthrie B, Saultz JW, Freeman GK, Haggerty JL. Continuity of care matters. *British Medical Journal* 2008; DOI: 10.1136/bmj.a867.
4. Hsiao CJ, Boult C. Effects of quality on outcomes in primary care: a review of the literature. *American Journal of Medical Quality* 2008; **23(4)**: 302–10.
5. Menec VH, Sirski M, Attawar D, Katz A. Does continuity of care with a family physician reduce hospitalizations among older adults? *Journal of Health Services Research and Policy* 2006; **11(4)**: 196–201.
6. Hansen AH, Halvorsen PA, Aaraas IJ, Førde OH. Continuity of GP care is related to reduced specialist healthcare use: a cross-sectional survey. *British Journal of General Practice* 2013; DOI: 10.3399/bjgp13X669202.
7. Shin DW, Cho J, Yang HK, *et al*. Impact of continuity of care on mortality and health care costs: a nationwide cohort study in Korea. *Annals of Family Medicine* 2014; **12(6)**: 534–41.
8. Franklin B. The impact of continuity of care on A1c levels in adult type 2 diabetic patients: a review of the literature. *Journal for Nurse Practitioners* 2014; DOI: http://dx.doi.org/10.1016/j.nurpra.2014.04.004.
9. Saultz JW, Albedaiwi W. Interpersonal continuity of care and patient satisfaction: a critical review. *Annals of Family Medicine* 2004; **2(5)**: 445–51.
10. Waibel S, Henao D, Aller MB, *et al*. What do we know about patients' perceptions of continuity of care? A meta-synthesis of qualitative studies. *International Journal for Quality in Health Care* 2012; **24(1)**: 39–48.
11. Turner D, Tarrant C, Windridge K, *et al*. Do patients value continuity of care in general practice? An investigation using stated preference discrete choice experiments. *Journal of Health Services Research Policy* 2007; **12(3)**: 132–7.

12. Rubin G, Bate A, George A, *et al*. Preferences for access to the GP: a discrete choice experiment. *British Journal of General Practice* 2006; **56(531)**: 743–8.
13. Rhodes P, Sanders C, Campbell S. Relationship continuity: when and why do primary care patients think it is safer? *British Journal of General Practice* 2014; DOI: 10.3399/bjgp14X682825.
14. Stokes T, Tarrant C, Mainous AG 3rd, *et al*. Continuity of care: is the personal doctor still important? A survey of general practitioners and family physicians in England and Wales, the United States, and the Netherlands. *Annals of Family Medicine* 2005; **3(4)**: 353–9.
15. Schers H, Bor H, van den Bosch W, Grol R. GPs' attitudes to personal continuity: findings from everyday practice differ from postal surveys. *British Journal of General Practice* 2006; **56(528)**: 536–8.
16. Ridd M, Shaw A, Salisbury C. 'Two sides of the coin' – the value of personal continuity to GPs: a qualitative interview study. *Family Practice* 2006; **23(4)**: 461–8.
17. Balint M. *The Doctor, His Patient, and the Illness*. London: Pitman, 1957.
18. Roland M. Continuity of care: betrayed values or misplaced nostalgia. *International Journal of Integrated Care* 2012; **12**: e200.
19. Aboulghate A, Abel G, Elliott MN, *et al*. Do English patients want continuity of care, and do they receive it? *British Journal of General Practice* 2012; DOI: 10.3399/bjgp12X653624.
20. NHS England. *Everyone Counts: planning for patients 2014/15 to 2018/19*. Leeds: NHS England, 2014, www.england.nhs.uk/wp-content/uploads/2013/12/5yr-strat-plann-guid-wa.pdf [accessed 10 June 2015].
21. Royal College of General Practitioners. *Continuity of Care Toolkit: helping clinicians and practices maximise relationship continuity*. London: RCGP, 2014, www.rcgp.org.uk/policy/rcgp-policy-areas/~/media/Files/Policy/A-Z-policy/Continuity%20of%20Care%20Toolkit.ashx [accessed 12 March 2014].

CHAPTER 25

INTELLIGENT KINDNESS

Developing and sustaining the effective *and* compassionate practitioner

John Ballatt

THE CHALLENGES

The enormous challenges faced by modern health care, and the very size of the enterprise, lead, inevitably, to preoccupations with efficiency, consistency and value for money. The focus can move towards industrialising the ways in which health care is organised: considering the people, resources, time and procedures as a production line; setting, measuring and regulating the performance of this machine-like enterprise. To complicate, and further dehumanise this mechanistic picture, the healthcare task can become that of delivering numbers of fragmented commodities to consumers, at a price, within a competitive market.

All these processes can make the healthcare task difficult, not least because they squeeze out awareness of and attention to the core truth about clinical care: it is a *relational task*. Its effectiveness, its efficiency, and the care and compassion experienced by patients depend on clinical staff *bringing together* their 'technical' knowledge and skills with a sophisticated psychosocial understanding and expertise. That the anxieties and processes at work in the wider culture of health care conspire to ignore and drive out this reality is bad enough, but do education, training, continuing professional development and healthcare leadership give due regard to the need for high-level *relational skills*? Do we collude with a dangerous split between 'important', 'professional' and 'scientific' skills and 'soft', 'sentimental', 'fuzzy' and 'secondary' human qualities. Indeed, do we even have a clear sense of what these latter capabilities are, and what promotes and sustains them in working settings?

It is not a question simply of interpersonal skills such as building rapport, listening, communicating and many others, though these are obviously important. Clinicians depend, for accurate diagnosis, effective treatment and the avoidance of error, on being able to manage themselves, emotionally and psychologically, in relationships with patients and colleagues. They must sustain attentiveness and goodwill within a wider 'relational system' that has to manage intense anxiety, complexity, repetitive routine, pressure of demand, competing priorities and limits to resources. Failure to manage in this way will impact, crucially, on patient experience, both in terms of clinical outcomes, and of the compassion and concern they meet in the services they need.

Reintegrating the psychosocial with the technical

A way of reintegrating the psychosocial with the technical in our view of health care is to think about the system, and the individual and group relationships within it, from the point of view of *kinship*. It is from this root that our much denigrated word *kindness* – a word that appears in nearly all positive patient 'reviews' of their experience – emerges. In a kinship system, individuals recognise their interdependency, their need to look out for, and put themselves out for, each other, to combine their efforts, and to protect and care for each other. Moved by this recognition, they are inclined towards an attitude of kindness, which directs them to pay *attention* to each other in particular ways.

Trust in the system

This kind of attention (very obvious in bonding between infants and parents, but also evident in sports teams, musical groups, military groups and, often, in clinical teams) leads to *attunement*. In this state, there has been an emotional and cognitive engagement, and understanding, developed between people that can lead to empathy, ease of communication and anticipation of need. Out of this attunement is built *trust*, which promotes honesty, openness and relief of anxiety. On the basis of this trust, close and effective cooperative activity emerges – in the healthcare setting, an effective *therapeutic alliance* is built. This 'psychosocial system' does not just lead to people feeling they are being treated kindly and with care and dignity: because of the quality of attention, communication and working relationships, the *outcomes* of treatment are likely to be optimal.

Kinship, kindness and optimism

Research shows that wounds can heal quicker when anxiety is minimised, that frequent attendance at A&E can be reduced by providing 'compassionate treatment', and that the outcomes of psychotherapy depend more on the quality of the therapeutic alliance than on the model of treatment used. A crucial aspect of this system – illustrated in Figure 25.1 – is that it is *self-reinforcing*: when it works, it further nourishes the sense of kinship, kindness and optimism. There is a 'virtuous circle' at work.

Vitally, this circle, and its component qualities, is as relevant to the way staff relate to each other, as to how they engage with patients. Indeed, it can be argued that the latter depends on the quality of the former.

'Technical skills'

To engage with and become an active member of such a positive kinship system requires that staff, equipped with their 'technical' skills:

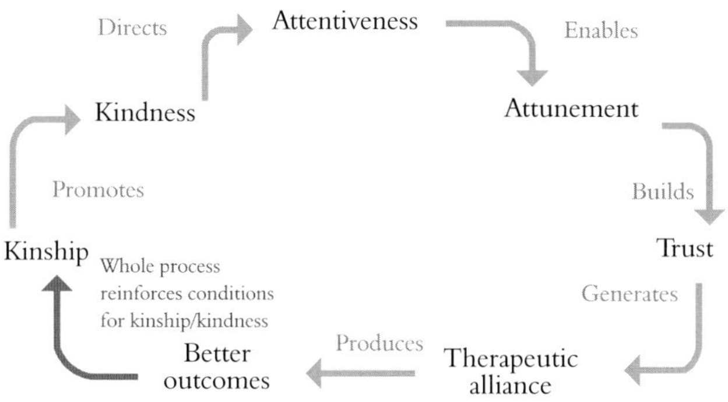

Figure 25.1: Kinship in action – a virtuous circle
Source: Ballatt J, Campling P. *Intelligent Kindness: reforming the culture of healthcare.*[1] © John Ballatt and Penelope Campling.

- are able to bear each other, and the patient, in mind
- can use their imagination to understand how their role or intervention can contribute to the needs of others
- have a sense of freedom and agency, so as to be able to act upon their awareness, feelings and understanding.

As important as helping people understand this kinship system is equipping them to manage the sheer difficulty of participating in, and sustaining, it. In all kinship systems conflict, neglect, competition and exclusivity can emerge: indeed ethology seems to teach us that the most open, benign and emotionally rich kinship systems are *more* vulnerable to breaking down than more rigid, insensitive, 'closed down' systems. The healthcare environment presents particular challenges to maintaining the virtuous circle above.

Ill-being of patients

At the core of the challenge is the sheer unpleasantness, the often frightening nature, the uncertainty and the complexity of meeting the *ill-being* of patients. That ill-being includes the illness and symptoms themselves, the emotional and psychosocial experience of the patient and those around him or her, the patient's capacity to communicate, the way the patient manages his or her anxiety and dependency. We train and support staff poorly if we minimise the need for what Raymond Tallis, geriatrician and philosopher, calls constant *self-overcoming*. Tallis highlights the *cognitive* self-overcoming involved in being able to think about the workings and disorders of our interiors. There is, though, an equally challenging *emotional and psychological* self-overcoming involved for clinical staff in the face of feelings of fear, grief and disgust, the urge to turn away, to close down, to resort to rote behaviour.[2] It is all too common to hear of trainees in all professions being encouraged to 'get over' this (as almost a one-off developmental task), rather than to learn to stay open to, live with, and constantly manage it.

Our individual responses to ill-being are very much rooted in our personalities. How we meet anxiety, grief, disgust and fear, how we deal with feelings of hopelessness and confusion, of dependency and fear of failure or error, are all very personal things. Our motives for entering our professions, our self-image and expectations from such membership, and our attitudes to other people all influence our relationship with our work and our patients. Crucially, our own ability to connect with and attach to others in the virtuous circle is very much influenced by our own psychosocial development. There is a range of models for understanding these factors, and it can be argued that some basic understanding of them should be part of the training of every practitioner.

Clinicians – managing themselves

What is certain is that effective and compassionate clinicians must *manage themselves* well to engage in the virtuous circle. It is important that practitioners develop habits and skills in reflective practice that help them maintain awareness of themselves in their roles in this context. Such approaches as Balint groups have helped develop this competency, but there is a range of helpful interventions, from supervision through to whole-system reflection such as Schwartz Rounds. Crucially, reflective practice is not occasional, not just for trainees, and not just for medical revalidation.

Reintegration of the relational with the technical

Here, we meet another challenge in the reintegration of the relational with the technical: it is not just, or even mainly, about individuals. Much is said about the need for 'cultures' that sustain compassionate practice but, too often, what we know about human groups and systems is ignored in this rhetoric. Again, reference to what we know about kinship systems is valuable.

The challenge of widening to include individuals and groups who are not 'blood kin' (one of, or exactly like, us) has always been complex, and has required agreement and the management of potential for selfishness or conflict. The ambitious and, to this writer, admirable, aim of the NHS in the UK to provide free care to all confronts society as a whole with the anxiety of sharing limited resources, with questions of whether people are deserving, truly 'like us', people we want in our family.

Resource limitation

Society is becoming more complex and diverse, inequality is increasing, and the success of medical science is leading to the survival of people with increasingly complex and challenging needs. As a result, we are confronted with the challenge to connect with, include and be generous to people whose culture, lifestyle and language, whose communication skills, dependency, complexity of need, and the risks they present or face, can evoke strong social anxiety and ambivalence.

Practitioners may share these uncertainties – whether or not they do, they work in systems where the funding, organisation and culture of services can often express them. The problems faced by people with learning disabilities or serious mental health problems in society are disturbingly echoed in our hospitals and services. Older people, with complex and multiple difficulties, challenge the organisation, pace, efficiency and priorities of our primary, community and acute services.

Management of anxiety by organisations

A central reality of the organisations and systems in which staff work is how they manage *anxiety*. This includes, but is by no means limited to, the anxiety of the 'primary task' of working together with ill-being, though this can lead to problems in morale, behaviour and relationships within the system. Public anxiety, expressed through government and policy, about illness and death, about best or fair use of resources, about the quality of care available, infects policy priorities, regulation and performance management.

These processes may be inevitable and necessary, but the degree to which they can inject dangerous distraction, anxiety and coercive behaviour into the system, into the front-line clinical team, needs constant attention. This is an ethical and practical challenge for managers and leaders, but individual practitioners, teams and professional organisations need to be aware of, and develop strategies for managing, these processes and their emotional impact. A particularly important dimension is the effect this anxiety has on *interdisciplinary* relationships, at team level, and at the level of how professions relate to each other and make common purpose to address difficulties and challenges.

Implications for training

Without overburdening curricula, it is entirely feasible to equip healthcare practitioners in training with understanding of and skills in managing some of these realities. There is a vast body of knowledge in relation to the way groups, teams and organisations behave. Social psychologists, like Asch,[3] Milgram[4] and Zimbardo,[5] have demonstrated the way group pressure, authority and role pressures can skew, even pervert, the behaviour, emotional experience and attitudes of individuals, and the relationships between teams in wider systems.

Support from within teams

The group relations tradition sheds light on how teams can be places that help their members remain open, attentive, cooperative and resilient, if anxiety, passivity, conflict and authority are managed well, and if team members learn to manage themselves and participate effectively. There is increasing understanding, rooted in neuroscience and in psychology, of ways of helping people manage themselves consciously and humanely in stressful systems, in such approaches as mindfulness and compassionate mind training.

Leadership and 'intelligent kindness'

There is a challenge here for leaders – of education and training, of healthcare services, and of professional bodies. If they take seriously the 'parity of esteem' between technical expertise and relational capability argued for here, then they must equip themselves with understanding and skill. They must look at their roles in creating the cultures, priorities and expectations (implicit and explicit) in their organisations and examine whether they lead and manage in a way that develops and sustains people, teams and practice that integrates these perspectives. Vitally, they must manage with courage, awareness and skill the anxieties and the pressures from industrialisation, regulation and marketisation that can close down, devalue or even kill off the personal, team and organisational 'intelligent kindness' required for effective, compassionate care.

References

1. Ballatt J, Campling P. *Intelligent Kindness: reforming the culture of healthcare*. London: RCPsych Publications, 2011.
2. Tallis R. *Hippocratic Oaths: medicine and its discontents*. London: Atlantic Books, 2005.
3. Asch SE. Effects of group pressure upon the modification and distortion of judgments. In: H Guetzkow (ed.). *Groups, Leadership and Men*. Pittsburgh: Carnegie Press, 1951, pp. 177–90.
4. Milgram S. Behavioural study of obedience. *Journal of Abnormal and Social Psychology* 1963; **67**: 371–8.
5. Haney C, Bank WC, Zimbardo PG. Interpersonal dynamics in a simulated prison. *International Journal of Criminology and Penology* 1973; **1**: 69–97.

Further reading

- Chance MRA. *Social Fabrics of the Mind*. London: Lawrence Erlbaum Associates Publishers, 1988.
- Cole-King A, Harding KG. Psychological factors and delayed healing in chronic wounds. *Psychosomatic Medicine* 2001; **63(2)**: 216–20.
- Commissioning Board Chief Nursing Officer and DH Chief Nursing Adviser. *Compassion in Practice: nursing, midwifery and care staff. Our vision and strategy*. Leeds: NHS, 2012, www.england.nhs.uk/wp-content/uploads/2012/12/compassion-in-practice.pdf [accessed 15 June 2015].
- Cooper M. *Essential Research Findings in Counselling and Psychotherapy*. London: Sage Publications, 2008.
- Department of Health. *Transforming Care: a national response to Winterbourne View Hospital*. London: HMSO, 2012, www.gov.uk/government/uploads/system/uploads/attachment_data/file/213215/final-report.pdf [accessed 15 June 2015].
- Francis R. *Independent Inquiry into Care Provided by Mid Staffordshire NHS Foundation Trust, January 2005–March 2009*. London: TSO, 2010, www.gov.uk/government/publications/independent-inquiry-into-care-provided-by-mid-staffordshire-nhs-foundation-trust-january-2001-to-march-2009 [accessed 15 June 2015].
- Gilbert P. *The Compassionate Mind: a new approach to life's challenges*. London: Constable & Robinson, 2009.
- Goodrich J, Cornwell J. *Seeing the Person in the Patient: the Point of Care review paper*. London: King's Fund, 2008, www.kingsfund.org.uk/sites/files/kf/Seeing-the-person-in-the-patient-The-Point-of-Care-review-paper-Goodrich-Cornwell-Kings-Fund-December-2008.pdf [accessed 15 June 2015].
- Holmes J. *John Bowlby and Attachment Theory*. London and New York: Routledge, 1993.
- Menzies Lyth I. The functions of social systems as a defence against anxiety: a report on a study of the nursing service of a general hospital. *Human Relations* 1959; **13**: 95–121 [reprinted in *Containing Anxiety in Institutions: Selected Essays Vol. 1*. London: Free Association Books, 1988].
- Patient Opinion, www.patientopinion.org.uk.
- Redelmeier DA, Molin J, Tibshirani RJ. A randomised trial of compassionate care for the homeless in an emergency department. *Lancet* 1995; **345(8958)**: 1131–4.
- Weinman J, Ebrecht M, Scott S, *et al*. Enhanced wound healing after emotional disclosure intervention. *British Journal of Health Psychology* 2008; **13(1)**: 95–102.

CHAPTER 26

HOW TO DISCOURAGE A DOCTOR

A view from the US

Richard B. Gunderman

Not accustomed to visiting hospital executive suites, I took my seat in the waiting room somewhat warily.

Seated across from me was a handsome man in a well-tailored three-piece suit, whose thoroughly professional appearance made me – in my rumpled white coat, sheaves of dog-eared paper bulging from both pockets – feel out of place.

Within a minute, an administrative secretary came out and escorted him into one of the offices. Exhausted from a long call shift and lulled by the quiet, I started to doze off. Soon roused by the sound of my own snoring, I started and looked about.

That was when I spotted the document on an adjacent chair. Its title immediately caught my eye: *How to Discourage a Doctor*.

No one else was about, so I reached over, picked it up, and began to leaf through its pages. It became apparent immediately that it was one of the most remarkable things I had ever read, clearly not meant for my eyes. It seemed to be the product of a healthcare consulting company, presumably the well-dressed man's employer. Fearing that he would return any moment to retrieve it, I perused it as quickly as possible. My recollection of its contents is naturally somewhat imperfect, but I can reproduce the gist of what it said.

> 'The stresses on today's hospital executive are enormous. They include a rapidly shifting regulatory environment, downward pressures on reimbursement rates, and seismic shifts in payment mechanisms. Many leaders naturally feel as though they are building a hospital in the midst of an earthquake. With prospects for revenue enhancement highly uncertain, the best strategy for ensuring a favorable bottom line is to reduce costs. And for the foreseeable future, the most important driver of costs in virtually every hospital will be its medical staff.

> 'Though physician compensation accounts for only about 8% of healthcare spending, decisions that physicians strongly influence or make directly – such as what medication to prescribe, whether to perform surgery, and when to admit and

discharge a patient from the hospital – have been estimated to account for as much as 80% of the nation's healthcare budget. To maintain a favorable balance sheet, hospital executives need to gain control of their physicians. Most hospitals have already taken an important step in this direction by employing a growing proportion of their medical staff.

'Transforming previously independent physicians into employees has increased hospital influence over their decision making, an effect that has been successfully augmented in many centers by tying physician compensation directly to the execution of hospital strategic initiatives. But physicians have invested many years in learning their craft, they hold their professional autonomy in high esteem, and they take seriously the considerable respect and trust with which many patients still regard them.

'As a result, the challenge of managing hospital medical staff continues to resemble herding cats.

'Merely controlling the purse strings is not enough. To truly seize the reins of medicine, it is necessary to do more, to get into the heads and hearts of physicians. And the way to do this is to show physicians that they are not nearly so important as they think they are. Physicians have long seen the patient–physician relationship as the very center of the healthcare solar system. As we go forward, they must be made to feel that this relationship is not the sun around which everything else orbits, but rather one of the dimmer peripheral planets, a Neptune or perhaps Uranus.

'How can this goal be achieved? A complete list of proven tactics and strategies is available to our clients, but some of the more notable include the following:

'Make healthcare incomprehensible to physicians. It is no easy task to baffle the most intelligent people in the organization, but it can be done. For example, make physicians increasingly dependent on complex systems outside their domain of expertise, such as information technology and coding and billing software. Ensure that such systems are very costly, so that solo practitioners and small groups, who naturally cannot afford them, must turn to the hospital. And augment their sense of incompetence by making such systems user-unfriendly and unreliable. Where possible, change vendors frequently.

'Promote a sense of insecurity among the medical staff. A comfortable physician is a confident physician, and a confident physician usually proves difficult to control. To undermine confidence, let it be known that physicians' jobs are in jeopardy and their compensation is likely to decline. Fire one or more physicians, ensuring that the entire medical staff knows about it. Hire replacements with a minimum of fanfare. Place a significant percentage of compensation 'at risk', so that physicians begin to feel beholden to hospital administration for what they manage to eke out.

'Transform physicians from decision makers to decision implementers. Convince them that their professional judgment regarding particular patients no longer constitutes a reliable compass.

'Refer to such decisions as anecdotal, idiosyncratic, or simply insufficiently evidence based. Make them feel that their mission is not to balance benefits and risks against their knowledge of particular patients, but instead to apply broad practice guidelines to the care of all patients. Hiring, firing, promotion, and all rewards should be based on conformity to hospital-mandated policies and procedures.

'Subject physicians to escalating productivity expectations. Borrow terminology and methods from the manufacturing industry to make them think of themselves as production-line workers, then convince them that they are not working sufficiently hard and fast. Show them industry standards and benchmarks in comparison to which their output is subpar. On the off chance that their productivity compares favorably, cite numerous reasons that such benchmarks are biased and move the bar progressively higher, from the 75th to the 95th percentile.

'Increase physicians' responsibility while decreasing their authority. For example, hold physicians responsible for patient satisfaction scores, but ensure that such scores are influenced by a variety of factors over which physicians have little or no control, such as information technology, hospitality of staff members, and parking. The goal of such measures is to induce a state that psychologists refer to as 'learned helplessness', a growing sense among physicians that whatever they do, they cannot meaningfully influence healthcare, which is to say the operations of the hospital.

'Above all, introduce barriers between physicians and their patients. The more directly physicians and patients feel connected to one another, the greater the threat to the hospital's control.

'When physicians think about the work they do, the first image that comes to mind should be the hospital, and when patients realize they need care, they should turn first to the hospital, not a particular physician. One effective technique is to ensure that patient–physician relationships are frequently disrupted, so that the hospital remains the one constant. Another is. …'

The sound of a door roused me again. The man in the three-piece suit emerged from the office, he and the hospital executive to whom he had been speaking shaking hands and smiling. As he turned, I looked about. Where was *How to Discourage a Doctor*? It was not on the table, nor was it on the chair where I had first found it. 'Will he think I took it?' I wondered. But instead of stopping to look for it, he simply walked out of the office. As I watched him go, one thing became clear: having read that document, I suddenly felt a lot less discouraged.

Further reading

- The Health Care Blog, http://thehealthcareblog.com/blog/2014/09/18/how-to-discourage-a-doctor/.

CHAPTER 27

PROFESSIONALISM
A changing tide

Richard Knox

Have we lost our way as a profession? Have we lost 'professionalism'? If so, how did this happen, and how can we get it back?

A simple dictionary definition of professionalism is as follows:

> The competence or skill expected of a professional:
> the key to quality and efficiency is professionalism

or

> The practising of an activity, especially a sport, by professional rather than amateur players:
> the trend towards professionalism[1]

When thinking about professionalism in general practice (or indeed any other healthcare profession), a simple dictionary definition is far from adequate. It may have been appropriate in yesteryear, when we were more concerned with defending boundaries and restricting access, but the concept has so many more connotations now.

THE 'SEARCH' FOR REDEFINING PROFESSIONALISM

We are not alone in our 'search' for redefining professionalism. A brief survey of the literature uncovers similar questions about this concept across the multidisciplinary team. Although we should champion our individual professional roles within the team, there is much that can be learned from our colleagues' self-discovery.

In 2014, the Nursing and Midwifery Council (NMC) convened a consultation about its role as a regulator in 'professionalism'.[2] The then Chair of the House of Commons Health Committee, Stephen Dorrell, spoke at its 'high level roundtable' discussion and 'identified three characteristics of professionalism':[2]

1 The core relationship is between the professional and the service user. The professional has an individual responsibility in that relationship
2 To be a professional is to be always looking for a better way – 'divine discontent'. Professionals have a responsibility to keep a record and account for their own practice, and to measure their own practice against the best
3 Professionals have a collective responsibility; a responsibility to report poor or unsafe practice in others and to raise concerns.

While being a useful reminder of any healthcare professional's responsibilities, and a useful framing point for the NMC's deliberations, there can be problems if professionalism is solely considered from this perspective. Members of the professional group may be concerned that their 'professionalism' is just a means of being held to account when things go wrong, rather than truly using their knowledge and skills for the benefit of patients.

Regulating professionals

The Health and Care Professions Council (HCPC) is the body responsible for regulating 16 groups of professionals including paramedics, physiotherapists and dieticians. They recently commissioned a focus group study with education (or training) providers and students looking at the concept of professionalism. One of their conclusions was that the concept can be:[3]

> regarded as a meta-skill of situational awareness and contextual judgement, allowing individuals to draw on a range of communication, technical and practical skills, and apply the appropriate skills for a given professional scenario. The true skill of professionalism may be not so much in knowing what to do, but when to do it.

The authors go on to talk about professionalism being 'a judgment rather than a skill'.[3]

This description speaks directly to the heart of what many of us try to do on a day-to-day basis. Interacting with our patients will often require complex communication skills married with up-to-date clinical knowledge, and the competence (and confidence) to know when and how to act. As someone who is trying to redevelop a medical school's professionalism curriculum, this is a useful reminder that an important skill is to be able to 'take one step back' and review the situation, and a strong reinforcement of the limitation of the utility of reductionist check-list approaches to assessment.

Professionalism and the medical profession

But what about an overarching definition of professionalism with respect to the medical profession. Is that possible? The simple answer is no.

A systematic review of the topic concluded that there was no internationally agreed definition of professionalism,[4] and a recent Association for Medical Education in

Europe (AMEE) guide suggests that each education provider should develop its own definition.[5]

Our colleagues at the Royal College of Physicians have provided a useful description, which we have adopted in subsequent documents: 'A set of values, behaviours and relationships that underpin the trust the public has in doctors.'[6]

THE DOCTOR–PATIENT RELATIONSHIP

The public does have trust in doctors: despite recent events, we are still considered one of the most trusted professions. We're even considered more trustworthy than primary school teachers.[7] However, there is a danger that the trust can be slowly chipped away. When our values seem less than honourable, our behaviours questionable and relationships marred, there is understandable public outrage.

Why does that happen? Maybe it actually goes back to that first characteristic of professionalism that was described in the NMC document: the doctor–patient relationship. When we lose sight of the centrality of the patient, when there is a dip in compassion, things can start to go wrong.

> When we lose sight of the centrality of the patient, when there is a dip in compassion, things can start to go wrong.

COMPASSION

Compassion can be described as a 'deep awareness of the suffering of another coupled with the wish to relieve it'.[8] It is a state of mind that goes beyond empathy, and can only be universally outworked in a facilitative working environment.[9] The working environment described in the Francis Report was far from facilitative[10] – and although that in no way excuses the behaviours reported, it may go some way to explain why this may happen. One may argue that in encountering such a working environment, the honourable thing to do would be to whistle-blow or at least remove yourself from the environment – some did – with varying effect.

But what if you feel that the 'environment' is actually the state of the NHS today? The fact that we are seeing record numbers of GPs leaving the profession (and not enough joining) could indeed be indicative of this. The survey of GPs presented in the RCGP's *Put Patients First: back general practice* campaign leaflet makes for stark reading:[11]

- four in five GPs say it will become increasingly difficult to deliver continuity of care to vulnerable elderly people in the next two years
- 49% of GPs say they feel they can no longer guarantee safe care to their patients
- 80% of GPs say they now have insufficient resources to provide high-quality patient care.

There has been an exponential rise in demand for UK general practice, but without a similar rise in funding. Many GPs genuinely feel unable to provide care to the quality they would like to. If GPs are exhibiting behaviours that reflect the constraints of a working environment, rather than the ideals of medical practice, then the Royal College of Physicians definition starts to lose its foundations, patient care is compromised, and the professionalism of UK general practice implodes.

Developing a 'new professionalism'

Can we develop a 'new professionalism'? One that is honourable, and patient focused, while being fit for purpose in the twenty-first century? There is no use looking back with rose-tinted spectacles. The world of primary care is very different from that inhabited by Dr Finlay. With the complexity of care available, the pace of change and the range of treatment options, it wouldn't be feasible for the single-handed compassionate GP (or indeed average partnership) to provide round-the-clock cover to their patients.

As a profession, focusing on our patients is, however, something that we are hard-wired to do. At a base level it is evident in our College exam objectives, but it cuts deeper than that. As GPs, we are our patients' advocates, and a first point of call for many diverse health and social care needs.

We might have 'paved paradise' (to quote Joni Mitchell) with out-of-hours clinics, phone-in services and telemedicine, but we are still highly trained experts in the delivery of patient-centred primary care. To provide modern primary care in the UK setting, we may, however, have to make some radical changes. This may involve increasing co-working with members of the multiprofessional team. It would also seem sensible to tease out what it is that we bring to the table as GPs. This could include championing our role as the expert generalist as an increasing number of our patients have active multi-morbidities.[12,13]

It is even possible that the proliferation of disease-specific quality assurance targets has led to a decrease in the capacity for the delivery of truly patient-centred care. As we move towards a more patient-focused management system,[14] we have the opportunity to regain our professionalism that demonstrates 'situational awareness and contextual judgement'.[3] Part of our professional role may also be declining developments that could further jeopardise a patient-centred approach.

> We also need to inspire the next generation of UK GPs to continue the journey.

Maybe our role as true professionals can only be realised if we are able to deliver on this modified definition of professionalism:

> The ability to deliver compassionate, patient-centred care and to prevent the delivery of care that is neither compassionate nor patient-centred.

References

1. Oxford English Dictionary online. Professionalism. 2015. www.oxforddictionaries.com/definition/english/professionalism [accessed 11 June 2015].

2. Nursing and Midwifery Council. *Roundtable on Professionalism*. London: NMC, 2014, www.nmc-uk.org/Documents/Legislation/Roundtable%20on%20professionalism%20notes.pdf [accessed 11 June 2015].
3. Health and Care Professions Council. *Professionalism in Healthcare Professions*. London: HCPC, 2014, www.hpc-uk.org/assets/documents/10003771Professionalisminhealthcareprofessionals.pdf [accessed 11 June 2015].
4. Rogers W, Ballantyne A. Towards a practical definition of professional behaviour. *Journal of Medical Ethics* 2010; **36(4)**: 250–4.
5. O'Sullivan H, Van Mook W, Fewtrell R, Wass V. Integrating professionalism into the curriculum: AMEE Guide No. 61. *Medical Teacher* 2012; DOI: 10.3109/0142159X.2012.655610.
6. Royal College of Physicians. *Doctors in Society: medical professionalism in a changing world*. London: RCP, 2005.
7. Ipsos MORI. Trust in professions poll 2015. www.ipsos-mori.com/researchpublications/researcharchive/15/Trust-in-Professions.aspx [accessed 11 June 2015].
8. Chochinov HM. Dignity and the essence of medicine: the A, B, C, and D of dignity conserving care. *British Medical Journal* 2007; **335(7612)**: 184–7.
9. De Zuleta P. Reflecting on the Francis Report: how can we develop more human systems of care. *Nursing Ethics* 2013; **20(7)**: 838–42.
10. Francis R. *Report of the Mid Staffordshire NHS Foundation Trust Public Inquiry*. London: TSO, 2013, www.midstaffspublicinquiry.com/report [accessed 27 April 2015].
11. Royal College of General Practitioners. *Put Patients First: back general practice*. London: RCGP, 2013. www.rcgp.org.uk/campaign-home/~/media/Files/PPF/Put-patients-first-campaign-brief.ashx [accessed 11 June 2015].
12. Salisbury C, Johnson L, Purdy S, *et al.* Epidemiology and impact of multimorbidity in primary care: a retrospective cohort study. *British Journal of General Practice* 2011; DOI: 10.3399/bjgp11X548929.
13. Goodwin N, Curry N, Naylor C, *et al. Managing People with Long-Term Conditions*. London: King's Fund, 2010, www.kingsfund.org.uk/sites/files/kf/field/field_document/managing-people-long-term-conditions-gp-inquiry-research-paper-mar11.pdf [accessed 11 June 2015].
14. NHS Improvement. *Managing Multimorbidiy in Practice: what lessons can be learnt from the care of people with COPD and co-morbidities*. Leicester: NHS Improvement, 2013, www.educationforhealth.org/wp-content/uploads/2015/03/COPD_MultiMorbidities.pdf [accessed 11 June 2015].

CHAPTER 28

COMPASSION AND THE COLLEGE MOTTO

Cum scientia caritas – past, present and future

Rodger Charlton

There is nothing like being a patient when it comes to focusing our minds to remind us how important access is to a doctor and why, when illness strikes. Access to physicians is changing worldwide, not least through social media, the use of email and smartphones. But, the basic tenet of the doctor–patient relationship, the consultation, is essentially the same. However, the equity of access to physicians varies from country to country and also within countries where socioeconomic status is a large determinant. This is something we must always be mindful of through the work of Dr Julian Tudor Hart and what he described in the *Lancet* in 1971 as the 'inverse care law'.[1]

The role of doctors is increased when they see the same patient on many occasions and learn a new part of the patient's life story or narrative in relation to his or her health and possible illness. It is the ability of the doctor to provide continuity of care through the episodic nature of the illness and ongoing proactive and reactive care for those with long-term conditions that is most valued by patients.

Doctors, whether in primary or secondary care, are generally held in very high esteem by the public and it is for this reason that patients have considerable expectations in relation to the consultation and getting satisfaction from each meeting with a doctor or any healthcare professional. I attended a lecture many years ago by a doctor who worked for social services and I still recall the four points that she made about the possible outcomes of the consultation. These were: being given a prescription; getting a referral to a specialist; being given a sick note; and the fourth, which is perhaps the most important, receiving a bit of love. The best doctor is the one who has perhaps been there him or herself with illness and so is able to understand, or, failing this, the one who tries to understand a patient's plight and circumstances.

Times of distress, which may be brought on by illness or complicated by psychosocial issues in patients' lives, are times of extreme vulnerability, and our patients may hang on to every word that a doctor says. However, it is not just the words that the doctor utters which matter, but the manner in which they are delivered. This determines if the doctor is seen as sympathetic and, where possible, empathetic. So frequently in medical teaching we emphasise communication, both verbal and non-verbal, but do we ensure it is always delivered to the highest quality possible?[2]

A new consultation model

Prof. David Haslam, who has written a foreword to this book and is both past Chair of RCGP Council and past President of the College, has come up with a new consultation model (which has not yet been published). There are many consultation models, and it could be argued that there is no ideal model and eventually each doctor develops his or her own individual style. His alternative model, which is very straightforward, and has come about following considerable reflection is: shut up, listen, care and know something. It is the last model that is so important and is contained within the College mottos of the UK, New Zealand and Australian Royal Colleges of General Practice – '*Cum scientia caritas*', which means scientific care with loving kindness.[3]

A 'new professionalism'

But it is more than sympathy, empathy and care, and the term that now gets much of our attention in medical education is professionalism. Sadly, it is possible sometimes to demonstrate professionalism without truly caring. And perhaps it might be best to go back to the phrase 'bedside manner', which has been superseded by the word professionalism. True professionalism must include compassion and should perhaps be the 'new professionalism'.

Compassion is almost undefinable, but the current pace and pressure of modern medicine means it is squeezed out as we see more patients, more frequently and with shorter consultations. Compassion is more than empathy; it is the wish to relieve suffering, where the degree of compassion is our desire to want to help and so, in turn, show kindness, love and care. This is the embodiment of altruism in health care. *Caritas*, continuity and compassion are what GPs do best and it is time to embed these as themes in health care for the foreseeable future. With an increasingly frail elderly population with multiple co-morbidities through long-term conditions, the emphasis should be on *caritas* balanced appropriately with *scientia*. The 3Cs for us in the future should be continuity, caring and compassion, and could again be viewed as the new professionalism.

Difference between illness and disease

Much of my time is spent teaching both undergraduates and postgraduates, and I regularly have to remind them that medicine is not an exact science and that there is a difference between illness and disease. The role of the doctor has been compared with that of both a priest and an engineer. However, with increasing technological advances in medical science the public now perceives the profession more and more as engineers. A greater expectation is therefore put on the scientific aspect of medicine. Until recently this idea of the doctor as an engineer has been fostered within medical schools where students concentrated on the scientific and technological aspects of medicine rather than the improvement of communication skills and 'bedside manner'.

This concept is well described in a paper in 1981 by the late Cecil Helman, a London GP who wrote from the perspective of a GP and an anthropologist.[4]

> Illness is what the patient feels when he goes to the doctor and disease is what he has on the way home from the doctor's office. Disease, then, is something an organ has; illness is something a man has. Illness refers to the subjective response of the patient to being unwell; how he, and those around him, perceive the origin and significance of this event; how it effects his behaviour or relationships with other people; and the steps he takes to remedy this situation. It includes not only his experience of ill-health, but the meaning he gives to that experience. Even responses to physical symptoms, such as pain, can be influenced by social and cultural factors; these factors can in turn affect the presentation of the symptoms and the behaviour of the patient and his family.

Furthermore, Helman goes on to say that, 'Illness can occur in the absence of disease.'

If a doctor observes a patient from the perspective of an engineer then it may be forgotten that each patient is first and foremost a living being with an illness, which is far more important than his or her disease. Each patient has hopes and fears like any of us and is particularly vulnerable when he or she comes to consult a doctor. Whether or not the patient has a disease, it is these hopes and fears that can lead to an illness.

A mission statement of Prof. Bill Shannon of the Royal College of Surgeons of Ireland was reported in the *Irish Medical Times* as: 'It is often more important for a doctor to know the person who has the disease than the disease the person has.'[5] The key is to know patients as individuals and get to know their story or narrative and so how best to manage their illness, where they may or may not have an obvious disease.

Evidence-based medicine

In the current era of evidence-based medicine (EBM) and guidelines, the assumption is being made that medicine is an exact science and that all patients are part of a population and not individuals who have clearly defined disease. And for some patients this may be the case, but for many patients they have undifferentiated illness. It is important for GPs and those we train in the art of medicine not to evolve into doctors who fervently insist on always following evidence-based guidelines with algorithms, which are not always what is best for patients. Rather, what is required is making difficult judgements while at the same time being an advocate for the patient, whether that is in relation to cure, continuing care or perhaps palliation.

It is important to return to the College motto, '*Cum scientia caritas*' – scientific care with loving kindness – and remind ourselves that the role of doctors as they practise now through the doctor–patient relationship is not limited to that of a mechanistic rule-book. This is particularly pertinent as it has been estimated that many people visiting a GP, and thus perceiving themselves as being ill, have no serious disease[6] and this is where the majority of patients are seen with what we often refer to as 'undifferentiated' illness. EBM is important, but it is not, as it is often heralded, always the way forward.

What compassion is not

In the preface I stated that many of the authors have provided a personal view. So too in this paragraph I present very much my own personal view. So often I attend meetings as an academic or as a GP, or in another capacity, and the discussion that is missing is that which refers to patients or the patient. I have quoted that as medical educators we have failed if our trainees are not better doctors than we are, as we are not perfect, and they are tomorrow's doctors. Our health service is often said to be failing or at fault. The answer to this in the last few years has been that we need to send colleagues on leadership courses, or more recently resilience training. This may occasionally have reference to patients but totally neglects that the success of the Health Service depends on the goodwill of staff, who are valued by their employees and patients alike, and by always referring to the patient, who should be at the centre. This is what we so often refer to as patient-centred medicine. We need to be compassionate both to the needs of our staff and patients.

Ideally, when treating a patient it should be as you yourself would wish to be treated or a member of your family. So often in medical training, it is emphasised how important it is to have personal detachment between you and the patient, and not to get emotionally involved. If that is the case, what of compassion? We are told this is to desensitise us and aid objectivity. Defining what is a 'good doctor' is not easy. However, there are two types of doctors: those who are technically good and those who are kind with their patients and listen to their patients. As a patient one needs both qualities in a doctor, which is captured by the College and its motto: '*Cum scientia caritas*'.

Compassion – a bit of kindness

The art of medicine is how to apply the science. This is not the mystique of the 'Church of Medicine', but the role of the 'good doctor'. This book is a compilation of the views and reflections of many well-known and respected leaders in health care and a resource for those seeking to learn more about what compassion is. There is no absolute definition and it means different things to different patients. It cannot be measured or administered from a bottle. Maybe it is what Rabbi Lionel Blue described in his *Thought for the Day* on BBC Radio 4; 'A bit of kindness' in his experience as a patient:[7]

> With relief I discuss with a passing nurse a piece of news I do know something about: nurses will get three-year degrees, not two-year diplomas, a step up we agree they deserve, for medical technology gets more complex monthly.
>
> But there's a problem here too – I've found the kindness of nurses as essential as technology, but how do you teach kindness on a degree course? For vulnerable

oldies, and youngsters too, hospitals become a way of life, and kindness is the difference between heaven and hell.

He goes on to say:

In my experience you learn kindness by remembering the kindnesses and unkindnesses you've encountered and how both felt; also the kindnesses you've shown and the unkindnesses you've inflicted and how you catch kindness from people like measles, not just from books.

'Compassion is like the sun, it just shines'

As I concluded in the preface, compassion is not something that you can learn or just switch on. A description that I find fitting comes from my research assistant, Jane Coomber. Jane, a nurse by training, describes compassion as 'emotional labour that has taken a back seat during the medical scientific advances of the twentieth century, and is now re-emerging to ensure all the needs of the patient are met'. When the effort is made in an ever busy and demanding health service, 'Compassion is like the sun, it just shines' – as written in the addendum to the piece written by Dr Clive Weston.

I recommend that you read and re-read this book, and consider the different personal views of my fellow authors. As editor, I have left their views largely unabridged. This is because the authors are speaking from the heart about something that is their own interpretation and based on many years of experience and their understanding of their role in and towards the College and its motto: '*Cum scientia caritas*'.

Dame Annis Gillie, RCGP President from 1964–7, approved the following 14-word interdenominational grace to be used at College functions and dinners. It echoes the College motto in which skills match *scientia* and compassion matches *caritas*:

God be praised for food and friends
Inspire our skills
Kindle our compassion. Amen

'There is a connotation that the general practitioner's fire of compassion, once lit, will burn brightly.'[8]

References

1. Tudor Hart J. The inverse care law. *Lancet* 1971; **1(7696)**: 405–12.
2. Charlton R. Editorial: We are all patients. *Hong Kong Practitioner* 2014; **36(3)**: 81–2.
3. McCulloch GL. *Cum scientia caritas*. *Journal of the Royal College of General Practitioners* 1969; **18(89)**: 315–20.
4. Helman CG. Disease versus illness in general practice. *Journal of the Royal College of General Practitioners* 1981; **31(230)**: 548–52.
5. Shannon W. *Irish Medical Times*, April 2005.
6. Bass C, Murphy M. Editorial: The chronic somatiser and the Government White Paper. *Journal of the Royal Society of Medicine* 1990; **83(4)**: 203–5.

7. Blue L. *Thought for the Day*, 18 January 2010. BBC Radio 4.
8. Pereira Gray DJ. Ceremonies and insignia. In: DJ Pereira Gray (ed.). *Forty Years On: the story of the first forty years of the Royal College of General Practitioners*. London: RCGP, 1992, pp. 171–8.

Index

Note: page numbers in *italics* refer to figures and tables.